THERAPEUTIC RECREATION PROCESSES AND TECHNIQUES

THERAPEUTIC RECREATION PROCESSES AND TECHNIQUES

David R. Austin

Indiana University

John Wiley & Sons

New York   Chichester   Brisbane   Toronto   Singapore

Austin, David R., 1941–
    Therapeutic recreation processes and techniques.

    Includes indexes.
    1. Recreational therapy.   I. Title.
RM736.7.A97   615.8'5153   82-2833
ISBN 0-471-08666-5   AACR2

Printed in the United States of America
10 9 8 7 6 5 4 3 2 1

To
Ron,
Dorothy,
Joan,
and
Janet

FOREWORD

Therapeutic recreation is an emerging professional specialization within the recreation field; it is concerned with the alleviation of human suffering and the promotion and facilitation of optimal human functioning. It is an emerging health-related discipline that is unique in its ability to use the recreative activity and environment as a modality of intervention for remediation, restoration, and rehabilitation of individuals who are experiencing some measure of dependency due to illness, disability, or maladaptation. Therapeutic recreation is a health-related service characterized by its humanistic orientation and its concern with the importance of recreation and leisure as a component of total wellness and self-actualization of the human spirit.

Some textbooks in therapeutic recreation have chosen to approach the field from a very broad perspective. They have based their approach on a definition that states that therapeutic recreation is essentially "the delivery of recreation and leisure services for special population." Such an approach often leaves readers confused as to the primary role of therapeutic recreation in relation to other health-related disciplines and other areas of specialization within the broad range of park and recreation occupations.

Therapeutic Recreation Processes and Techniques is the first major text to confront this issue clearly and concisely without getting bogged down in a meaningless philosophical debate. The author states clearly that "the overriding mission (of therapeutic recreation) is the provision of purposeful intervention designed to help the clients grow and to assist them to prevent or relieve problems through recreation and leisure."

What is purposeful intervention? According to Dr. Austin, it is a "systematic method of problem solving through a progression of phases." It includes (1) assessment, (2) planning, (3) implementation, and (4) evaluation. It is what he refers to as the *TR process,* and it begins where the client (or group of clients) is at any point along the illness-wellness continuum. It is not a limited or restricted concept of service carried out only within the constraints of traditional institutionalized care, but is a client-centered model that reflects a concern for the total well-being of the individual.

Within this framework, Dr. Austin takes the readers through the TR process with remarkable clarity and simplicity. Building on a well-established foundation in the behavioral sciences, readers are provided with a bridge between theory and practice and are supplied with sound, well-tested techniques that have practical application for the therapeutic recreation practitioner.

For the first time in any existing textbook on the subject, readers are guided through the steps in the systematic application of therapeutic recreation in a readable and easy-to-follow manner. The skillful way in which this task is accomplished is a reflection of the many years of practical experience the author has had in working with disabled populations in various settings.

Therapeutic Recreation Processes and Techniques is a scholarly yet practical contribution to the therapeutic recreation literature. It sets a new standard that will be welcomed by beginning students, experienced practitioners, and educators.

Therapeutic recreation is acknowledged to be an emerging profession with much room for growth, development, and refinement of technique; however, this text is an excellent example of the growing maturity of this field. It will go far in advancing the knowledge and skills for those who are dedicated to the alleviation of human suffering and the promotion of the human spirit through the systematic application of therapeutic recreation as a health-oriented service.

Jerry D. Kelley
University of Maryland

PREFACE

Most therapeutic recreation textbooks have been written for the introductory course market (e.g., Frye & Peters, 1972; Avedon, 1974; Kraus, 1978; O'Morrow, 1980). Until Gunn and Peterson's (1978) book on program design became available, no textbook existed for upper-level undergraduate courses or graduate-level courses in therapeutic recreation. Instructors of therapeutic recreation courses dealing with processes and techniques have relied on journal articles or textbooks written for allied fields for readings.

I wrote this book because there was a need for a book geared toward the actual practice, or the *how,* of therapeutic recreation. Instead of providing information *about* therapeutic recreation services or client characteristics, I wrote a book that emphasizes substantive concerns involved in therapeutic recreation practice. Therefore there are many practical guidelines, exercises, and concrete examples throughout this book. Also, I have discussed not only theory but also the implications of theories to actual practice in therapeutic recreation.

Second, I wanted this book to go beyond a "commonsense" approach utilizing knowledge gained primarily from personal experiences. To do this, I have drawn on literature of professions such as psychiatry, education, nursing, and counseling as well as academic disciplines representing the behavioral sciences. This, I hope, will provide a broad and scholarly basis for understanding therapeutic recreation processes and techniques.

Finally, I wished to provide a book which is readable and easy to follow. Each chapter adheres to a set format that includes objectives to guide the students' learning. This structure is explained in detail in Chapter 1.

A word about the choice of terms for this book is in order. The term "client" has been used because it is widely accepted in the world of therapeutic recreation today and is a more universal term than patient, student, or resident. Also, the terms therapeutic recreation specialist and

TR specialist were consistently applied when referring to therapeutic recreation professionals.

I am indebted to many individuals and institutions for aid in the preparation of this book. I am particularly grateful for the work of my wife, Joan; in addition to authoring Chapter 7, she made many suggestions and edited drafts of the manuscript. Finally, I thank my friend, Vickie Robb, who assisted with the final preparation of the manuscript.

David R. Austin

CONTENTS

1

BASIC
CONCEPTS

PURPOSE OF THE CHAPTER

OBJECTIVES

ON HELPING OTHERS

WHAT MAJOR TOPICS ARE COVERED IN THIS BOOK?
Theoretical Knowledge—Theories and Therapies
The Therapeutic Recreation Process
Helping Others
Communication Skills
Being a Leader
Health and Safety Considerations

WHAT IS THE FORMAT FOR EACH CHAPTER?

WHERE IS THE FOCUS OF INSTRUCTION FOR THIS BOOK?

HOW ARE OBJECTIVES USED?

KEY WORDS

READING COMPREHENSION QUESTIONS

REFERENCE

PURPOSE OF THE CHAPTER

Therapeutic recreation service accomplishes its goals through the actions of specialists who serve clients as helping professionals. To become a competent helping professional, the therapeutic recreation specialist must gain both the theoretical and technical knowledge necessary for successful practice. Within this chapter an introduction to helping others and to the content and format of the book is presented.

OBJECTIVES

- Comprehend the nature of the content contained within this book.
- Grasp what makes the TR specialist different from the layperson.
- Know the major topics to be covered in this book.
- Understand the format followed in each chapter.
- Recognize that the approach taken within this book is to make the student the focus for instruction.

Since there are other books on therapeutic recreation, one might ask, "Why add another one to the collection?" One reason might be that an improved version of prior works is needed. However, there are already several well-prepared works among the current therapeutic recreation textbooks. I have written this book because I believe there is a great deal of information regarding therapeutic recreation that has not been covered in previously published textbooks.

Introductory therapeutic recreation textbooks necessarily provide information about TR services and client characteristics but do not deal extensively with the actual delivery of direct client service. This book marks a departure from the "survey" type of textbooks that have served the profession well as literature for introductory courses in therapeutic recreation. It is aimed toward the *how* of TR. Although it is based largely on theory, the book covers basic helping skills required in the practice of therapeutic recreation.

ON HELPING OTHERS

We, in therapeutic recreation, are at a point in our evolution when we require literature that will expand our knowledge of the processes and techniques so central to the delivery of direct client services. In successful helping relationships we assist the client to meet a problem or need. If we are able to do a better job at this than the client can do alone or with family or friends, we must possess more than good intentions. The difference between a layperson's approach to the client and that of the trained practitioner is that the practitioner bases his or her service on processes and techniques drawn from the theoretical, scientific, and experiential knowledge of his or her profession. People rely on therapeutic recreation practitioners to have the theory and skills that will enable them to do things they could not accomplish themselves.

It is therefore critical that basic processes and techniques of therapeutic recreation be thoroughly understood and skillfully applied by those practicing in the profession. This book will provide professional information that will assist those developing themselves for careers in therapeutic recreation to gain competencies necessary for the provision of quality therapeutic recreation services.

WHAT MAJOR TOPICS ARE COVERED IN THIS BOOK?

THEORETICAL KNOWLEDGE—THEORIES AND THERAPIES

One distinction between the layperson and the professional is that the professional draws on theory as a basis for action. The professional operates from the theoretical framework from which practice springs. Differentiating among psychoanalytic, behavioristic, growth psychology, and other theories—and therapeutic approaches related to these orientations—provides a fundamental level of knowledge for the TR specialist.

THE THERAPEUTIC RECREATION PROCESS

The TR process is a systematic method of problem solving applied to therapeutic recreation. Through a progression of steps involving assessment, planning, implementation, and evaluation, the TR process is utilized to bring about changes in the client and the client's environment.

HELPING OTHERS

Therapeutic recreation takes place through interpersonal relations. Helping people is a complex act, an act that calls for an understanding of human behavior and of the effective helper and the helping relationship. This understanding is an essential ingredient for the TR specialist in order to bring about the therapeutic use of self. Also vital to TR specialists is the development of self-awareness. To know ourselves is a basic competency necessary in helping others. Self-awareness is a prerequisite for entering into a helping relationship if we believe we must know ourselves in order to help others.

COMMUNICATION SKILLS

All interpersonal relationships depend on communication. Without communication, no relationship can ever exist, since relationships depend on a two-way sharing of ideas and experiences (Sundeen et al., 1975). This is unquestionably true in helping relationships in therapeutic recreation, where our clients are not passive puppets on strings waiting to be manipulated, but active participants who interact with therapeutic recreation specialists to facilitate change.

BEING A LEADER

One of the most critical elements in therapeutic recreation is leadership. The interactions that occur between the leader and the client, and among clients, are central to the success of TR programs. Skills in leadership provide the TR specialist with the means to employ therapeutic interventions or facilitate client growth. Leadership in TR calls for competencies in dealing with both individuals and groups.

HEALTH AND SAFETY CONSIDERATIONS

Theory forms the underpinnings for professional practice; however, TR professionals also must possess certain technical knowledge and skills. Among the areas of technical knowledge that may be required in TR are the employment of first aid and safety procedures with members of specific client groups, the proper use of mechanical aids, procedures for transfers, and assistive techniques, and information on the effects of commonly employed psychotropic and anticonvulsant drugs.

WHAT IS THE FORMAT FOR EACH CHAPTER?

Each chapter begins with a brief *statement of purpose*, which is followed by a listing of the major *objectives* for the chapter. At the conclusion of the chapter there is a *key words* section in which terms essential to the chapter are defined. In addition to the traditional listing of references for the chapter, *reading comprehension questions* are provided in order to guide the student's reading within each chapter. They will also serve the instructor and students as class discussion questions.

Within the chapter the student will find questions or statements heading each section. These questions or statements are often designed to break down further the objectives for the chapter into smaller, more digestible parts.

4

Thus each chapter will begin with a statement of purpose followed by: (1) objectives for the chapter, (2) questions or statements heading each section of the chapter, (3) key words, (4) reading comprehension questions, and (5) references for the chapter.

WHERE IS THE FOCUS OF INSTRUCTION FOR THIS BOOK?

You, the reader, are the central point of focus for this book. The focus is on *you* and the *objectives* you must achieve in order to possess competencies necessary to meet the personal and professional demands that will be made on you as a therapeutic recreation specialist. Your mastery of the skills, attitudes, and knowledge required for professional service in therapeutic recreation is critical to your personal success and that of your profession.

HOW ARE OBJECTIVES USED?

The objectives at the beginning of each chapter form a road map for learning. You will know the objectives that have been stipulated for attainment. Making clear and explicit the path to the goal or purpose of each chapter through the listing of major objectives will enhance learning and remove the mystique that sometimes accompanies, and plagues, instruction.

KEY WORDS

Therapeutic Recreation Specialist. A person prepared for the responsibility of applying appropriate strategies in order to facilitate growth and development and help prevent or relieve problems of clients from special populations groups through the provision of recreation or leisure services.

Helping Relationship. An interpersonal relationship between a person or persons with special problems or needs and a person skilled in techniques to help meet these problems or needs. The goal of the relationship is to facilitate clients in assuming responsibility for themselves; it is not to solve their problems for them. The relationship is directed toward maximizing the clients' growth potential and preventing or relieving problems.

Objectives. As applied here, objectives state the general learning outcomes expected from the study of each chapter. They describe student behavior, not what the instructor will do.

Theory. A systematically related set of statements stipulating relationships or underlying principles, including some lawlike generalizations from which testable hypotheses may be drawn. From a practical perspective, theory provides a unifying focus for the assumptions underlying practice and a basis for leadership action, since it provides the beliefs and assumptions that affect our approach to helping others.

Reading Comprehension Questions

1 How does this book claim to differ from the traditional "survey" textbooks often used in introductory TR courses?
2 Why does the TR practitioner need more than "good intentions" in order to practice sucessfully?
3 What makes the TR specialist, or any professional helper, different from the layperson?
4 Outline the parts or items found in each chapter.
5 Where is the focus of the book directed?

REFERENCE

Sundeen, S. J., Stuart, G. W., Rankin, E.D., & Cohen, S. P. 1975. *Nurse-client interaction: Implementing the nursing process.* Saint Louis: The C. V. Mosby Company.

KEY WORDS

2

THEORETICAL KNOWLEDGE— THEORIES AND THERAPIES

PURPOSE OF THE CHAPTER

OBJECTIVES

WHAT IS THE ECLECTIC APPROACH?

WHAT ARE THE MAJOR THEORIES OF HELPING?
Psychoanalytic Approach
Behavioristic Approach
Growth Psychology Approach

OTHER THERAPEUTIC APPROACHES

Rational-Emotive Therapy
Reality Therapy
Transactional Analysis
Psychodrama
Bibliotherpy
Therapeutic Community
Relaxation Training
Stress Reduction and Physical Activity
Assertiveness Training
Values Clarification
Reality Orientation
Remotivation
Resocialization
Sensory Training

A SUMMING UP

KEY WORDS

READING COMPREHENSION QUESTIONS

REFERENCES

PURPOSE OF THE CHAPTER

There is no one preferred therapeutic approach found in therapeutic recreation. Instead, a great variety of methods are applied in the clinical, rehabilitative, continued care, educational and recreational environments in which therapeutic recreation takes place. Understandably, the emerging TR specialist may be confused by the diversity of approaches in practice today. This chapter will help the reader to grasp a fundamental understanding of therapeutic approaches that apply to intervention and counseling in the diverse settings in which therapeutic recreation services are delivered.

OBJECTIVES

- Appreciate the role of theory in influencing the practice of therapeutic recreation.
- Know what is meant by the eclectic approach.
- Differentiate among psychoanalytic, behavioristic, and growth psychology theories of human nature.
- Assess selected therapeutic approaches to understand implications for practice in therapeutic recreation.
- Define basic terminology and concepts of therapeutic approaches related to therapeutic recreation.
- Accept responsibility to begin to formulate personal theoretical notions in harmony with abilities, beliefs, and interests.

Theory was defined in Chapter 1 as a unifying focus for the assumptions that underlie therapeutic approaches. Also in Chapter 1, a case was made for the necessity of theory to direct methods of practice. Following this reasoning, theory furnishes a basis for action, since it provides beliefs, concepts, and assumptions that directly bear on the selection of specific therapeutic techniques. Even without formally studying the the-

8

ories related to helping, each of us form personal beliefs and assumptions that operate to guide our everyday actions (Okun, 1976). No doubt you have already begun to develop your own theory for practice, although you may not have systematically analyzed your theory to determine if it consistently and comprehensively integrates the beliefs, concepts, and assumptions from which it is comprised.

WHAT IS THE ECLECTIC APPROACH?

Therapeutic recreation is characterized by electicism, or the utilization of approaches and techniques drawn from several sources. The rationale for this eclectic approach is that even though each of the widely accepted therapeutic approaches has strong points, no single one has all the answers. Therefore, instead of imposing a specific approach on all clients, methods are dictated by the nature of client needs under the eclectic approach. By gaining familiarity with major theories and approaches, the TR specialist can select and combine the most appropriate techniques from a variety of sources. Of course, techniques chosen for actual practice should be in harmony with the personal abilities, beliefs, and interests of the therapeutic recreation specialist as well as with the policies and practices of the agency in which he or she is employed.

A bewildering number of therapeutic approaches exist for the student of therapeutic recreation to absorb. I will first discuss the three major theoretical approaches to human behavior and techniques that relate to them. Then I will deal with each of the remaining therapeutic approaches in a separate section.

WHAT ARE THE MAJOR THEORIES OF HELPING?

The three major theories of human behavior related to helping are the psychoanalytic, behavioristic, and growth psychology theories. In this section each of these major theoretical orientations will be briefly described.

PSYCHOANALYTIC APPROACH

Sigmund Freud's work represents a great contribution to the world of psychiatry, clinical psychology, and psychological theory. As a physician who proposed a psychological view of mental disorders in contrast to the then traditional organic view, Freud was not accepted by his medical colleagues. For the greater part of his career, he was viewed by the medical community as an extremist obsessed by sex (Maddi, 1972). Yet no other individual had the profound influence on psychological theory and treatment that Freud ultimately produced through the development of his psychoanalytic approach.

Freud proposed that there are basic instincts common to all people. These instincts have biological origin, but they are at the core of personality because of the powerful influence they have on thought and behavior. When an instinct is felt, it is an indication that the person is in a state of deprivation. This state of deprivation produces tension that the individual must somehow handle. Therefore the goal of instincts is to relieve tension produced by biologically induced deprivation. These instinctual drives emergize humans into action (Maddi, 1972).

Central to Freud's view is the assumption that there exists within each person a basic tendency to allow the maximum gratification of the primitive instincts, while giving minimum attention to the demands of society. This clash between maximizing instinctual desires and minimizing punishment and guilt resulting from society's social controls is the source of all goal-directed behavior. Adjustments in life center around the ability to meet this conflict by working out a compromise among self-centered, selfish, instinctual demand and the requirements of society (Maddi, 1972; Alderman, 1974).

Freud proposed a balance model in order to conceptualize the dynamics underlying this basic conflict. Under his model he identified three divisions of personality: the *id, superego,* and *ego.* All goal-directed behavior results from the interaction of these three systems.

The *id* is the primitive part of us. It is propelled by three major instinctual, biological drives. The first, the *self-preservation* instinct, preserves biological life. It deals with our basic needs for food, water, and oxygen. The other two major forces are the *sexual instinct* and the *aggression instinct* (which Freud later developed into the death instinct).

Freud gave much attention to the sexual instinct, which played an integral part in his theory. He termed the energy for sexual urges the *libido,* which induces action when sexual expression has been deprived. According to Freud's early writings, complete gratification of the sexual instinct was produced only by having intercourse with a person of the opposite sex. Other sexual activity was seen to lead to only partial fulfillment (Maddi, 1972). Later, however, Freud broadened his view of the sexual instinct to include pleasurable sensation from the erogenous zones and unidentified "inner" responses that produce pleasurable sensations (Ford & Urban, 1963). Therefore it may be noted that Freud eventually broadly defined the term sex to refer to almost anything pleasurable. The sexual instinct was perceived by Freud to develop to an adult level of maturity through five psychosexual stages (oral, anal, phallic, latent, and

10

genital). However, if the child was overindulged or overrestricted during any stage, a partial fixation with that stage could develop. Such a fixation would later be revealed in adult life (Borden & Stone, 1976).

The aggressive instinct leads to free-floating aggressive energy that builds up to the point that aggression must be expressed. Even though it may be displaced or sublimated, the aggressive urge will rebuild and, once again, must be released. The release of aggression is therefore a continual process (Austin, 1971).

The sexual and aggressive urges and emotions of the id are extremely selfish and self-centered. The id is propelled by raw forces of biological necessity, without accompanying social refinement. The process of seeking immediate gratification without concern for reality or moral constraint was termed by Freud as *pleasure principle functioning.*

The second system of personality is the *superego.* The superego is the person's social conscience. Its crucial role is to incorporate societal values that balance the impulsiveness of the id. Through the superego we take in, or internalize, socializing forces. Not surprisingly, much of the content for internalization comes from our parents or parent figures. Other prime teachers of societal values and beliefs are family members, peer group members, and other significant people in our lives. Once the roles of society are internalized, individuals are no longer controlled primarily by threat of punishment but by the guilt they experience if they transgress against their personal moral codes. Young people commonly have not formed their own value systems. Having not yet learned the rules of society, they are more likely to function at the level of the pleasure principle and, therefore, must be controlled by threat from parents, police, and other authority figures who have the power to levy punishment. At the other extreme, "mental illness" may occur when the superego has become too strict or unrealistic, and the person cannot cope with the resulting conflict.

The final system of personality is the *ego.* The ego is the moderator between the id and superego. It balances the primitive forces of the id with the structures the superego attempts to impose. Two functions are thus performed by the ego. The first is to aid in the satisfaction of instincts within the reality demands of the external world. The second function is to allow the expression of instinctual urges consistent with the demands of the superego. In carrying out these functions, the ego is guided by *reality principle functioning,* which leads to the realistic integration of the id's urges by arriving at a compromise that will meet the requirements of society. Thus the ego is the socialized unit of personality that allows people to make intelligent choices, taking into consideration the demands of the id, superego, and the environment. It is the part of the mind that controls higher cognitive powers and engages in realistic thinking based on accumulated experiences and perceptions of the environment.

In order to meet the instinctual demands of the id while defending against the moral structures of the superego, the ego may turn to the use of *ego defense mechanisms*. Defense mechanisms function unconsciously to protect us when we feel a threat to the integrity of our ego, or sense of self-concept. They put up a protective shield against psychic pain by displacing the energy of instinctive urges of the id toward objects or actions other than those from which they originated (Alderman, 1974). Among the commonly employed defenses are denial, repression, displacement, projection, sublimation, rationalization, and intellectualization. These defense mechanisms are outlined in Table 2-1. All the defenses are covered in most abnormal psychology textbooks. For example, Coleman's (1980) abnormal psychology textbook lists 14 defense mechanisms.

Before turning to psychoanalytic views directly related to play and recreation, it may be appropriate to discuss briefly the distinction between *psychoanalysis* and treatment based on psychoanalytic principles. Psychoanalysis is a long, drawn out therapy based primarily on exploring

---

Table 2-1   Common Defenses

Denial. The source of distress is not acknowledged or perceived because it is too threatening. The person refuses to admit being frightened by an event or action of another individual.

Repression. Unacceptable or anxiety-provoking thoughts or feelings are blotted out of consciousness. People forget threatening occurences.

Displacement. Emotions are transferred from the original person or object to a less formidable, or safer, target. It is the "kick the cat" defense.

Sublimation. Directing a socially unacceptable desire or activity into a socially acceptable one. For example, releasing sexual urges through dance.

Projection. Rejecting an unacceptable thought or feeling by blaming it on another person. By attributing it to someone else, the unacceptable thought or feeling is removed from the person.

Intellectualization. Painful emotions or feelings associated with an event are explained away by the use of a rational explanation.

Rationalization. A socially acceptable reason is given to avoid having to face a nonacceptable belief about oneself.

---

the unconscious to make it conscious. In orthodox psychoanalysis the patient is encouraged to transfer unknowingly to the therapist (psychoanalyst) attitudes and feelings the patient has held toward significant others. Through this expression of attitudes and feelings, the therapist can examine the patient's reactions. This process of identifying the therapist with a person from the patient's past is called *transference*. Supposedly the awareness gained by the patient through transference allows him or her to become free from past confusion and conflict. The term *countertransference* is used to describe the process when the therapist responds to the client as though he or she were someone from the therapist's past. Countertransference is not sought and must be guarded against by the therapist so that the client is responded to genuinely and not like another person from the therapist's past. Psychoanalytic psychotherapy, on the other hand, does not deal with extensive probing of the unconscious but employs psychoanalytic principles in dealing with specific problems in living (Kovel, 1976; Blackham, 1977). Play therapy, as discussed in the next paragraph, is a type of psychoanalytic psychotherapy for children.

Children's play was seen by Freud as a partial means to master painful or tension-producing experiences by acting them out over and over again. The purpose of repetitious play, in which children portray events they have experienced, is to absorb and incorporate unpleasant experiences or excessive stimuli into the ego, according to Freud's theory. Through play, children grasp the situation and feel mastery, or control, over reality (Ellis, 1973). Play therapy, as developed by psychcanalytic theorists, is based on this basic idea that symbolic play offers a means for the child to bring real life problems to the surface in order to be able to deal with them and establish control over them. In play therapy children are allowed to play out traumatic experiences under the direction of a therapist schooled in psychoanalytic theory. This therapist applies psychoanalytic principles during play sessions to help the child to understand the meaning behind these play activities.*

Psychoanalytic theorists have presented the positive effects of play and recreation in helping people to lead happier lives. Among these theorists have been the eminent psychiatrists Karl and William Menninger, who have suggested recreation activities as a means to discharging sexual and aggressive impulses in a socially acceptable manner (Menninger, 1960; Gussen, 1967). The influence of psychoanalytic theory has also found its way into therapeutic recreation literature. Meyer (1962), in a paper entitled, "The Rationale of Recreation as Therapy," discussed the strength-

---

*Not all play therapists follow the psychoanalytic mode. Axline (1969), for instance, is a follower of Rogers' nondirective approach.

ening of defense mechanisms through recreation activities. Included was information on the substitution of acceptable activities for aggressive impulses, the sublimation of sexual urges through dance and other art forms, and the development of skills to compensate for real or imagined inadequacies. O'Morrow (1971) in an article entitled "The Whys of Recreation Activities for Psychiatric Patients," suggested that therapeutic recreation activities provide approved outlets for aggression and other emotions by facilitating sublimation and permitting unconscious conflicts to be expressed.

The idea that recreation can provide outlets for pent-up aggressive urges has been widely accepted. Ventilating aggression supposedly provides a safe opportunity to rid the individual of aggressive energy. Sports and competitive games have been seen as proper outlets through which to express aggression in order to bring about what has been termed a cathartic effect. Freud is credited with developing the cathartic theory although, from the days of Aristotle, people have felt that venting an emotion can free a person from that emotion. Two ideas underlie the cathartic notion. One is that the expression of aggression can provide relief from the tension or make a person feel better. The second is that the person who expresses aggression will have a tendency to be less aggressive (Austin, 1971).

Quanty (1976) and Berkowitz (1978) have completed extensive reviews of the evidence regarding the cathartic notion. Their research indicates that viewing aggressive sports does not drain any aggression but actually *increases* it. Likewise, both reported similar findings in regard to actual participation in aggressive activities. That is, participation in aggressive activities only made people more aggressive. There is, therefore, a great deal of suggestive evidence that while aggressive responses may have tension-reduction properties and make people feel better, they also lead to more aggressive behavior. Aggression when rewarded, or at least condoned, simply brings about further aggression. If children or adults are encouraged to behave aggressively during recreation participation it would be expected that they will become more aggressive, not less aggressive, as once hypothesized.

Quanty (1976) has pointed out that the social learning model (i.e., behavior can be socially reinforced) contains the implication that prosocial responses to frustration can be just as effectively reinforced as aggressive responses. Therefore nonaggressive responses to anger can produce tension reduction and lead to more healthy interpersonal relationships.

Although the cathartic notion that aggression may be reduced through participation in aggressive recreation activities has been brought to question by the authorities previously cited and others (e.g., Martens, 1975;

14 WHAT ARE THE MAJOR THEORIES OF HELPING?

Parke & Sawin, 1975), the general influence of psychoanalytic theory may be felt in the practice of therapeutic recreation today. Hunnicutt (1979) has called for a reexamination of Freudian and neo-Freudian views as a possible model for adult therapeutic recreation services.

Summary
Within this section, Freud's psychoanalytic theory has been presented as a conflict model involving three systems of personality (id, ego, and superego) and two primary instinctual drives (sex and aggression). His theory attached a great deal of significance to unconscious factors operating in the id and superego and to the mediating role of the ego. Freud's classic pschoanalytic theory also placed great emphasis on the biological determinism reflected in the instinctual urges that supposedly propel behavior (although neo-Freudians have placed greater emphasis on social and cultural aspects as determinants of behavior). Although it is no longer the sole form of psychotherapy as it once was, the psychoanalytic approach is usually what comes to mind when the average person thinks of therapy (Kovel, 1976), and it continues to represent an influence on therapeutic recreation.

Implications for Therapeutic Recreation
Therapeutic recreation specialists will not conduct psychoanalytically oriented psychotherapy, but the theoretical ideas represented by the psychoanalytic viewpoint will likely pervade the practice of TR specialists. Therapeutic recreation specialists must recognize that unconscious motivational factors may affect behavior, the use of defense mechanisms in protecting against threats to self-concept, and the effects the developmental years have on adult behavior (Okun, 1976). Therapeutic recreation specialists must review the evidence for themselves to determine if it is appropriate to encourage clients to discharge aggressive impulses through socially acceptable recreation activities, since previously accepted psychoanalytic principles have been refuted by numerous researchers and theorists. Ideas concerning the releasing of aggressive urges have commonsense appeal, but current evidence strongly suggests that these concepts may lack the validity once afforded them by therapeutic recreation specialists.

BEHAVIORISTIC APPROACH

In the 1960s there emerged a new form of intervention that became known as behavior therapy or behavior modification. Many use the terms interchangably; however, the term *behavior therapy* seems to be employed mostly in psychiatric practice, while *behavior modification* is associated with other client groups, such as the mentally retarded. No matter what terminology is used to describe the behavioristic approach, it is concerned with bringing about changes in behavior. The theory and techniques used to bring about behavioral changes are based on the psychological theory of behaviorism.

Behaviorism arose as a protest to the psychoanalytic model. In contrast to the psychoanalytic approach, where emphasis is on hidden, unconscious forces that underlie behavior, the basis for behaviorism comes from academic learning theory. John B. Watson is noted as the founder of behaviorism. In 1913 he wrote the paper "Psychology as The Behaviorist Sees It" (Watson, 1913), in which he set down basic positions of behaviorism. Watson attacked subjectivity, saying that psychology should not be concerned with subjective experiences but with overtly observable behavior.

Followers of this new school of psychology also rejected the concept of "mental illness." Instead, they assumed that abnormal behavior was not a disease; like most behavior—adaptive and maladaptive—it, too, was learned.

The basic concepts of behaviorism spring from the early work of Pavlov and Thorndike. Pavlov emphasized the simple association of events that become linked when they repeatedly occur together. This theory, which became known as *classical conditioning,* or *respondent conditioning,* involves substituting one stimulus-evoking response for another. In Pavlov's famous dog study there was the pairing of one stimulus to which there was already a set response (salivation to food) with a neutral stimulus (the sound of a bell). After a number of pairings, the neutral stimulus (in this case, the bell) begins to take on the characteristics of the first stimulus (food—bringing on salivation). The *unconditioned stimulus* (food) and the *conditioned stimulus* (bell) become connected to bring about the *response* (saliva).

Thorndike emphasized that behavior is controlled by its consequences. That is, rewards function to reinforce certain behaviors, whereas negative outcomes tend to eliminate the occurence of behavior. A reinforcer is basically anything that reinforces behavior. Commonly employed reinforcers include food, money, attention, affection, and approval or praise. The potency of a reinforcer depends on the need state of the person. For example, food would be a poor reinforcer after dinner. Candy would not be a good reinforcer for someone on a diet. B. F. Skinner has more recently been associated with this line of thought, which has been termed *operant conditioning* or *instrumental conditioning.* The terms come from the idea that it involves voluntary actions that operate on the environment instead of just responding to the environment as in respondent conditioning.

Pavlov's theory (classical or respondent conditioning) involves the *principle of association,* while Thorndike's theory (operant or instrumental conditioning) involves the *principle of reinforcement.* These two basic principles help to form the foundation for techniques of the behavioral approach (McDavid & Harari, 1968; Berkowitz, 1972).

What specific intervention techniques have resulted from the behavioral approach? Terms such as positive reinforcement, extinction, modeling, shaping, chaining, prompting, fading, time-out, token economies, and the Premack principle may be familiar as techniques that have a basis in the behavioral approach. The following section will briefly review each of these techniques based on information drawn primarily from Diebert and Harmon (1970), Hunter, and Carlson (1971), and Vernon (1972).

The idea of *positive reinforcement* is that people tend to repeat behaviors that provide rewards. Any behavior that is followed by a positive reinforcer (reward) is likely to be repeated. Teaching new behaviors or increasing the occurence of existing behaviors therefore depends on the participants finding the behaviors rewarding. Following this train of thought logically, even frequently repeated behavior that seems to be inappropriate or unproductive must somehow be rewarding for those who perform them.

While we may first think of M&M candies as a reinforcer, people find many things to be rewarding. As previously mentioned, rewards include food and money as well as social reinforcers such as attention, affection, and approval. (A list of social reinforcers is found in Table 2-2.) More subtle are rewards gained from discovery or learning that people may gain as outcomes of educational or recreational experiences (Vernon, 1972). According to Vernon, children are least affected by subtle reinforcers. Therefore food is often initially used as a reinforcer in programs serving children. After a short while, praise is given along with the food and, occasionally, praise is given alone. Gradually, praise is used more and more by itself as a reinforcer.

Attention can be a potent reinforcer whether provided in the form of praise or approval or just paying attention to the child. As a matter of fact, the leader must be on guard not to give too much attention to those who act out or behave inappropriately. Children who feel neglected may cause problems just to draw attention to themselves. Positive outlets must be found for these children so that they can receive rewards for appropriate behaviors.

If desirable behavior exists it has been reinforced. It follows that the

Table 2-2 Possible Social Reinforcers

Actions
  Pat on the back
  Nod
  Clap hands with nod
  Hug
  Wink
  Smile
  Laughing with the client
  Handshake
  Glance of recognition
  Gestures of approval
  Have client demonstrate
  Rub child's head
  Pat child on knee
  Hold child on lap
Words

Hooray	Groovy
Beautiful	Sharp
Right on	Super
Fantastic	Great
Wonderful	Yes
Yeah	Good
Unreal	Nice
Okay	Fine
Wow!	Exactly
Atta girl (boy)	All right
Perfect	Of course
Terrific	Fabulous
Marvelous	Congratulations
Clever	Charming
Delightful	Brilliant
Oh, yeah	Uh huh
Positively	Go ahead
Nifty	Correct
Far out	Thank you

Other Possibilities

That's really nice.	Very interesting.
Keep up the good work.	Good thinking.
You look great.	Out of sight.
You son of a gun!	Nice going.

18

Good for you.	You're the best I've seen today.
That's great.	You are really trying.
Good job!	You've got it!
That's better.	You make it look easy.
Excellent work.	Not bad for a professor.
You did it!	I'm glad you're here.

Source. Some words and phrases drawn from D. R. Austin, 1975. "75 ways to say good for you," *TRAPS, 19*(1), 15, and C. K. Madsen & C. H. Madsen, 1972. *Parents/children/discipline: A positive approach.* Boston: Allyn and Bacon, Inc.

simplest way to get rid of a behavior is to stop reinforcing it and it will go away. Each time a behavior is emitted without being reinforced, the strength or frequency of that behavior is diminished. This process of withholding reinforcement is termed *extinction.*

The timing of the delivery of reinforcers is critical to their success. To have the greatest effect, they should come immediately after the behavior occurs. For this reason, athletes in Special Olympics competitions are rewarded immediately following completion of their events. The frequency of reinforcers is likewise important. During the time when behaviors are first being established, a *continuous schedule* of reinforcement seems to be best. The reward should occur every time the person performs the behavior if at all practical. Once the behavior has been established, it is possible to change to a *partial schedule* of rewarding the person only once in a while. This should be done slowly by gradually reducing the frequency of giving reinforcement. Diebert and Harmon (1970) suggest first decreasing reinforcement patterns to reinforce 80 percent of the time, then 50 percent, then 30 percent and, finally, only once in a while.

Shaping is another technique in reinforcement or operant conditioning. It is the process by which reinforcement is differentially applied to the responses that are made toward approximating a desired behavior. Reinforcement is delivered only when a particular standard is reached. Once reached, the standard is continually raised until the person being rewarded makes a closer and closer approximation of the behavior that is being conditioned. Eventually, the final form of desired behavior is reached. *Chaining* is an associated concept that involves linking one learned response with another to build to a more complex response.

Modeling is a form of social learning that may employ reinforcement. Through modeling, new responses can be acquired more quickly if the learner can see a model demonstrate the desired behavior, especially if this is combined with positive reinforcement. Responses can be learned through modeling combined with either seeing the model rewarded or the learner directly receiving a reward. Rawson (1978) has reported success in the use of modeling and reinforcement to alter the behavior of behaviorally disordered children in a camping program.

Wehman and Rettie (1975) have used modeling and social reinforcement in developing play behaviors with severely retarded young women. Wehman (1977) has also reported using various other behavior modification techniques to help severely and profoundly retarded children develop play patterns. Among the techniques employed were *prompting* and *fading*. In prompting the leader physically guides the child through the desired play skill. For instance, the child is manually guided to pull a wagon or roll a ball. Successes are followed by praise and affection. Fading involves gradually removing the physical guidance of the prompts when the play skill has become learned.

A procedure often employed in behavior modification programs for children is *time-out*. Time-out is used as an alternative to punishment when the behavior of a child is disruptive or may be harmful to himself or herself or to the group. It involves simply removing the child for a short time from the setting in which others are able to gain positive reinforcement. This is done in matter of factly without berating the child. Typically, the time-out room is a small, plain room devoid of stimuli so that there is nothing for the child to do. Therefore time-out involves stimulus removal in contrast to punishment's stimulus delivery.

Token economies are found in residential settings. Tokens are given by staff members to the residents as rewards for performing selected behaviors that have been determined to be desirable. The tokens are made of plastic or some other inexpensive material and have no value in themselves, but they can be redeemed for items or privileges that have value to the residents. Recreation participation has been used in some facilities as a privilege that may be earned with tokens. Woods (1971) has described one such token economy program, called PAYREC, in a residential school for mentally retarded children.

The final behavior modification procedure to be discussed is the widely accepted *Premack principle*. Premack introduced the idea that naturally highly preferred behavior can be used to reinforce a less preferred behavior. For example, quiet activity of children (the less preferred behavior) might be reinforced by allowing the children to have outside play on the playground (a naturally highly preferred activity). This procedure has several obvious advantages. One is that highly preferred behaviors are easily observed, so appropriate reinforcers can be predicted relatively simply for a given individual. Second, because activities are used as rein-

WHAT ARE THE MAJOR THEORIES OF HELPING?

forcers, a behavior can be increased without depending on outside rewards such as candy or other food.

Schmokel (1980), in an unpublished student research project, has called to question the validity of the Premack principle alone to predict behavioral outcomes adequately. According to Schmokel, a better explanation is the Response Depreviation Hypothesis proposed by Timberlake and Allison (1974). Under this hypothesis either a highly preferred behavior *or* a less preferred (low-rate) behavior can serve as a reinforcer. The key is that the individual is deprived of his or her normal level of activity until he or she increases the sought behavior above its accustomed level. Even a relatively low-rate behavior can be used as a reinforcer if the person is deprived from participating in it at the accustomed level. On the other hand, a high-preference activity will not serve as a reinforcer unless the individual feels deprived of participation at the normal level of activity. Thus the Premack principle, by itself, does not seem to explain reinforcement patterns sufficiently.

Implications for Therapeutic Recreation

The focus of the behavioristic approach is clearly on the objective observation of overt behavior and the learning of new behaviors. This approach emphasizes the need to make precise behavioral observations and consider conditions that may alter behavior. Therapeutic recreation specialists must be accountable by providing outcome measures resulting from designated plans and continually examining reward systems that surround and influence client behavior (Okun, 1976). Specific behavior modification procedures may prove useful in diverse therapeutic recreation settings ranging from institutions to camps. Behavior modification is a particularly effective approach in TR programs serving institutionalized mentally retarded residents (Woods, 1971; Wehman & Rettie, 1975; Wehman, 1977) and behaviorally disordered children (Rawson, 1978).

GROWTH PSYCHOLOGY APPROACH

The term "growth psychology" is taken from Schultz's (1977) book *Growth Psychology: Models of the Healthy Personality,* in which he presents the nontraditional views of figures such as Maslow, Allport, Fromm, Jung, Rogers, and Perls (most of whom would be considered to be humanistic psychologists). It is a fresh, new way of looking at human nature that rejects what many consider to be the negative and deterministic views presented by the psychoanalytic and behavioristic approaches. Growth psychologists do not see people as being primarily driven by instinctual urges or conditioned by the environment in a robotlike manner. Growth psychology recognizes biological drives and the influence of past learning, but it goes beyond previous theories to see people as being self-aware, capable of accepting or rejecting environmental influences, and generally in conscious control of their own destiny. Furthermore, under the growth model the emphasis is not so much on past failures and conflicts but on tapping previously unused creative talents and energies. In short, growth psychology takes a positive view of human nature in contrast to the relatively pessimistic picture offered by psychoanalytic theory and behaviorism.

Humanistic psychologists have been critical of the psychoanalytic and behavioristic approaches. A number of these criticisms have been presented by Borden and Stone (1976) in their book on human communication. The discussion that follows highlights an extensive review of the subject by these authors. First, the orthodox Freudians emphasize biological determinism and the behaviorists follow an environmental determinism. Neither assume that people have the intellectual and emotional capacity to be aware of their self-concepts and to be in control of their own destiny, so that they may engage in self-determination. Second, the traditional theories view humans as passive organisms who do not possess the will and ability to pursue actively their potentials for growth in a self-directed way. Third, psychoanalytic theory sees people as being driven by sexual and aggressive instincts; behavioristic theory views people as being motivated to seek pleasure and avoid pain. In contrast, humanistic theorists see people as being motivated to attain self-fulfillment, yet being able to transcend their personal needs for the betterment of others. A fourth point of criticism is in regard to the ability to enter into meaningful relationships with others. Of primary concern to psychoanalytic theory is the self-gratification of instinctual drives, while behavioristic theory focuses on doing things for rewards, instead of for altruistic reasons. Humanistic theory views humans as being capable of enduring relationships and forgoing personal needs out of the love for another. Finally, neither psychoanalytically oriented theorists nor behaviorists believe people are truly responsible for their own behavior. Psychoanalytically oriented theorists believe behaviors result from unconscious drives. Behaviorists perceive people to be controlled by the environment. In contrast, humanistic theorists see people as being responsible for their behavior. Since people have freedom of choice, they must assume responsibility for their actions. All of these notions are central to growth psychology, which views people as having to strive toward self-fulfillment in a self-aware, self-directed manner.

Schultz (1977) has referred to growth psychology as "health psychology," since it is concerned with wellness. Growth psychologists view mental health as more than the mere absence of neurosis or psychosis. Healthy persons are self-aware. They realize their strengths and weaknesses, and they do not pretend to be something they are not. They live in the present instead of dwelling on the past or fantasizing about the future. They are not satisfied to maintain the status quo but seek challenges and experiences in life.

Client-Centered Therapy

One of the most widely accepted growth-oriented therapeutic approaches is the *client-centered therapy* of Carl Rogers. To Rogers, people have the capacity to be rational thinkers who can assume responsibility for themselves and whose behavior will be constructive when given the freedom to set directions in life. People are seen as motivated by a basic tendency to seek growth (to actualize potentials) and self-enhancement (to feel positive regard).

As each person grows up, a sense of self begins to form. A positive concept of self is developed when a person receives love (positive regard) from others. If parents and significant others freely give love (unconditional positive regard) there is no need for defensive behavior or to feel guilty or unworthy. The person will feel good about himself or herself and will experience congruence between positive self-concept and life experiences with others.

When incongruence between the concepts of self and life experiences occurs, it is disturbing and poses a threat to established self-perception. Anxiety results and defense mechanisms become aroused. Through defense mechanisms experiences are distorted or denied in order to bring them in line with self-perceptions. Therefore psychological problems arise when incongruences exist between life experiences and self-concepts. Intervention through client-centered therapy allows the person to reestablish congruence and once again begin to pursue self-actualization.

The role of the helping professional in client-centered therapy is to display unconditional positive regard (complete acceptance) for the client. The basic hypothesis on which client-centered therapy rests is that the support of an empathetic, genuine, accepting helper will enable the client to change. Techniques are secondary to attitude, since the helper is not an expert with insight who can condition the client but someone to strengthen and support the client in efforts to become responsible for his or her own life. The helper is nonjudgmental and nondirective, providing an accepting atmosphere that will allow the client to assume the same positive self-regard the helper has shown the client. Since the client is obviously valued and cared for by the helper, the client begins to feel he or she is a person worth being cared for. In such a nurturing climate feelings are brought into awareness, and the client learns to revise his or her concepts of self to bring them into congruence with life experiences. Once this process is complete, the client no longer feels threatened and is open to new experiences (Meador & Rogers, 1973; Okun, 1976; Schultz, 1977).

Gestalt Therapy

A second well-known growth-oriented approach is *Gestalt therapy*. Frederick (Fritz) Perls conceived Gestalt therapy after he became disenchanted with Freud and psychoanalysis. The term "Gestalt" is a German word that implies an organized whole or a sense of wholeness.

Perls felt that many people repress impulses and wishes so that they become aware of only parts of themselves instead of knowing the whole self. Preconceived perfectionistic ideas cause these people to inhibit their feelings and impulses and to become afraid to express them. They live as they believe others expect them to behave. Instead of following natural and spontaneous responses guided by a true awareness of self and the world, external controls move them in stereotyped, predetermined ways. In short, they are directed by their environment rather than being self-directed.

Since they are unable to accept their own impulses and feelings, they project these onto others. By distorting the situation, they do not have to own up to their feelings. They may also deny that parts of themselves exist. Nevertheless, their hidden impulses and feelings will seek release in some indirect form such as a nervous tic or an ulcer.

The goal of Gestalt therapy is to restore the personality to wholeness. This is done by helping the client to gain a full awareness of what is really happening to him or her so that the person may recognize that he or she can be free of external regulations (including those that have become internalized). Without such awareness the person will be unable to be himself or herself and will continue to assume roles that he or she feels others expect.

Techniques of Gestalt therapy are aimed at opening up direct, immediate experiences so that the client can become aware of what he or she is feeling, thinking, and doing. The emphasis is always on present behavior (the "here and now") and on the direct expression of impulses, thoughts, and feelings instead of on following stereotyped social roles that keep people from becoming aware of their needs and feelings. The critical aspect of Gestalt therapy is, therefore, opening the person's awareness of real needs and feelings (which avoidance mechanisms have excluded from awareness) and having the person assume the responsibility to act directly to express his or her impulses and feelings.

In addition to awareness of the self, Perls presented two other levels of awareness: (1) awareness of the world, and (2) awareness of intervening fantasy between the self and the world. Gestalt therapy helps persons to become aware of the aspects of the personality that contain fantasy and irrational prejudices and to discontinue them so that they are no longer barriers between the self and the real world. In becoming aware of intervening fantasy, people see things as they really exist. They can then experience the world in the present instead of consuming energy dealing with prejudices and fantasies.

The methods of Gestalt therapy revolve around training people to observe themselves by bringing experiences into awareness so they can be examined. Techniques such as role playing and group awareness exercises are used to help clients get in touch with what they are experiencing so that they may become more deeply aware of themselves. The therapist remains active during therapy in order to redirect the client when he or she tries to avoid problems. Thus the therapist must remain alert to signals in tone of voice, posture, or other nonverbal cues that indicate true feelings are being denied so that the client's attention may be drawn to them.

The facilitation of client awareness is seen as the therapist's main responsibility. Once healthy awareness of the self and the world are established, unhealthy processes that substitute for growth and block self-actualization are removed. The healthy person can then actualize his or her potentials by responding spontaneously and naturally to needs and feelings (Freedman et al., 1975; Okun, 1976; Matson, 1977; Schultz, 1977).

Implications for Therapeutic Recreation

As stated in Chapter 3, the general humanistic orientation reflected in growth psychology has been felt in the philosophy and practice of therapeutic recreation. Many implications of the humanistic view of human nature are highlighted in that discussion and, therefore, are not covered here. Implications for the two specific therapies covered under growth psychology are briefly reviewed in the following paragraph.

Many of the skills of client-centered therapy may be applied in the daily practice of therapeutic recreation. Healthy interpersonal relationships, empathetic listening without levying judgment, and a warm, accepting climate are elements basic to the practice of therapeutic recreation. Like Gestalt therapists, TR specialists are interested in clients talking but also gaining personal awareness through experiences—including trying out new expressions of impulses and feelings. While certain skills of Gestalt therapy may be helpful in the practice of therapeutic recreation (such as Gestalt awareness exercises in leisure counseling), the emerging therapeutic recreation specialist should be warned that Gestalt techniques tend to take on a gimmicky quality in the hands of persons who have not had training in their use.

OTHER THERAPEUTIC APPROACHES

Many therapeutic approaches are not based directly on the assumption of one of the three major theories, yet they have value in intervention and counseling. Approaches discussed in this section are diverse in content and in their level of theorizing. Some have been used primarily in psychiatric settings. Psychodrama, rational-emotive therapy, relaxation training, bibliotherapy, and therapeutic community fall into this group. Others, such as reality orientation, remotivation, resocialization, and sensory training, have been employed mostly with elderly persons. Still others, such as reality therapy, transactional analysis, assertiveness training, and values clarification, have been used in an array of settings with a variety of client groups. Since the approaches presented in this section do not fit together into neat packages, no attempt has been made to group or arrange them systematically (with the exception of those primarily employed with the elderly, which are placed together). Therefore the order in which a particular approach is presented has nothing to do with its importance or its possible value to therapeutic recreation.

RATIONAL-EMOTIVE THERAPY

Rational-emotive therapy (RET) is a system of philosophy, a theory of personality, and a psychological treatment approach (Ellis, 1976). Albert Ellis' rational-emotive therapy relies heavily on the cognitive processes, or people's thinking processes. Its philosophical origins go back to a notion first put forth by Epictelus, an early philosopher, who wrote, "Men are disturbed not by things, but by the view which they make of them." Later this same thought was expressed by Shakespeare in *Hamlet* when he wrote: "There's nothing either good or bad but thinking makes it so" (Ellis, 1973).

Ellis (1973, 1976) uses an A-B-C theory. The A is the activating experience (or what the person irrationally believes causes C). C stands for the consequences (e.g., feel upset, worthless, depressed). B represents beliefs about A. B is the critical intervening variable that influences the way we look at what happens to us. Ellis holds that we value, perceive, or conceptualize first; then we feel. Therefore it is what we bring to each experience in the way of our beliefs, concepts, and attitudes (or our way of thinking) that influences our feelings.

26

According to RET, we have a predisposition to expand ourselves, to be creative and to experience enjoyment in the here and now. Ellis (1976) has written:

> *RET clearly defines appropriate feelings and rational beliefs as those aiding human survival and happiness—particularly those enabling you to accept objective reality, live amicably in a social group, relate intimately to a few members of this group, engage in productive work, and enjoy selectively chosen recreational pursuits (p. 21).*

However, we can also engage in irrational thinking involving absolutes ("I must") or perfection ("I should") or other irrational beliefs leading to inappropriate feelings. In short, we can be rigid and intolerant of ourselves to the point of destroying our health and happiness (Ellis, 1973). By entering into self-defeating thinking, we may become the creators of our own psychological disturbances. It is the task of RET to assist in changing basic self-defeating beliefs and attitudes in order to correct irrational thinking. Once this is done, we are rid of the emotional blockages that have prevented us from reaching our true potentials. Thus the basic goal of RET is not helping the client to solve a particular problem but to develop a new philosophy of life.

During therapy, RET therapists help the client identify irrational beliefs; they attack these beliefs, show the client they cannot be validated, and ultimately teach the client to change his or her irrational belief system (Ellis, 1973, 1976). In addition to therapy sessions, homework assignments utilizing behavioral techniques are also employed with RET clients.

Implications for Therapeutic Recreation

The most obvious implications of RET for the TR specialist are: (1) the strong relationship between cognitive processes (beliefs and attitudes) and feelings, and (2) the need for people to discard irrational thinking that prevents enjoyment in the here and now. It is particularly important that those doing leisure counseling be aware that beliefs and attitudes may block leisure enjoyment for many persons. For example, some people cannot escape work and feel guilty about having free time. Such persons might profit by examining the thinking that prevents them from enjoying leisure.

REALITY THERAPY

The focus of the reality therapy of William Glasser is on present behavior, facing reality, and taking responsibility for one's own needs. Responsibility and reality are central to Glasser's approach. Responsibility deals with achieving personal needs without depriving others from fulfilling their needs. Reality has to do with facing instead of denying the world around us (Glasser, 1965).

According to Glasser, the basic human needs are to find love and worth—or relatedness and respect. Those who fail to meet these psychological needs (those who feel lonely and worthless) escape hurt and pain by denying the world of reality. Psychotic persons who cannot make it in the real world cope with loneliness and worthlessness by withdrawing and creating their own worlds of reality. Some deny the laws of society and engage in crime or antisocial acts. Others may become physically ill and seek help for backaches, headaches, or other illnesses. Still others drink to escape feelings of inadequacy. Anyone of these and other denying responses are seen by Glasser to be irresponsible coping behaviors that have been learned throughout life (Glasser, 1965).

Reality therapy does not dwell on feelings but, instead, helps clients to examine their present behavior, confront irresponsible actions, and establish commitment to change. Once a client makes a plan, the therapist does not accept any excuses from the client. No matter what has occurred in the past, no excuse is accepted for irresponsible behavior in the present. Therefore, unlike conventional therapy, reality therapy emphasizes the present, not the past. Even though personal insights may be interesting, the therapist's interest lies in the actual behavior of the client, not the unconscious motivations that may be offered as an excuse for irresponsible behavior (Glasser & Zunin, 1973).

Because clients have the need to love and be loved and to feel worthwhile to themselves and others, it is necessary that the therapist build a firm relationship with the client. Involvement on the part of the therapist begins immediately to reduce the client's loneliness and worthlessness. Therefore a warm, caring attitude is mandated on the part of the therapist. Nevertheless, cautions Glasser (1976), the helping professional must be careful never to promise more involvement than he or she plans to provide.

Reality therapy has been used in a number of settings, including homes for delinquent children, outpatient mental health services, psychiatric hospitals, and public schools. Exhaustive training is not necessary in order to apply the principles of reality therapy. Parents, teachers, ministers, and work supervisors have successfully employed Glasser's approach (Glasser, 1976).

Implications for Therapeutic Recreation
Perhaps the major implication of reality therapy for therapeutic recreation specialists is that all helping relationships demand an accepting and understanding attitude and that positive involvement by the helper may

28

immediately reduce client feelings of loneliness and worthlessness. Through his or her personal relationship with the client, the TR specialist can provide a feeling of involvement and being cared for. The client can then become actively involved with others through participation in TR groups, ultimately leading to expanded involvements within ongoing recreation groups. Without such involvements people cannot help themselves to fulfill their needs to feel cared for and to care for others. A second implication is that clients can take responsibility to alter irresponsible behavior. Therapeutic recreation specialists must provide opportunities for clients to learn and try out social behaviors that will lead to new relationships and more satisfying involvements. The climate created in therapeutic recreation should provide an accepting atmosphere that encourages positive social interaction. The final implication from reality therapy is to help clients to live in the present. Therapeutic recreation, like reality therapy, is geared primarily toward helping people function in the here and now.

TRANSACTIONAL ANALYSIS

Transactional analysis (TA) is a theory of personality and social interaction conceived by Eric Berne. It is most commonly used as a basis for group therapy. Along with rational-emotive therapy and reality therapy, TA emerged in the 1950s. It was not, however, until Berne's book, *Games People Play* (1964), became a best-seller in the middle of the 1960s that transactional analysis gained popularity.

According to Berne's theory, there are four primary methods to understand human behavior: structural analysis (to understand ego states within a given individual); transactional analysis (to understand interactions between two people's ego states); racket and game analysis (to understand repetitive transactions that are useless and of a devious nature); and script analysis (to understand life plans formed in childhood on which adults base choices on how their lives should be lived) (Harris, 1976; Woollams et al., 1976).

Structural Analysis
People have the capacity to store recordings, or "tapes," of past experiences in the brain. From these, they can recall both information and feelings related to specific events, the most significant of which occur during the preschool years. Different tapes play back depending on which of three ego states a person is operating in—the Parent, Child, or Adult (Harris, 1976). Through structural analysis the ego state that is operating in a given individual at a particular time is identified.

The source of the *Parent ego state* is a massive tape of external experiences absorbed during the most formative years (birth to age 6). An enormous store of attitudes, beliefs, values, and rules for living learned primarily from parents (or parent substitutes) direct patterns of behavior of the Parent. A person's Parent can be nurturing or controlling and critical. In either case, these attitudes can be expressed directly in the individual's words, demeanor, voice tone, and expressions or gestures—or indirectly as an effect on the Adult or Child. Associated with the Controlling Parent would be words such as "bad," "should," "ought," and "always," a stern and judgmental demeanor, a critical or condescending tone of voice, and gestures such as pointing the index finger. The Nurturing Parent would use words such as "good," "nice," "cute," and "I love you," a caring demeanor, a warm tone of voice, and expressions and gestures such as smiling and open arms.

The *Child ego state* is based on another tape that has been made simultaneously with the Parent tape. This tape has recorded the internal reactions or feelings of the child to external events (Harris, 1976). Thus the Child ego state is made up of all the emotions that spring from early experiences in addition to natural or innate feelings. As with the Parent, the Child can be divided into two major parts: the Adapted Child and the Natural Child (or Free Child). The Adapted Child responds in ways that gain acceptance from "big people." The Natural Child is spontaneous and free from worry about pleasing others (Woollams et al., 1976).

The *Adult ego state* is the rational part of the person that weighs facts before making decisions. It begins to develop late in the first year of life. Through exploration and testing, the infant begins to take in and respond to information (as the Parent and Child) and to gain control over the environment. The Adult ego state is the computerlike data processor that makes decisions based on information from the Parent, the Child, and from data the Adult has collected and continues to gather (Harris, 1976). By the time the person has reached 12 years of age, the Adult has matured to the point of becoming fully functional (Woollams et al., 1976).

The emotionally healthy individual can function appropriately from the ego state of his or her choosing, whether it is serving as a Nurturing Parent to a youngster, the Adult making a decision, or the Natural Child enjoying recreation (Woollams et al., 1976). Problems develop when a person is unable to work from the appropriate ego state in a particular situation. For example, the person who lets the Controlling Parent pattern his or her behavior during leisure deprives himself or herself of a true recreational experience and may be a disruptive force in the recreational enjoyment of others.

Transactional Analysis

Transactions are interactions between two people's ego states. For example, two mature persons might interact on an Adult-to-Adult level. Through transactional analysis, such interactions are examined. In the example given a parallel transaction exists. In such parallel transactions the response comes from the ego state at which it was directed, and the returned response is aimed at the original ego state that initiated the transaction. In parallel transactions the flow of communication continues. In contrast, nonparallel (crossed) transactions always cause a breakdown in communication. For example, one person may ask from the Adult, "Where are the cards?" Another person responds, "Why can't you take care of things?" The second person responded from his or her Parent to the Child of the first. It is easy to see how this transaction could lead to a communication breakdown.

Both parallel and crossed transactions are diagramed in Figure 2-1. In the first transaction the Adult-to-Adult parallel transaction is shown. In the second diagram a parallel transaction exists between Parent and Child. The crossed transaction discussed in the preceding paragraph is shown in the third diagram. Finally, a Parent-to-Child transaction is responded to with an Adult-to-Adult reply, creating a crossed transaction in the fourth diagram.

Rackets and Games

The phrase *collecting stamps* is used to describe the process by which people collect feelings, much as shoppers might collect trading stamps. These stamps (feelings) are later cashed in to justify some behavior. People cash in their stamps toward any number of things, from getting drunk to attempting suicide. Their logic is that they deserve whatever "prize" they desire (Woollams et al., 1976).

Figure 2-1   Parallel and crossed transactions.

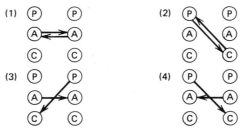

Healthy persons do not collect stamps. Instead, they deal with feelings as they occur. Unhealthy persons save up stamps in order to justify acts that fit into their life position of feeling they are no good. The actual act of pursuing and saving stamps is the person's *racket*. Different rackets exist, including anger rackets and depression rackets in which people collect anger stamps or depression stamps, depending on their particular racket.

Games substitute for intimate relations. Essentially they are a series of dishonest transactions people repeat over and over in order to accomplish ulterior motives. Games follow set formats, so that those who play them may reach the payoff they seek in terms of collecting bad feelings or stamps.

Scripts

Early in life most people determine a life plan by which they live their lives. This plan, or script, preordains the roles they will assume in later life (Steiner, 1974). If the script results mostly in positive strokes (recognition) it is a winner's script. If the strokes are generally negative it is a loser's script. Routine, boring scripts that look good superficially but in which people actually do not take chances and avoid emotionally charged situations are termed nonwinning or banal scripts. An example of a banal script is the hardworking businessman who relies on his Adult but does not seek intimacy or release his Natural Child (Woollams et al., 1976). Since scripts are self-determined, they may be altered. Once understood, a person can focus on his or her script and change it.

Scripts are closely related to *life positions* because scripts are formed out of the vantage point of one of four life positions. These are: (1) I'm OK—You're OK, (2) I'm OK—You're not OK, (3) I'm not OK—You're OK, and (4) I'm not OK—You're not OK. When an infant enters the world, he or she naturally assume the healthy I'm OK—You're OK position. This position is maintained as long as the person receives positive strokes (recognition). These can be nonverbal (a pat on the back) or verbal ("You're beautiful"). When a person's stroke bank is full, a stroke reserve is built to draw on and the person feels OK. When the reserve is depleted, the person feels not OK (Campos & McCormick, 1974).

The need for people to gain strokes is called stimulus-hunger. Structure-hunger (the need to structure time) is an extension of exchanging or avoiding strokes (Woollams et al., 1976). There are six ways of structuring time: (1) withdrawal, (2) rituals, (3) pastimes, (4) games, (5) activities, and (6) intimacy. *Withdrawal* is removing oneself from others. By withdrawal, people avoid strokes. *Rituals* are predictable exchanges of strokes, while *pastimes* are goal-directed communications. Both are superficial and result in minimum stroking. *Games* are useless time fillers that substitute for intimate relations. They result only in negative strokes. *Activities* have to do with accomplishing things people want to do or have to do. *Intimacy* is represented in genuine caring relationships that are totally free from games or exploitation. Activities and intimacy provide positive strokes that reinforce OK feelings (James & Jongeward, 1971).

Implications for Therapeutic Recreation

Every person needs positive stroking. Positive stroking encourages young persons to grow into the winner roles they were born to assume. Ignoring individuals or giving negative strokes pushes young persons toward losers' scripts and reinforces losers' scripts for older people (James & Jongeward, 1971). By structuring opportunities for activities and intimacy, therapeutic recreation specialists will lead people to give and obtain positive strokes. TR specialists can also help people release the script-free Natural Child in order to be able to experience the freedom and joy found in play and recreation. TA also can be used to help clients improve interpersonal communications. Since TA is not the private domain of any single professional group, it can be employed by therapeutic recreation specialists who have studied its theories and processes.

TA offers the leisure counselor a commonsense, understandable approach through which clients can gain insights and make choices to change leisure behavior. James and Jongeward (1971), in their best-selling book on transactional analysis, *Born to Win*, have presented exercises related both to people's childhood and current play that are appropriate for use in leisure counseling. Gunn (1977) has written of using TA approaches in a major work on leisure counseling edited by Epperson, Witt, and Hitzhusen.

PSYCHODRAMA

Psychodrama is a form of psychiatric treatment developed by Jacob L. Moreno. The goal of psychodrama is to help the client gain increased awareness of feelings and behaviors through personal insights and the perceptions of others resulting from dramatizing situations centering around past, current, or anticipated difficulties. The client discovers more about his or her difficulties and learns to cope with them by means of the cathartic expression of acting out problems.

Elements involved in psychodrama include the stage, director, subject (client), alter ego, and auxiliary ego. The psychodrama takes place on a stage and is directed by the leader, who may interject comments when necessary and who interprets the drama. It is also the leader's job to convey a warm, caring, and supportive attitude conducive to encouraging spontaneity. The subject has the opportunity of playing the leading role, which may be himself or herself or someone else. This person, or any character in the drama, may have an alter ego (or double) who stands immediately behind the person and states aloud whatever that character is probably thinking (in contrast to what the person is actually saying). Thus the alter ego is an extension of the person's ego. The auxiliary ego is a person who portrays a significant other in the life of the subject (Matson, 1977; Cohen & Lipkin, 1979).

Implications for Therapeutic Recreation
Therapeutic recreation specialists should not be tempted to conduct psychodrama without extensive preparation. The psychodrama leader must obtain a high level of training under expert direction. Nevertheless, aspects of psychodrama such as role playing and role reversal may be used by therapeutic recreation specialists. Like the leader of psychodrama, the TR specialist should also attempt to create a warm, accepting atmosphere so clients feel free to express themselves.

BIBLIOTHERAPY

Bibliotherapy employs reading materials such as novels, plays, short stories, booklets, and pamphlets to help clients become aware that others share problems similar to theirs and to help bring new insights into being. Bibliotherapy is usually used in psychiatric settings. Particular readings are selected for the client that contain characters with problems related to the client's problems. The client will then supposedly identify with the characters and project himself or herself into the story. This process results in an emotional reaction that can then be discussed with a helping professional (Eisenberg & Delaney, 1977; Coleman, 1980).

Implications for Therapeutic Recreation
Bibliotherapy has not become a popular technique among therapeutic recreation specialists, but it does reinforce the importance of structuring ways for clients to help themselves. Clients can engage in self-help activities without direct assistance from TR specialists if proper structures are provided.

THERAPEUTIC COMMUNITY

Maxwell Jones originated the term "therapeutic community," which describes a way of operating a relatively small unit within a general hospital, large psychiatric hospital, or other institution. Therapeutic communities have been used primarily on psychiatric services and with nursing home residents in the treatment of emotional and behavioral problems.

Therapeutic communities are based on the concept that the entire social milieu may be used as an intervention, since clients change and grow as a result of involvement in interpersonal relationships. It is reasoned that since client problems have resulted from faulty social learning, positive social learning can build the individual's ability to cope. The goal is for persons to help themselves by helping others, ultimately learning to be responsible for themselves. In the therapeutic community staff and clients interact freely in work and recreation within an understanding atmosphere designed to utilize the total impact of group processes. The concept of therapeutic community stands in contrast to the hierarchical, authoritarian organization often associated with hospitals and institutions. The student of therapeutic recreation may recognize that the therapeutic community has much in common with the moral therapy of the nineteenth century (Barns et al., 1973).

Implications for Therapeutic Recreation

Even though there are problems related to the therapeutic community concept, including its abstractness and staff role blurring, the approach has implications for therapeutic recreation specialists. One is the importance of all staff in facilitating change, since all client experiences have therapeutic value and all transactions between clients and staff are seen as having therapeutic potential. Since TR specialists are regularly very involved with the daily activities of institutionalized clients, their potential impact on the social milieu is obvious, calling for them to have extensively developed skills in interpersonal communications and group dynamics. The therapeutic community approach also shows that therapeutic recreation specialists must learn to function harmoniously in a team effort with staff and clients in order to create a positive social structure to enhance treatment.

RELAXATION TRAINING

Progressive relaxation training is a technique by which helping professionals train clients in achieving relaxation. Edmund Jacobson's name is usually associated with relaxation training. His progressive relaxation is based on becoming aware of the amount of tension in the body. By having people tense and release their muscles and attend to the resulting sensation of tension and relaxation, Jacobson discovered that a feeling of deep relaxation could be achieved. Joseph Wolpe, the noted behaviorist, later further refined Jacobson's original relaxation procedure. Today a number of variations of relaxation training exist.

Relaxation training is generally done with clients who are experiencing high levels of stress and tension. It takes place in a quiet room in which the windows and doors have been shut and the blinds or drapes drawn. This removes distracting stimuli. To create further a tranquil environment, lights in the room are kept dim. Soft background music may be played if desired. Clients assume a comfortable position in a chair or on a couch, or they may lie on their backs on the floor. Comfortable, nonbinding clothing is worn by clients. Glasses, jewelry, belts, shoes, and other such items are taken off, and clients are instructed to close their eyes during the actual relaxation exercises.

The helping professional's voice is also used to create the proper atmosphere in which to bring about relaxation. Voice volume and tone are instrumental in the process. An initial conversational level gives way to progressive reductions in volume as the session continues. Likewise, the pace of presentation is reduced, or slowed, as the session goes on. Although the tone of voice is not hypnotic or seductive, it remains smooth and even.

The basic procedure is to move the client through the tensing and relaxing of a series of muscle groups. A similar five-step sequence is suggested by Bernstein and Borkovec (1973) for relaxing each group of muscles. First, the client is told to focus attention on the muscle group. On signal, the muscle group is tensed. Tension is held for 5 to 7 seconds. Tension is then released on the cue of the helping professional. Finally, the client's attention is focused on the muscle group as it is relaxed.

Specific relaxation techniques have been developed by various individuals. Bernstein and Borkovec (1973) follow a technique in which 16 muscle groups are relaxed, beginning with the dominant hand forearm. The set order for exercising the muscle groups follows.

1. Dominant hand and forearm.
2. Dominant biceps.
3. Nondominant hand and forearm.
4. Nondominant biceps.
5. Forehead.
6. Upper cheeks and nose.
7. Lower cheeks and jaws.
8. Neck and throat.
9. Chest, shoulders, and upper back.
10. Abdominal or stomach region.
11. Dominant thigh.

36

12. Dominant calf.
13. Dominant foot.
14. Nondominant thigh.
15. Nondominant calf.
16. Nondominant foot.

Girdano and Everly (1979) propose a technique that begins with breathing exercises. The order for their relaxation exercises follows.

1. Very deep breathing.
2. Deep breathing.
3. Normal breathing.
4. Dorsiflexion of ankle joints.
5. Plantar flexion of ankle joints.
6. Extension of knee and hip.
7. Muscles of the spine.
8. Abdominal muscles.
9. Extension of wrist and fingers of both extremities.
10. Wrist and finger contraction (flexion).
11. Straightening arms against sides.
12. Shoulder shrug.
13. Head rotation.
14. Facial exercise.

Girdano and Everly (1979) suggest that as each gross movement relaxation exercise is completed, the client breath in during muscle contraction and out during muscle relaxation.

Learning relaxation skills is just like learning any new behavior. In order to get better at it, practice is necessary. There really is nothing particularly magical or mysterious about it. And, as with any new skill, some will pick it up quicker than others.

An example of an actual instruction by the leader of a relaxation training session follows.

Slowly and easily take a deep breath through your nose. Fill up your lungs as much as you can. Hold it briefly being aware of the contractions of the back and chest muscles. . . . Now breathe out slowly. . . . Keep this slow deep breathing going. Breathe deeply in . . . and deeply out. As the air leaves your lungs, say to yourself, "relax," and notice how your muscles relax.

Interested readers are referred to *Progressive Relaxation Training: A Manual for the Helping Professional* by Bernstein and Borkovec (1973), *Stress Power!* by Anderson (1978), and *Controlling Stress & Tension: A*

Holistic Approach by Girdano and Everly (1979) for detailed information on relaxation training procedures. These books were the major sources for this section.

Implications for Therapeutic Recreation

Traditionally, psychologists and psychiatrists have conducted relaxation training. However, other helping professionals, including therapeutic recreation specialists, may also find this technique helpful with tense clients. Brammer (1979) has stated that relaxation training is a simple skill to learn and possesses few hazards for clients.

Other methods to facilitate stress reduction include meditation, biofeedback, and physical exercise. Meditation and biofeedback are not covered in this chapter. Many sources contain information on these methods, including the Anderson (1978) and Girdano and Everly (1979) books previously mentioned in the discussion of relaxation training. Physical activity as a means to stress reduction is discussed in the following section.

STRESS REDUCTION AND PHYSICAL ACTIVITY

Perhaps the most natural way to bring about the control of stress is through participation in physical activity. Physical exercise may be conceived to be nature's tranqualizer.

Conflicts, frustration, threats, and insults may bring about psychological stress. In reaction to stress the body activates itself for the occurrence of an anticipated "fight or flight" response. That is, the body becomes physiologically mobilized in anticipation of protective actions to deal with or remove danger. As a result, a widespread physical reaction is brought about. There is a general overall increase in arousal level to heighten alertness. The cardiovascular system shows increased activation, and respiration is increased. Adrenal cells secrete hormones into the blood, and the flow of blood is increased to the brain, heart, and skeletal muscles (Sundeen et al., 1976; Dusek-Girdano, 1979). In short, the body becomes ready for a *physical* reaction to stress.

When the stress reaction occurs, Dusek-Girdano (1979) has proposed that physical activity can help handle stress by alleviating the stress state. She has written:

> *This is not a time to sit and feel all of these sensations tearing away at the body's systems and eroding good health. This is the time to* move, *to use up the products, to relieve the body of the destructive forces of stress on a sedentary system. Appropriate activity in this case would be total body exercise such as swimming, running, dancing, biking, or an active indi-*

vidual, dual, or team sport that lasts at least an hour. . . . Such activities will use up the stress products that might otherwise be harmful and that are likely to play a part in a degenerative disease process such as cardiovascular disease or ulcers (p. 222).

Research reported to date (e.g., Ismail & Trachlman, 1973; Muller & Armstrong, 1975; Palmer & Sadler, 1979) holds promise that running and jogging, in particular, may help many people by reducing stress and fostering positive psychological effects. (Treatment programs using these forms of exercise are sometimes referred to as "running therapy.") It might be speculated that the high level of interest in running in recent years may be correlated to people's need to cope with the stress of modern life.

Implications for Therapeutic Recreation

Physical activity has long been a popular program area in therapeutic recreation. The recent emergence of running on the American scene along with the increasing amount of attention being given to "running therapy" has, however, brought newfound recognition of the psychological benefits to be gained from physical activity. Running would seem to have particular promise for therapeutic recreation, since it is not a costly activity and can be done almost anywhere. Other physical activities such as swimming, boating, biking, and hiking seem to be particularly well suited to helping people handle stress because they are not normally approached on a competitive basis, which might lead to further threat, conflict, and frustration for participants.

ASSERTIVENESS TRAINING

Assertiveness training is an offshoot of behavioral therapy that helps people to become more assertive in social relationships, sexual expression, work-related interactions, or other social situations. Assertiveness training assists persons to change habits or behaviors, allowing them to stand up for their legitimate rights and the rights of others. This new assertiveness, in turn, makes people feel better about themselves, thus increasing feelings of self-esteem.

Nonassertive behaviors are usually reflected by submissive actions, inability to communicate in social situations, difficulty in maintaining eye contact, and fear of rejection. Learning to respond in an assertive fashion begins with the client identifying situations in which he or she wishes to respond more assertively. The helper then assists the client to examine irrational beliefs behind timid behavior and to identify more rational beliefs. Once this is completed, the helper and client identify proper assertive responses that may be made. Role-playing, rehearsal, modeling, and reinforcement techniques are used to establish new assertive responses. When the client has demonstrated assertive responses repeatedly within assertiveness training sessions, he or she is encouraged to try out their behavior in real-life situations. Successful clients put aside their inhibitions about responding assertively in all types of circumstances as newly learned behavioral tendencies generalize to other situations (Hackney & Nye, 1973; Eisenberg & Delaney, 1977; Matson, 1977).

Implications for Therapeutic Recreation

Assertiveness training provides a model for helping people reduce anxiety by developing responses that will enable them to say and do what they wish. TR specialists can easily allow for opportunities for clients to practice healthy assertiveness and can reinforce this behavior. Therapeutic recreation specialists may also wish to gain skills to conduct assertiveness training. Assertiveness training has been suggested as a technique to be used in leisure counseling (Connolly, 1977).

VALUES CLARIFICATION

Values clarification has been employed in various counseling situations, including leisure counseling. Counselors help clients explore and make decisions regarding values (important beliefs and principles by which people live their lives).

Prominent among authorities associated with values clarification is Sidney B. Simon, who has presented an approach to valuing made up of seven steps. These seven steps fall under three major categories (choosing, cherishing, acting), each of which represents a plateau. The first category or plateau deals with choosing one's beliefs and behaviors. It has three subprocesses: option exploration or determining alternatives; appraising the consequences of a particular choice; and freely choosing a value after rational consideration. The second plateau deals with cherishing beliefs and behaviors. It contains the fourth step, which asks if you feel good or are happy with your choice and you are ready to let others know of your choice. The third plateau contains the final two steps. Step six is determining action or what you are willing to do about your value. Step seven is making the value a regular part of your life (Simon & Olds, 1977).

Simon has also presented a number of values clarification strategies. Included among these are many that directly concern leisure choices (Simon et al., 1972; Simon & Olds, 1977).

Among exercises from the book by Simon, Howe, and Kirschenbaum

OTHER THERAPEUTIC APPROACHES

(1972) that I have used with groups are "The Pie of Life" (strategy 33), in which persons are asked to draw a circle that they divide into segments representing what they do in a 24-hour period, and "Two Ideal Days" (strategy 57), in which participants write a brief paper about what they fantasize to be an ideal 48-hour period. Other exercises I have used from the 1972 Simon book are strategies 1, 3, 4, 23, 27, 28, and 71. With some of these the leader must choose parts or adapt them in a way that emphasizes leisure aspects. A very helpful strategy to use in conjunction with a number of the exercises is strategy 15, "I Learned Statements." This exercise stimulates group discussion about the previous strategy by allowing participants to complete phrases such as "I learned that I . . . ," "I realized that I . . . ," and "I was surprised that I. . . . "

Implications for Therapeutic Recreation

Values clarification has direct implications for therapeutic recreation specialists who may employ values clarification strategies in leisure education and leisure counseling programs. Through these exercises individuals can discover leisure values and initiate plans to act on their values. Usually exercises are completed in a group, with the leader providing the instructions for each exercise. No particular equipment is necessary, although it is helpful to have a blackboard available. Participants may need paper and pencils to complete some exercises.

REALITY ORIENTATION

James Folsom is credited with designing reality orientation (RO) as a technique to meet the needs of elderly patients possessing moderate to severe degrees of disorientation and confusion. RO has been used primarily in homes for the aged, nursing homes, and geriatric units in psychiatric hospitals.

RO involves the technique of regular repetition of basic facts and constant orientation to time, place, names, events of the day, and things in the environment. Everyone who comes in contact with residents uses RO 24 hours a day to combat confusion, depression, and apathy and generally to move the person toward reality. All staff address residents by name, encourage them to use each others' names, and drill them on essential information such as place, time of day, date and day of week, the next meal, and object identification. Typical staff questions would be: "What is your name?" "What is the name of this facility?" "What city are we in?" "What is your hometown?" "How is the weather today?" Personnel may also engage in environmental engineering to provide stimulation by ths use of bright colors, signs, clocks, and calendars.

In addition to the continuing informal RO, daily RO classes are conducted. Four or five residents generally meet for 30-minute class at a routine time each day; again, the residents are provided with repetition and constant orientation. The course begins with simple name, date, and place recognition—usually using an RO board on which the name of the facility is posted along with the year, day of week and date, the weather for the day, the next holiday, and the upcoming meal. As time goes on, the staff person introduces the identification of various common objects such as utensils, food, and clothes. As the class progresses, residents may be asked to classify objects by shape and color and, perhaps, abstract qualities (Folsom, 1968; Barns, et, al., 1973).

Implications for Therapeutic Recreation

The technique of reality orientation suggests that the confusion experienced by some elderly persons may be due to factors other than organic cause, such as social deprivation and lack of stimulation. Minimizing social deprivation and increasing stimulation for older people can promote improvement in persons who otherwise might be termed "senile" and simply be forgotten. The too common, stereotyped "bingo and birthday party" programming that prevails in some facilities becomes just another part of the monotonous institutional atomsphere. Such programming should not be tolerated. It must be replaced by creative programs that put variety into the residents' daily lives.

REMOTIVATION

Remotivation was originated by Dorothy Haskins Smith to be employed with moderately confused elderly residents. It is often used to augment other therapies with clients who have successfully completed an RO program. Clarke (1967) has reported the use of the remotivation technique with aging, mentally retarded clients.

The remotivation technique involves a group interaction process, usually conducted by a trained aide-level staff member. Groups are composed of 10 to 15 residents. The basic concept on which remotivation is based is that there are always well parts in the mind that can be activated if given stimulation within a supportive atmosphere. Remotivation participants are encouraged to take a renewed interest in their environment through a series of carefully planned group conversations that stress simple, objective features of everyday life not related to the residents' emotional difficulties. The group meetings follow a five-phase process. Each session begins with the staff person warmly greeting each participant with a handshake while addressing the person by name and making some comment in regard to the resident's appearance. This is called creating a *climate of acceptance.* The second step is the *bridge to reality,* which is built by the staff person, and perhaps some of the residents, reading lively, rhythmical poetry. *Sharing the world we live in* is the third step; it involves conversation about the particular topic of discussion for the day. A diversity of topics may be chosen from baseball to gardening; the only restriction is that controversial subjects such as sex, politics, religion, or marital relations may not be discussed. The fourth step, an *appreciation of the work of the world,* naturally follows the subjects discussed during the third step. Topics usually spark a reminder of past hobbies or occupations that the client is encouraged to rediscover. The last step is that of establishing a *climate of appreciation* at the completion of each group session. Here the staff person thanks each resident for coming, makes a comment about the participation of each individual, and informs the group about the plans for the next session (Barns et al., 1973; Kraus & Bates, 1975; Coleman, 1980).

Implications for Therapeutic Recreation

The ideas expressed in the remotivation technique of establishing a warm, accepting atmosphere, dealing with the well parts of clients, and encouraging the rediscovery of interests have obvious merit in therapeutic recreation programming for older persons. Therapeutic recreation programs should help clients to feel wanted and comfortable in a group, assist in the development of positive attributes, help encourage the reawakening of the interests that have brought gratification in the past.

As aging clients begin to take a renewed interest in themselves and their environment, it is critical that they are allowed to establish a sense of control over their leisure activities. Iso-Ahola (1980) has presented convincing evidence to support the contention that the sense of personal responsibility and control gained by clients over their behaviors and environment is the most important result of recreation participation for residents of nursing homes. According to this author, being able to pick and choose activities allows clients to experience responsibility for themselves. Through participation in self-selected activities, feelings of helplessness give way to feelings of mastery or control.

RESOCIALIZATION

Resocialization is a technique to increase the social functioning of residents in geriatric settings. Its goal is to increase awareness of self and others by helping clients to form relationships, establish friendships, and discover new interests. Through the group process, isolated individuals are encouraged to rediscover their surroundings, values, and potentials.

Resocialization groups are conducted by a staff member for groups of 5 to 17 residents, depending on the mental and physical abilities of the participants. Refreshments are served at group meetings, which take place three times a week. Sessions usually last 30 to 60 minutes. The leader serves as a role model by showing acceptance of participants, making nonjudgmental comments, displaying flexibility, and raising discussion questions. The focus of the group is on building relationships, discussing problems of living together in their social community, and reliving of happy experiences. The leader attempts to maintain a free and accepting group atmosphere where participants will feel at liberty to discuss interpersonal problems (Barns et al., 1973).

Implications for Therapeutic Recreation

The restoration of social functioning through group processes is a common goal of TR specialists working with older clients who exhibit symptons of withdrawal. Many recreation programs for older people follow structures and objectives similar to those of the remotivation technique. However, in recreation groups the emphasis is not usually centered around discussions but around activities in which group members can find satisfaction. Programs attempt to provide opportunities for relatively isolated and lonely clients to establish involvements with staff and other clients. Through such social involvements clients hopefully develop the ability to interact effectively with their environments by acquiring skills and attitudes necessary to function successfully in social roles with others. Such programming requires a basic knowledge of group dynamics, interpersonal communications, and social learning on the part of the therapeutic recreation specialist.

SENSORY TRAINING

Originally developed to work with children with perceptual-motor problems, sensory training has been used extensively with regressed and disoriented older persons in psychiatric facilities and nursing homes. Sensory training attempts to maintain and improve the functioning of regressed patients through a program of stimulus bombardment directed toward all five senses. Its goal is to improve the individual's perception and alertness in responding to the environment.

Patients meet with a leader in groups of four to seven for sessions lasting 30 to 60 minutes. Each session begins with the group sitting in a circle. The leader introduces himself or herself and asks the participants

OTHER THERAPEUTIC APPROACHES

to introduce themselves. The purposes of the session are explained, perhaps using a blackboard or bulletin board to note major points; then the leader conducts a series of activities requiring use of all the senses. At the conclusion of the session, the leader thanks each participant for taking part and reminds them when the following session will be held. Kraus and Bates (1975) suggest that the leader should shake hands with each participant at the beginning and end of each session and that name tags be used. They state that after the introductions, the leader should orient participants to time, place, date, day of the week, and that they are at the treatment facility because they need specialized care and treatment. Finally, they stress the need for the leader to use a loud speaking voice and to speak slowly and clearly, repeating statements when required.

Actual activities include: kinesthetic awareness exercises (in which participants name and flex and extend parts of their bodies from a sitting position); tactile stimulation activities (in which patients feel objects such as balls, sponges, or pieces of wood while being asked questions about the sensations received, preferences, and feelings); smelling activities (in which participants smell sharp or distinct-smelling substances and are questioned about feelings regarding them and uses the substances have); listening activities (providing a number of sounds through media such as records, simple instruments, clapping, and singing); tasting activities (using different foods such as candy and pickles to establish contrasts); and visual activities (employing mirrors and colorful objects) (Barns et al., 1973; Kraus & Bates, 1975).

Implications for Therapeutic Recreation

Sensory training provides input to activate perception and increase alertness. It is important to recognize that older people can become more functional if they receive the proper stimuli to activate their senses. Therapeutic recreation specialists can conduct sensory training as well as recreation programs that emphasize the use of the senses. Through such programming, aging clients may be able to reactivate senses that have not received adequate stimulation from the dull, routine environments that exist in many long-term care facilities.

A SUMMING UP

Therapeutic recreation is diverse in the types of populations it serves and the nature of the settings in which it is delivered. Diversity is therefore demanded in its methods. In this chapter a wide variety of therapeutic approaches have been reviewed that have implications for, or direct application in, the practice of therapeutic recreation.

Some approaches covered in the chapter, such as psychoanalytic psychotherapy or psychodrama, are beyond the normal bounds of therapeutic recreation and are utilized by other helping professions. Nevertheless, theoretical notions or actual techniques drawn from these approaches may have application in therapeutic recreation. Other approaches, such as behavior modification, transactional analysis, and values clarification, are more likely to be used in therapeutic recreation intervention and leisure counseling. The information in this chapter will hopefully act as a catalyst for the interested reader to develop expertise in several of these therapeutic approaches.

Influential in the actual application of any particular approach will be the characteristics of the clients to be served and the setting in which the service will be delivered. For instance, a cognitively oriented approach such as rational-emotive therapy would be inappropriate within a residential program for mentally retarded children. A behavior modification approach, however, might be quite appropriately employed. In all likelihood, in actual practice the therapeutic recreation specialist will combine several methods to form an eclectic approach.

No matter what methods or techniques are used, it is wise to keep in mind that therapeutic recreation is a very human enterprise. Any helping interaction must begin with the building of a person-to-person relationship based on mutual respect and a shared confidence in the abilities of both persons to meet the client's problems or needs. Good person-to-person relationships remain at the heart of therapeutic recreation, regardless of which particular approach is used.

KEY WORDS

Electic Approach. The utilization of therapeutic approaches and techniques selected from various sources or theoretical orientations.

Intervention. The carrying out of a plan of action derived during the planning stage of the therapeutic recreation process. Interventions may be based on various therapeutic approaches.

Reading Comprehension Questions

1 Provide an example from your own experience that shows how theory affects practice.
2 What is meant by the eclectic approach? Do you agree that therapeutic recreation is characterized by eclecticism?
3 Differentiate between the psychoanalytic and behavioristic approaches. Contrast these with the growth psychology approach.

46

4 What are the id, ego, and superego?

5 Think of possible conflicts you have personally experienced between your id and superego.

6 What is psychoanalysis? Transference? Countertransference?

7 Do you accept the cathartic notion? Why or why not?

8 Describe play therapy.

9 How do behaviorists view "mental illness?"

10 Compare classical conditioning with operant conditioning.

11 Discuss what is meant by shaping, prompting, and fading.

12 What is modeling? Suggest ways to use it in TR.

13 What is time-out? Do you think it should be used by therapeutic recreators as a behavior modification technique?

14 What are token economies?

15 Should recreation be used as a privilege to be earned with tokens?

16 Explain the Premack principle. Do you think the response deprevation hypothesis is a better explanation of reinforcement patterns?

17 What is growth psychology? Who is associated with growth psychology?

18 What do you consider to be the major implications of Rogers' client-centered therapy for practice in TR?

19 Briefly describe Gestalt therapy. Do you see any way its techniques could be used in leisure counseling?

20 Which of the three major orientations do you personally favor (psychoanalytic, behavioristic, growth psychology)? Why?

21 Do you agree that rational-emotive therapy can have useful application in leisure counseling?

22 Do you agree with Glasser's basic propositions regarding responsibility and reality? Would you place the same level of importance on involvements as Glasser does in his theory?

23 What are the four primary methods by which those using TA attempt to understand behavior?

24 What are the TA ego states?

25 Do you allow your Natural Child to come out in play and recreation?

26 What are positive strokes?

27 Does psychodrama have implications for therapeutic recreation?

28 Do you feel TRs should use bibliotherapy? Why or why not?

29 Do you see therapeutic recreation as playing a critical role in the therapeutic community? Please explain.

30 Should relaxation training or assertiveness training be used by therapeutic recreation specialists?

31 Do you personally favor using values clarification exercises as a major part of leisure education or leisure counseling with special populations?

32 Compare and contrast reality orientation, remotivation, resocialization, and sensory training. List implications of these techniques.

REFERENCES

Alderman, R. B. 1974. *Psychological behavior in sport*. Philadelphia: W. B. Saunders Company.

Anderson, R. A. 1976. *Stress power!* New York: Human Sciences Press.

Austin, D. R. 1971. Catharsis theory: How valid in therapeutic recreation? *Therapeutic Recreation Journal*. 5(1), 30, 31, 44, 45.

Austin, D. R. 1975. "75 ways to say good for you," TRAPS, *19*(1), 15.

Axline, V. 1969. *Play therapy*. New York: Ballantine.

Barnes, E. K., Sack, A., & Shore, H. 1973. Guidelines to treatment approaches: Modalities and methods for use with the aged. *The Gerontologist*. *13*, 515–522.

Berkowitz, L. 1972. *Social psychology*. Glenview, Ill.: Scott, Foresman and Company.

Berkowitz, L. 1978. Sports competition and aggression. In W. F. Straub (ed.), *An analysis of athlete behavior*. Ithaca, N. Y.: Movement Publications.

Berne, E. 1964. *Games people play: The psychology human relationships*. New York: Grove Press, Inc.

Bernstein, D. A., & Borkovec, T. D. 1973. *Progressive relaxation training: A manual for the helping professions*. Champaign, Ill.: Research Press.

Blackham, G. J. 1977. *Counseling: Theory, process, and practice*. Belmont, Calif.: Wadsworth Publishing Company, Inc.

Borden, G. A., & Stone, J. D. 1976. *Human communication: The process of relating*. Menlo Park, Calif.: Cummings Publishing Company.

Brammer, L. M. 1979. *The helping relationship: Process and skills* (2nd edition). Englewood Cliffs, N. J.: Prentice Hall, Inc.

Campos, L., & McCormick, P. 1972. *Introduce yourself to transactional analysis: A TA primer*. Stockton, Calif.: San Joaquin TA Institute.

Clarke, W. 1967. Remotivation technique: A therapeutic modality. *Therapeutic Recreation Journal*. *1*(1), 31, 35, 36.

Cohen, R. G., & Lipkin, G. B. 1979. *Therapeutic group work for health professionals*. New York: Springer Publishing Company.

Coleman, J. C., Butcher, J. N., & Carson, R. C., 1980. *Abnormal psychology and modern life* (6th edition). Chicago: Scott, Foresman and Company.

Connolly, M. L. 1977. Leisure counseling: A values clarification and assertive training approach. In A. Epperson, P. A. Witt, & G. Hitzhusen (eds.), *Leisure counseling: An aspect of leisure education.* Springfield, Ill.: Charles C. Thomas, Publishers.

Diebert, A. N., & Harmon, A. J. 1970. *New tools for changing behavior.* Champaign, Ill.: Research Press Company.

Dusek-Girdano, D. 1979. Stress reduction through physical activity. In D. Girdano, & G. Everly (eds.), *Controlling stress & tension: A holistic approach.* Englewood Cliffs, N. J.: Prentice-Hall, Inc.

Eisenberg, S., & Delaney, D. J. 1977. *The counseling process* (2nd edition). Chicago: Rand McNally College Publishing Company.

Ellis, A. 1973. Rational-emotive therapy. In R. Corsini (ed.), *Current psychotherapies.* Itasca, Ill.: F. E. Peacock Publishers, Inc.

Ellis, A. 1976. Rational-emotive therapy. In V. Binder, A. Binder, & B. Rimland (eds.), *Modern therapies.* Englewood Cliffs, N. J.: Prentice-Hall, Inc.

Ellis, M. J. 1973. *Why people play.* Englewood Cliffs, N. J.: Prentice-Hall, Inc.

Folsom, J. C. 1968. Reality orientation for the elderly mental patient. *Journal of Geriatric Psychiatry. 1,* 291–307.

Ford, D. H., & Urban, H. B. 1963. *A Systems of psychotherapy.* New York: John Wiley & Sons, Inc.

Freedman, A. M., Kaplan, H. I., & Sadock, B. J. (eds.) 1975. *Comprehensive textbook of psychology/II* (2nd edition). Baltimore: The Williams & Wilkins Company.

Girdano, D. & Everly, G. 1979. *Controlling stress & tension: A holistic approach.* Englewood Cliffs, N. J.: Prentice-Hall, Inc.

Glasser, W. 1965. *Reality therapy: A new approach to psychiatry.* New York: Harper & Row, Publishers.

Glasser, W. 1976. Reality therapy. In V. Binder, A. Binder, & B. Rimland (eds.), *Modern therapies.* Englewood Cliffs, N. J.: Prentice-Hall, Inc.

Glasser, W., & Zunin, L. M. 1973. Reality therapy. In R. Corsini (ed.) *Current psychotherapies.* Itasca, Ill.: F. E. Peacock Publishers, Inc.

Gunn, S. L. 1977. Leisure counseling: An analysis of play behavior and attitudes using transactional analysis and gestalt awareness. In A. Epperson, P. A. Witt, & G. Hitzhusen (eds.), *Leisure counseling: An aspect of leisure education.* Springfield, Ill.: Charles C. Thomas, Publisher.

Gussen, J. 1967. The psychodynamics of leisure. In P. A. Martin (ed.), *Leisure and mental health: A psychiatric viewpoint.* Washington, D. C.: American Psychiatric Association.

Hackney, H., & Nye, S. 1973. *Counseling strategies and objectives.* Englewood Cliffs, N. J.: Prentice-Hall, Inc.

Harris, T. A. 1976. Transactional analysis: An introduction. In V. Binder, A. Binder, & B. Rimland (eds.), *Modern therapies.* Englewood Cliffs, N. J.: Prentice-Hall, Inc.

Hunnicutt, B. K. 1979. Freudian and Neofreudian views of adult play and their implications for leisure research and therapeutic service delivery. *Therapeutic Recreation Journal, 13*(2), 3–13.

Hunter, M. C., & Carlson, P. V. 1971. *Improving your child's behavior.* Glendale, Calif.: Bomar.

Ismail, A. H., & Trachtman, L. E. 1973. Jogging the imgaination. *Psychology Today. 6*(10), 78–82.

Iso-Ahola, S. E. 1980. Perceived control and responsibility as mediators of the effects of therapeutic recreation on the institutionalized aged. *Therapeutic Recreation Journal. 14*(1), 36–43.

James, M., & Jongward, D. 1971. *Born to win: Transactional analysis with gestalt experiments.* Reading, Mass.: Addison-Wesley Publishing Company.

Kovel, J. 1976. *A complete guide to therapy: From psychoanalysis to behavior modification.* New York: Pantheon Books.

Kraus, R. G., & Bates, B. J. 1975. *Recreation leadership and supervision: Guidelines for professional development.* Philadelphia: W. B. Saunders Company.

Maddi, S. R. 1972. *Personality theories: A comparative analysis.* Homewood, Ill.: The Dorsey Press.

Madsen. C. K., & Madsen, C. H. 1972. *Parents/children/discipline: A positive approach.* Boston: Allyn and Bacon, Inc.

Martens, R. 1975. *Social psychology and physical activity.* New York: Harper & Row, Publishers.

Matson, K. 1977. *The psychology today omnibook of personal development.* New York: William Morrow and Company, Inc.

50

McDavid, J. W., & Harari, H. 1968. *Social psychology, individuals, groups, societies.* New York: Harper & Row, Publishers.

Meador, B. D., & Rogers, C. R. 1973. Client-centered therapy. In R. Corsini (ed.), *Current psychotherapies.* Itasca, Ill.: F. E. Peacock Publishers, Inc.

Menninger, W. C. 1960. Recreation and mental health. *Recreation and psychiatry.* New York: National Recreation Association.

Meyer, M. W. 1962. The rationale of recreation as therapy. *Recreation in treatment centers* (Vol. 1). Washington, D. C.: National Therapeutic Recreation Society, National Recreation and Park Association.

Muller, B., & Armstrong, H. 1975. A further note on the "running treatment" for anxiety. *Psychotherapy: Theory, Research and Practice. 12*(4), 385–367.

Okun, B. F. 1976. *Effective helping: Interviewing & counseling techniques.* North Scituate, Mass.: Duxbury Press.

O'Morrow, G. S. 1971. The whys of recreation activities for psychiatric patients. *Therapeutic Recreation Journal. 5*(3), 97–103+.

Palmer, L. L., & Sadler, R. R. 1979. The effects of a running program on depression in rehabilitation clients. Unpublished research report. Fisherville, Va.: Research Utilization Laboratory, Woodrow Wilson Rehabilitation Center.

Parke, R. D., & Sawin, D. B. 1975. *Aggression: Causes and controls.* Homewood, Ill.: Learning Systems Company.

Quanty, M. B. 1976. Aggression catharsis: experimental investigations and implications. In R. G. Green & E. C. O'Neal (eds.), *Perspectives on aggression.* New York: Academic Press.

Rawson, H. E. 1978. Short-term residential therapeutic camping for behaviorally disordered children ages 6–12: An academic remediation and behavioral modification approach. *Therapeutic Recreation Journal. 12*(4), 17–23.

Schmokel, C. 1980. An alternative to the Premack principle. Unpublished paper. Bloomington, Ind.

Schultz, D. 1977. *Growth psychology: Models of the healthy personality.* New York: D. Van Nostrand Company.

Simon, S. B., Howe, L. W., & Kirschenbaum, H. 1972. *Values clarification: A handbook of practical strategies for teachers and students.* New York: Hart Publishing Company, Inc.

Simon, S. B., & Olds, S. W. 1977. *Helping your child learn right from wrong: A guide to values clarification.* New York: McGraw-Hill Book Company.

Steiner, C. M. 1974. *Scripts people live: Transactional analysis of life scripts.* New York: Grove Press, Inc.

Sundeen, J., Stuart, W., Rankin, D., & Cohen, P. 1975. *Nurse-client interaction: Implementing the nursing process.* St. Louis: The C. V. Mosby Company.

Timberlake, W., & Allison, J. 1974. Response deprivation: An empirical approach to instrumental performance. *Psychological Review. 81,* 146–164.

Vernon, W. M. 1972. *Motivating children: Behavior modification in the classroom.* New York: Holt, Rinehart and Winston, Inc.

Watson, J. B. 1913. Psychology as the behaviorist views it. *Psychological Review. 20,* 158–177.

Wehman, P. & Rettie, C. 1975. Increasing actions on play materials by severely retarded women through social reinforcement. *Therapeutic Recreation Journal. 9,*(4), 173–178.

Wehman, P. 1977. Application of behavior modification techniques to play problems of the severely and profoundly retarded. *Therapeutic Recreation Journal. 11*(1), 16–21.

Woods, M. L. 1971. Development of a pay for recreation procedure in a token economy. *Mental Retardation. 2*(1), 54–57.

Woollams, S., Brown, M. & Huige, K. 1976. *Transactional analysis in brief.* Ann Arbor, Mich.: Huron Valley Institute.

3

THE
THERAPEUTIC
RECREATION
PROCESS

PURPOSE OF THE CHAPTER

OBJECTIVES

THE PERSON—A HUMANISTIC PERSPECTIVE

DOES TR REFLECT THE HUMANISTIC APPROACH?

WHAT IS HIGH-LEVEL WELLNESS?

ARE THERAPEUTIC RECREATION AND HIGH-LEVEL WELLNESS
SIMILAR?

THE GUNN/PETERSON MODEL

WHAT IS THE THERAPEUTIC RECREATION PROCESS?

WHAT IS INVOLVED IN COMPLETING CLIENT ASSESSMENT?

WHAT ARE SOURCES OF ASSESSMENT INFORMATION?

WHAT ARE METHODS OF ASSESSING CLIENTS?
The Observation Method
The Interview Method

WHAT ARE SOME SECONDARY SOURCES OF INFORMATION?
Medical Records
Educational Records
Standardized Testing
Interviews with Family or Friends

PURPOSE OF THE CHAPTER

It is critical that TR specialists become aware of basic philosophical beliefs that prevail in therapeutic recreation. Beliefs affect theoretical notions that, in turn, affect the principles on which professionals operate. It is equally important that a thorough understanding of the therapeutic recreation process be gained, since this process underlies the delivery of all TR services. This chapter will help the student to develop a more comprehensive and systematic perspective on these fundamental concerns that will ultimately pervade the student's delivery of services to clients.

54

OBJECTIVES

- Understand the humanistic perspective as it relates to TR.
- Recognize the relationship between therapeutic recreation and high-level wellness.
- Describe the Gunn/Peterson model.
- Appreciate the need to employ a systematic method of problem solving known as the therapeutic recreation process.
- Reduce the therapeutic recreation process to a series of logical steps, defining each in terms of its role in the total process.
- Explain methods of client assessment.
- Describe the setting of priorities to meet client needs.
- Relate guidelines for formulating client goals and objectives.
- Describe the elements of an individual (personalized) program plan.
- Know the importance of clearly defined implementation procedures.
- Recognize approaches to evaluation.
- State a rationale for involvement of clients in the entire therapeutic recreation process.

THE PERSON—A HUMANISTIC PERSPECTIVE

Therapeutic recreation may be perceived as a field of specialization within the broad profession of recreation and leisure service. During the 1970s the recreation and leisure service profession began to assume a humanistic perspective that recognized that people have the ability to be self-directed, make wise choices, and develop themselves during leisure. This philosophical position has been reflected in the writings of Gray (1975) and Murphy (1973, 1975), among others.

From the humanistic position Murphy (1975) has stated:

> *Recreation and leisure agencies which incorporate a humanistic approach to service seek to promote the capacity and ability of groups and individuals to make self-determined and responsible choices—in light of their needs to grow, to explore new possibilities, and to realize their full potential (p. 2).*

Murphy (1975) goes on to discuss the ramifications of the humanistic perspective for leisure service personnel. He states:

> *. . . leisure service personnel need to have unconditionally positive regards for their clientele. They must relate person-to-person. The participants are respected for what they are, and accepted for that, with all their potentialities. Such unconditional relationships, which have often*

been fostered in therapeutic settings, are seen as fundamental to all *areas of recreation and leisure service (p. 3).*

Among other concepts, those embracing the humanistic approach: (1) take a holistic view of the person, (2) believe both children and adults are capable of change, (3) see people as being in dynamic interaction with the environment, not just reacting to the external world, and (4) view people as healthy who strive for personal satisfaction, yet go beyond their own needs to understand and care about others (Chapman & Chapman, 1975; Ringness, 1975; Borden & Stone, 1976; Sundeen et al., 1976).

DOES TR REFLECT THE HUMANISTIC APPROACH?

Therapeutic recreation seems to epitomize the humanistic concepts brought forth in the writing of Gray (1975) and Murphy (1973, 1975) directed toward the recreation and leisure profession. As O'Morrow (1980) has stated: "Present-day therapeutic recreation specialists emphasize the concept that the 'whole person' is involved" (p. 151). Therapeutic recreation specialists take a holistic approach with their clients. They see each client as an individual possessing a unique biological, psychological, and social background from which to react to the environment as a total person or whole being.

Gunn and Peterson (1978) have made reference to the person as an integrated whole in their discussion of the biopsychosocial components of client behavior. They write:

No aspect of human behavior stands alone. Meaningful social behavior requires some degree of emotional stability, physical and mental involvement, and sexual awareness. Likewise, meaningful intellectual behavior relies on the existence of other aspects of the personality for support. To be lacking in any of the biopsychosocial areas affects the behavior of the person (p. 33).

Also central to the humanistic orientation of therapeutic recreation are the beliefs that people have the freedom to change, make decisions, and assume responsibility for their own actions—particularly in regard to leisure. This "freedom to become" or ability to develop oneself more fully is in keeping with the provision of therapeutic recreation activities. Through activities clients express their natural motivation toward stimulus seeking in positive recreative experiences in contrast to waiting passively for the environment to act on them. Within the accepting atmosphere provided in therapeutic recreation, clients have the opportunity to reach unexplored potentials.

Finally, therapeutic recreation is interested in helping people feel good about themselves through personal satisfaction gained in recreation. The therapeutic recreation specialist assumes a caring, understanding attitude toward the client and attempts to create a free and open recreational environment where the client can experience positive interactions with others. Good person-to-person relationships are at the heart of therapeutic recreation, as are opportunities for self-expression and creative accomplishment. Through such experiences persons may enhance positive self-concepts and learn to grow beyond themselves to care about others.

The humanistic approach exemplified in the philosophy of therapeutic recreation provides an excellent theoretical framework from which to help clients grow and to assist them to prevent or relieve problems. And in what better atmosphere than that achieved in recreation and leisure could growth be fostered and problems met?

WHAT IS HIGH-LEVEL WELLNESS?

The humanitic perspective has also helped to bring about the concept of "high-level wellness" championed by Dunn (1961) and Ardell (1977). High-level wellness is defined by Dunn (1961) as " . . . an integrated method of functioning which is oriented toward maximizing the potential of which the individual is capable" (p. 4). Dunn's approach, which centers around the wholeness of the individual, calls for not only an absence of physical illness but implies a psychological and environmental wellness. Thus the physical well-being of the total person is joined by mental and social well-being in forming the concept of health under the notion of high-level wellness.

High-level wellness is gained, according to Dunn (1961), when we exist in a "very favorable environment" and enjoy "peak wellness" (where illness and wellness are conceived along a continuum, with death on one end and peak wellness at the other). When limitations hinder the obtainment of peak wellness, an optimal level of high-level wellness may be achieved by making the individual's environment as conducive to growth as possible. For example, intellectual potentials are difficult to alter, but we may enhance the opportunity for intellectual growth by providing a deprived child with a stimulating play environment.

The holistic medicine proposed under the banner of high-level wellness treats the person, not the disease. Like therapeutic recreation, holistic medicine is concerned with the "whole person" and with allowing individuals to assume responsibility for their own health and well-being. According to Ardell (1977), the ultimate aim of "well medicine" (in contrast to the "traditional medicine" normally practiced by the medical community) is moving clients toward self-actualization and, therefore, the achievement of high-level wellness. While traditional medicine deals solely with illness according to Ardell (1977), well medicine deals with wellness or health enhancement.

ARE THERAPEUTIC RECREATION AND HIGH-LEVEL WELLNESS SIMILAR?

The similarity between therapeutic recreation and the concepts expressed by Dunn (1961) and Ardell (1977) in their separate works entitled *High Level Wellness* is striking. Both have health enhancement and self-actualization as major goals, and both have seemingly been heavily influenced by the humanistic viewpoint.

Therapeutic recreation, like traditional medical practice, has long dealt with the problem of illness. Unlike traditional medicine, however, therapeutic recreation has not dealt exclusively with illness. Therapeutic recreation has historically promoted the goal of self-actualization, or the facilitation of the fullest possible growth and development of the client. Therefore therapeutic recreation may be conceived to be much like traditional, medically oriented, allied health professions in its concern for preventing and alleviating illness. At the same time, therapeutic recreation specialists join both other leisure service professionals and physicians practicing "well medicine" in their desire to bring about the self-actualization of their clients. Thus therapeutic recreation specialists may be perceived to have concern for the full range of the illness-wellness continuum (Figure 3-1).

It may be seen by observing Figure 3-1 that the therapeutic recreation specialist may assume several different functions, depending on the needs and desires of the client. At one point, the function of the TR specialist may be to join with other clinical staff to help a client alleviate illness. For example, the TR specialist may function as a member of a treatment team in a psychiatric hospital. Moving along the continuum toward wellness, we may find the TR specialist conducting a leisure counseling program at a comprehensive mental health center for clients who reside in the community. Even further along the continuum, the TR specialist might be found working with a community-based recreator on a community recreation program aimed at bringing about stress reduction for health enhancement.

Similar examples may be provided in all areas of therapeutic recreation service. For instance, the TR specialist may initially assist the patient undergoing physical rehabilitation to prevent, curtail, or reverse secondary disabilities such as muscle atrophy or decubitus ulcers, which may be caused by inadequate care, neglect, or disuse (Avedon, 1974). This pro-

Illness		Wellness	
(concern with disease)		(concern with growth)	
Death			Peak health

Figure 3-1 Illness-wellness continuum.

gramming usually occurs within the hospital or rehabilitation center. Later, as the patient moves along the wellness continuum, the therapeutic recreation specialist may provide a resocialization program to begin to foster social and leisure skills necessary for community living. Still later, the patient may be introduced to organized, community-based recreation programs as a part of a leisure counseling program.

THE GUNN/PETERSON MODEL

Gunn and Peterson (1977, 1978) have conceptualized a model in which therapeutic recreation service is seen as existing along a continuum from client-oriented therapy at one end to special recreation programs at the other. This continuum may be divided into three components: (1) therapy or rehabilitation, (2) leisure education, and (3) special recreation. The *therapy or rehabilitation* component is directed primarily toward treatment and restoration. Therapeutic recreation specialists function chiefly as therapists who help clients gain basic functional abilities. Recreation activities are means toward reaching treatment goals. The *leisure education* component deals with the development of activity skills and social interaction skills as well as issues for leisure counseling. Therapeutic recreation specialists function primarily as teachers and counselors. In therapeutic recreation programs clients develop their leisure and social skills. Through leisure counseling clients explore leisure-related problems and attitudes in order to determine future directions. The third component, *special recreation,* concerns the provision of recreation programs for members of special population groups. Therapeutic recreation specialists function as recreators who provide individuals from special population groups with opportunities for leisure participation. The emphasis is on leisure opportunities, not behavioral or attitudinal change.

I object to the suggestion that a *primary* role of therapeutic recreation specialist is that of "a recreator for special populations" (Gunn & Peterson, 1978, p. 23). If the major function of special recreation is the provision of opportunies for self-directed leisure, then those charged with the responsibility for the delivery of leisure service—community recreation personnel—should operate recreation programs for special populations.

If, however, there is a need to intervene with a special recreation program because certain special population group members are not willing or able to enter into self-directed leisure pursuit, the therapeutic recreation specialist should be responsible for the program.

An analogy to special education may be used to explain the primary role of the therapeutic recreation specialist. Most parents and educators would object to the stipulation that the provision of educational opportunities for all children with disabilities was the primary domain of special educators. Skills of special educators are reserved for particular instances when an educational intervention is necessary. Special educators are not simply "educators for special populations," but specialists who prescribe or direct interventions. Likewise, therapeutic recreation specialists are not "recreators for special populations," but helping professionals who utilize the therapeutic recreation process to intervene in the lives of clients.

This is not to say that therapeutic recreation specialists have no connection with recreation for special populations. Therapeutic recreation specialists may assist their clients to enter recreation and leisure service agency programs directed toward the provision of opportunities for self-directed leisure. Therapeutic recreation specialists may also occasionally share their expertise through consultation to community-based recreators responsible for recreation programs for special populations. In institutional settings therapeutic recreation specialists may be called on to conduct programs directed toward the provision of leisure opportunities for clients either because these programs are seen as a vital part of the total treatment milieu or because it would be impractical to employ others for the sole purpose of conducting recreation programs for the population residing at the institution. But the provision of leisure opportunities is not the principal reason for the existence of TR specialists in clinical or rehabilitation settings.

Since the therapeutic recreation specialists are foremost involved with purposeful intervention, the setting in which help is given is of little significance. Therapeutic recreation may be performed in virtually any setting. The concern of therapeutic recreation specialists should not be hospital therapeutic recreation, community therapeutic recreation, or any other type of therapeutic recreation—except *people* therapeutic recreation. No matter where therapeutic recreation specialists are based, their overriding mission is the provision of purposeful intervention designed to help clients grow and to assist them to prevent or relieve problems through recreation and leisure. Purposeful intervention in therapeutic recreation is brought about through the employment of the TR process.

WHAT IS THE THERAPEUTIC RECREATION PROCESS?

WHAT IS THE THERAPEUTIC RECREATION PROCESS?

The therapeutic recreation process may be used with a client or group of clients at any point along the illness-wellness continuum. The needs of the client dictate where the process will be directed. No matter where along the continuum the client's needs lie, the TR process provides a systematic method of problem solving through a progression of phases. O'Morrow (1980) has listed four steps in the therapeutic recreation process: (1) assessment, (2) planning, (3) implementation, and (4) evaluation.

WHAT IS INVOLVED IN COMPLETING CLIENT ASSESSMENT?

The first step in the therapeutic recreation process, assessment, is concerned with data collection and analysis in order to determine the status of the client. Once assessment information is available, the therapeutic recreation specialist can identify and define the client's problems and strengths. With this information a plan of action may be formulated.

Stephens (1976) has discussed the fact that for years teachers have been told to start "where the child is," but rarely has anyone informed the teacher of how to determine the specific beginning point. This situation is not unlike that which exists in therapeutic recreation. That is, TR specialists have been told they must assess clients, but few means have been suggested. I do not pretend to have *the* answer as to how to do assessment in every specific and unique therapeutic recreation setting, but perhaps the following guidelines will be helpful.

To begin, the purpose of TR assessment must remain clear. Therapeutic recreation assessment is not conducted in order to label or categorize the client. Instead, we assess to gain information that is useful in helping the client profit from our services. Assessment should aid us to determine client strengths, interests, and expectations and to identify the nature and extent of problems.

Through assessment, the therapeutic recreation specialist attempts to obtain as complete a picture as possible of the client's life situation. In order to accomplish this, the client's history, present condition, and expectations for the future must be examined.

WHAT ARE SOURCES OF ASSESSMENT INFORMATION?

The primary source of information is usually the client. Secondary sources are, however, almost always used as well. Secondary sources include medical or educational records, results of testing (e.g., psychological testing), interviews with family or friends, the social history (usually taken by a social worker), case recordings or progress notes that staff have charted, and conferences and team meetings with other staff. Occasionally, TR specialists also assess the client's home and community to determine leisure patterns of the client or to survey for recreation opportunities. Knowledge of the potential recreation environment found in the client's home and community are useful in understanding the client and to future planning with the client.

WHAT ARE METHODS OF ASSESSING CLIENTS?

Observing and interviewing are the two most used methods of client assessment. Both observations and interviews offer a number of perspectives from which to approach client assessment.

THE OBSERVATION METHOD

Schulman (1978) has outlined several methods of observation. Among these are what he has termed casual observation, naturalistic observation, specific goal observation, and standardized observation.

Casual Observation

Casual observation is the type of nonsystematic observation in which we engage on a daily basis. It is responding to our environment in a somewhat random fashion and out of our personal bias and background. It is not "skilled observation" in that it is not directed or purposeful.

Naturalistic Observation

Other methods of observation outlined by Schulman (1978) involve "skilled observation," including naturalistic observation. In naturalistic observation there is no attempt to manipulate or change the natural environment. This method calls for keeping an ongoing account of the client's behavior through written anecdotal notes, photographs, film, videotape, or a combination of these techniques. In therapeutic recreation, naturalistic observation might be accomplished while watching the hospitalized client interact during unstructured recreation on the ward or by observing handicapped children on the playground in a free play situation.

Specific Goal Observation

This type of observation requires precision in planning, since the observer sets definite goals for observation to meet a particular purpose or to assess a well-defined behavior. Here the therapeutic recreation specialist may observe how cooperative the client is in a corecreational game situation or the client's response to frustration in an athletic contest.

With children, the TR specialist may confirm other information concerning the child while viewing the child at play. Takata (1974) has provided a list of questions to guide such observation. They are:

- With what does the child play?
- How does the child play?
- What type of play is avoided or liked the least?
- With whom does the child play?
- How does the child play with others?
- What body posture does the child use during play?
- How long does the child play?
- Where does the child play?
- When does the child play?

Examples of goal observations calling for specific behaviors might include observing an adult playing a card game such as bridge or an adolescent square dancing. These activities make certain cognitive, psychomotor, or social demands on the client. The therapeutic recreation specialist observes to determine how the client meets these specific demands and records this information.

Standardized Observation

Standardized observations take two major forms (Schulman, 1978). One is the standardized (norm-referenced) test. An example of a standardized test that a therapeutic recreation specialist might administer would be a physical fitness test or a play skills inventory. Although standardized tests are not extensively employed by therapeutic recreation specialists, results of standardized tests given by other staff are often utilized in TR assessment. Instruments administered by psychologists would be one such example.

Another type of standardized observation is that of time-interval observations. In this assessment technique clients are observed at predetermined times during the day. These time samples may be for 15 minutes, 30 minutes, or any period of time. During the observation, the therapeutic recreation specialist looks for a specific behavior and records frequency counts when that behavior occurs. For instance, the number of verbal interactions with other clients or the number of times a client behaves in an aggressive manner could be recorded.

THE INTERVIEW METHOD

The therapeutic recreation specialist will generally attempt to conduct at least one interview with every new client. The interview usually has three purposes. First, the interview provides an opportunity to gain information from the client and to observe the client. Second, the TR specialist wishes to begin to develop a relationship, or gain rapport, with the client. Finally, orientation to the program or programs available to the client may be provided.

Gaining Information

A prime purpose of the interview is, of course, to gather information regarding the client and to provide the client with an opportunity to begin to identify his or her needs and how these may be met. This may be accomplished by talking with the client and observing the client's condition and behavior.

The client's leisure behaviors and interests are regularly the focus of discussion during the interview. The therapeutic recreation specialist will likely ask the client about past leisure patterns, including the amount of time given to leisure, the activities in which he or she has participated, and who has taken part in recreation with the client. Additionally, an attempt is usually made to help the client identify recreational interests for possible future participation.

Common techniques to facilitate the interview are (1) a list of open-ended questions related to leisure patterns, and (2) formal leisure interest instruments. Typically, the open-ended questions appear on an interview form with a brief space following each one in which the client's response may be recorded. Leisure interest instruments are normally in a checklist format so that the client may complete them with the help of a therapeutic recreation specialist, or the TR specialist may read the items to the client and check the appropriate place on the forms. The following are representative of the open-ended questions.

- What kinds of things do you do for fun in your spare time?
- What are some of your hobbies?
- What would you like to do?
- Do you own any recreational equipment such as golf clubs, a tennis racket or canoe?
- Do you watch television and, if so, what programs do you watch?
- What things do you do with your family (spouse, children)?
- With whom do you take part in recreation?
- When do you usually participate in recreation?
- Would you rather do things with others or alone?

- Of the things you do in your free time, which do you like best?
- Do you like outdoor activities such as fishing or camping?
- Do you take vacations and, if so, what do you usually do on vacation?
- What would be your ideal vacation?

It is important that these or similar questions be used only to form as a guideline for interviewing and not be strictly adhered to. Instead the interviewer should feel free to deviate from any set of questions in order to follow up on a client's statement or probe more deeply into a particular area.

Most agencies or institutions offering therapeutic recreation service will adopt or develop some type of leisure interest instrument appropriate for use with their clients. As previously stated, the usual format for these instruments is a checklist. The instruments ask the client to review a listing of possible recreation activities and, for each one, respond if they now take part in the activity or if they would like to try it. Some instruments, such as the Mirenda Leisure Interest Finder (Mirenda, 1973), ask the client to indicate *how much* they like or dislike particular activities. In addition to Mirenda's instrument, other tools available for use in assessing client's interests include the Self Leisure Interest Profile (SLIP) (McDowell, 1974), Leisure Activities Blank (LAB) (McKechnie, n.d.; 1974), and the Avocational Activities Inventory (AAI) (Overs, 1970).

Whatever the approach, clients should be given the opportunity to express themselves in regard to their perceptions of strengths, weaknesses, and problems. Knowing how each client views himself or herself, the environment, and his or her place in that environment is necessary to understand completely the client's behavior. An attempt should be made to acquire this knowledge when occasions arise throughout the interview process.

Children

For children, traditional interview methods may not be appropriate. When feasible, the therapeutic recreation specialist may begin assessment procedures with an interview with each child's parents. Stanley and Kasson (n.d.) have produced materials to be used by those faced with the task of interviewing parents of handicapped children. These materials contain a series of questions that may be directed toward the parents regarding their child's play and social patterns. Questions based on those posed by Stanley and Kasson (n.d.) follow.

- What kinds of things does (child's name) do after school? On the weekends?

- Who does (child's name) play with? Other children? Parents? By himself or herself?
- If (child's name) does play with other children in the neighborhood, do they invite him or her to play?
- Does (child's name) indicate a preference for certain activities, such as sports, art, or music?
- What recreation equipment does (child's name) have?
- What sorts of recreation equipment or toys does (child's name) like to buy?
- Does (child's name) get excited easily or is he or she calm and easygoing?
- Does (child's name) like to try new things?
- Does (child's name) stick to projects or give up easily?
- Does (child's name) tend to be a self-starter or does he or she rely on others to get things started?
- Is (child's name) outgoing or shy?
- Does (child's name) enjoy helping around the house?
- Does (child's name) like to make decisions?

Stanley and Kasson (n.d.) also provide a list of suggested questions that might be used when interviewing the child. The following questions are adapted from that list.

- What sorts of things does your family do together for fun?
- If you weren't allowed to watch TV, what would you do in that time?
- What sort of hobby would you like to learn?
- Tell me the best birthday or Christmas present you ever got. What made it so good?
- What things do you do after school? On the weekend? With whom do you play?
- Did you like your summer vacation? What was good about it?
- What are your three favorite things to do?
- If you get an allowance, what do you spend it on?

When interviewing children, it is wise to consider conducting the interview in an area conducive to creating a relaxed, friendly environment. A play area may help create this atmosphere and has the added feature of allowing for possible observation of the child at play. Stanley and Kasson (n.d.) have suggested that the interviewer should make sure that various age-appropiate playthings are available so the child may play in a variety of modes during the interview. They go on to state that if the interviewer invites the child to play, this should always be done in a friendly and sincere manner so that the child is not given the impression of being tested. For the shy child or the child who has difficulty with verbal expression, Stanley and

WHAT ARE METHODS OF ASSESSING CLIENTS?

Kasson (n.d.) propose the use of pictures illustrating children taking part in various play or recreation activities. The child can be asked to choose those that he or she likes or would enjoy exploring. With all clients, nonverbal language is often the best indicator of the client's true feelings. Clues provided by bodily movement, gestures, and posture can prove to be more revealing than verbal expression. Few people would disagree that the child's smile is a good indicator that he or she likes something.

Developing a Relationship

A second purpose of the interview is to develop a relationship with the client. Developing rapport is not usually a major hurtle for the therapeutic recreation specialist, who is customarily seen by clients as a nonthreatening person. In highly clinical settings clients may feel particularly alienated by the surroundings and too frightened to approach the doctor or nurse. In such situations the unique role of the therapeutic recreation specialist often comes to the forefront. With the therapeutic recreation specialist clients usually feel that they can relax, "drop their guards," and "be themselves." In the clinical atmosphere a TR specialist may become a "professional friend," since he or she is viewed as someone who enters into a mutual participation with clients instead of as someone who does something *to* clients.

Orientation to the Program

Finally, the interview is sometimes also used to acquaint the client with the program or services provided by the therapeutic recreation service. Even though this orientation is often limited and necessarily brief, the interview allows the opportunity to inform the client of basic program offerings. The therapeutic recreation specialist must exercise judgment in determining how extensive an orientation is appropriate for the individual client. This may range from a few general statements regarding the availability of selected programs to a review of the complete therapeutic recreation offerings provided by the agency or institution.

WHAT ARE SOME SECONDARY SOURCES OF INFORMATION?

MEDICAL RECORDS

Medical records include the results of the physician's examination report, along with information on the client's medical history, physical assessment, and diagnostic studies. Also contained in the medical record is the medical diagnosis, a prognosis, a plan for medical treatment, physician's orders, progress reports, and other relevant medical information (Marriner, 1975; Murry & Zentner, 1975).

EDUCATIONAL RECORDS

In educational settings, educational records may be a basis for client assessment. According to Stephens (1976), assessment information for children with learning or behavioral handicaps should include an assessment of academic skills, a determination of which sensory modes are most effective in learning, an evaluation of the level of social skills, and an appraisal of the child's reinforcement system. Other information that might be found in educational records includes educational diagnoses and teacher and physician reports.

STANDARDIZED TESTING

Testing provides objective data about the client. Results from tests administered by psychologists or staff from other allied disciplines can be useful to therapeutic recreation assessment.

INTERVIEWS WITH FAMILY OR FRIENDS

Much can be learned about the client and his or her relationships with others by interviewing family or friends who may possess knowledge about the client's past leisure interests and behaviors. Information may also be gained in regard to future expectations and anticipated resources for the client's leisure participation.

SOCIAL HISTORY

The social history is normally completed by the social worker. It contains information on where the client was born, raised, and educated, the client's home and family, past occupations, family income, recreational pursuits, and religious affilation.

CASE RECORDINGS OR PROGRESS NOTES

Notes written by various staff contain objective comments regarding the client's behaviors as they deviate from normal. Charting is commonly accomplished daily in treatment and rehabilitation facilities by staff members, including nursing service and activity therapy personnel.

CONFERENCES AND TEAM MEETINGS

Where treatment teams exist, the therapeutic recreation specialist will likely be an integral part of the team. In this capacity he or she will confer regularly with other staff, both within and outside of formal team meetings. The formal and informal sharing of information with other staff will provide information that may be applied in therapeutic recreation assessment.

SURVEY OF CLIENT'S HOME AND COMMUNITY

A great deal may be learned by visiting the client's home and community. What are the social and recreational opportunities accessible to the client? What specific recreational outlets are evident in the home? Are parks, community centers, libraries, or other recreational facilities available in the client's neighborhood or community? Some treatment facilities maintain an up-to-date inventory of recreational programs and facilities available in the communities they serve.

WHAT GENERAL CLIENT INFORMATION IS COLLECTED?

General information that the therapeutic recreation specialist might wish to have on hand as soon as possible would include:

- Client's full name, address, and telephone number.
- Sex, age, and marital status.
- Date admitted.
- Education completed.
- Language(s) spoken.
- Occupation.
- Leisure interests briefly noted.
- Limitations or precautions (e.g., physical restrictions; suicidal).
- Medications.
- Why the client is seeking service.

In a clinically oriented facility it would also be appropriate to note the names of the client's physician, social worker, and primary therapist when recording initial assessment information. In a community-based program it would be advantageous to list with whom the client is living and who should be contacted in case of emergency. This insures that the information is readily available when required. Other information needed on the client will differ, depending on the type of setting in which therapeutic recreation service is delivered.

CONCLUDING STATEMENT ON ASSESSMENT

Adequate assessment is a prerequisite to the provision of individual program planning. However, assessment is a continuing process that does not end after the initial work-up on the client. Clients, like all human beings, are in a dynamic state of change necessitating that ongoing assessment be conducted with every client.

By assembling all available assessment data, the therapeutic recreation specialist will gain an overall picture of the client from which a statement of problems and needs may be made. Both *objective* data from various sources and *subjective* information gained directly from the client are usually required in order to formulate a clear definition of the client's needs.

Objective information includes data from medical records, educational records, results of standardized testing, interviews with family and friends, social history, case recordings or progress notes, information from staff conferences or team meetings, community survey information, systematic observations, and general client information, including demographic data.

Subjective assessment data is gathered directly from the client. Gunn and Peterson (1978) write:

> *Traditionally, subjective data include information about: (1) hours of available free time, (2) hobbies, (3) membership in organizations or groups, and (4) possible future interests. Additionally, it is important that constituents be allowed to express (1) what they believe their problems to be, (2) what their limitations are, (3) what their strengths are, and (4) what they hope to gain from participation (pp. 77–78).*

Client assessment employing objective and subjective data allows the TR specialist to explore both client strengths and weaknesses and then identify client needs. Once the initial assessment procedures have been completed, the TR specialist has formed the basis for individual program planning and can move to the second step in the therapeutic recreation process, the development or planning phase.

WHAT CONSTITUTES THE DEVELOPMENT OR PLANNING PHASE?

After identifying the client's needs, they are examined to determine priorities, goals are formulated, and a plan of action is determined. As a result of this planning phase, the client's personalized therapeutic recreation program emerges.

A four-step procedure may be conceptualized for the planning phase:

(1) setting priorities following examination of the client's needs; (2) formulating goals or general objectives; (3) determining strategies or actions to meet the goals; and (4) selecting methods to assess progress made toward the goals.

SETTING PRIORITIES

After the client's needs have been identified, the therapeutic recreation specialist should examine them carefully to determine if TR services can be helpful and to set priorities for dealing with the client's needs. Marriner (1975) suggests that for nursing plans it should be determined which needs the client can handle independently, which require professional help and what kind of help is indicated, and which needs are most urgent. She goes on to recommend that Maslow's needs hierarchy may serve as a guide to setting priorities. It would seem that Marriner's (1975) thoughts translate well to therapeutic recreation planning.

Maslow, the father of humanistic psychology, pictured humans as constantly striving toward self-actualization, or self-fulfillment, the highest level of need. Maslow's (1970) hierarchy contains five basic needs. At the lower levels are physiological needs (thurst, hunger, etc.) and safety needs (security, protection from threat of danger, freedom from fear). Next are social needs (belongingness and love needs) and self-esteem or ego needs (for self-respect, status, recognition). At the top of Maslow's hierarchy is the need for self-actualization (or the need to fulfill one's potentials). (See Chapter 4 for a more thorough explanation of Maslow's hierarchy.)

Once a need has been met it no longer evokes behavior. Satisfaction of lower-level physiological and safety needs provides a firm foundation from which the individual can move forward toward developing his or her potentials. Generally, there are fewer problems with these lower-levels needs than with the other needs, although physiological and safety needs certainly must be considered by the therapeutic recreation specialist. One area where this is particularly true is in dealing with the client's need for psychological safety. Psychological safety may be a problem if the client does not feel free from the fear of being labeled or discriminated against because of a disability or illness (Ringless, 1975). Neurotic anxieties also may threaten psychological safety (Maslow, 1970).

Recreation and leisure offer natural means by which the client's higher-level needs for belonging, self-esteem, and self-actualization may be met. Through gratifying recreation experiences, clients gain acceptance, validate their personal worth, and grow toward their potentials.

Employing Maslow's hierarchy, the therapeutic recreation specialist can analyze the client's needs and set priorities for the needs that require professional help. The client should be included in this planning if possible, although physical or mental conditions may prohibit the client's participation at times. Nevertheless, it is desirable to seek this involvement as soon as the client is ready to join the TR specialist in the planning process. Like all of us, clients are apt to become more committed to plans that they have helped to form. In recreation, where self-direction and independent decision making are hallmarks, client involvement becomes paramount.

FORMULATING GENERAL OBJECTIVES OR GOALS

Having general objectives or goals provides us with a sound basis for selecting activities or programs appropriate for client needs. General objectives or goals also are useful to evaluation, since they represent clear statements of sought outcomes. Finally, general objectives or goals give direction to the therapeutic recreation specialist and allow others to know what outcomes are intended.

It should be clear that general objectives or goals reflect sought outcomes that are directed toward satisfaction of our clients' needs. Therefore goals are written in terms of the clients' behavior and not the activities or processes of the therapeutic recreation specialist.

The critical nature of clearly formed goals in therapeutic recreation planning is reflected in a statement by O'Morrow (1980). He has written: "Without goals or objectives, the plan has lost its therapeutic value" (p. 205).

What are General Objectives or Goals?

Goals and general objectives describe proposed changes in the individual client or in the client's environment. When goals or general objectives are spelled out, the client knows just what is expected and will likely feel a real sense of accomplishment when goals are achieved.

Within this discussion, the terms goal and general objective are used to mean the same thing. They may be used interchangably. Goals or general objectives may be contrasted with specific objectives, which deal with very specific behaviors.

Goals or general objectives are written at the level of specificity needed to direct action but not be overly restricting. Gronlund (1970) speaks of general objectives in terms of *educational* outcomes and likens specific objectives to the *training* level. General objectives provide direction toward a general type or class of behavior, while specific objectives deal with a narrow band of behavior. In fact, one way to conceptualize the difference between a general objective and a specific objective is to think in terms of having to realize several specific objectives in order to reach one general objective. Therefore we may evaluate progress toward general objectives by sampling from a number of specific objectives that fall under the general objective.

We usually begin our therapeutic recreation planning by goal formulation, or stating general objectives. Then we stipulate specific objectives that will enable the client to achieve the long-range goal. The specific objectives of learning to breathe correctly in water and to float in water, for example, move the child toward the more general objective of swimming using particular strokes.

WHAT ARE CHARACTERISTICS OF USEFUL OBJECTIVES?

The chief characteristics of the useful objective is that it states what the client will *do* or, said another way, it identifies the kind of *behavior expected*. The lone exception to this would be the objectives having to do with changing the client's environment instead of seeking changes from within the client. Even with environmental goals, however, we should remain cognizant of the need to be explicit. But, in the main, the therapeutic recreation specialist will be working with behavioral changes; therefore the discussion of objectives will stress behavioral objectives.

Some rules for stating objectives, drawn primarily from Gronlund (1970), are:

1. *Begin with an action verb* instead of with a phrase such as, "The client will. . . ." By placing the verb first, the focus of the reader is placed on the sought outcome from the beginning.
2. *State the objective to reflect client behavior* instead of mixing client objectives with process objectives you may have for yourself in helping the client to reach goal satisfaction.
3. *Only state one terminal behavior per* objective instead of placing several behaviors in the same objective. This allows you to tell more easily if the objective has been fully realized. Putting two or more behaviors in the same objective is confusing and creates problems in evaluation when one behavior has been achieved but the other has not.
4. *Aim the objective at the appropriate level of specificity* instead of being too broad or too narrow. This is a difficult rule to follow, since it involves a certain amount of "feeling" or "intuitiveness" to stipulate objectives at the proper level. General objectives should be definable by stating specific types of behaviors that fall under them. Specific objectives should be relevant to a more general objective.

Mager (1962) has suggested that specific objectives may also stipulate conditions under which the behavior is to be performed and criteria for performance. To use Mager's (1962) terms, a condition is a "given" or a "restriction." These further define terminal behaviors by stipulating exact conditions imposed on the individual who is striving for the objective. Criteria, on the other hand, state a standard, or "how well" the individual is expected to perform.

Some brief examples may help clarify the concepts of criteria and conditions. Say you have a specific objective reading:

Locate the show times for films playing at local theaters.

You could begin by imposing a *condition* of the source information. So the specific objective might now read:

Given a copy of the Herald-Telephone *daily newspaper*, locate the show times for films playing at local theaters.

In addition to this *given* you might add another condition to the objective. This could be a *restriction* such as:

Without the help of the TR specialist, and given a copy of the *Herald-Telephone* daily newspaper, locate the show times for films playing at local theaters.

If you really want to become specific about your objective, you might add a *criteria*. The objective might then read like this.

Without the help of the TR specialist, and given a copy of the *Herald-Telephone* daily newspaper, locate the show times for films playing at local theaters *within a 3-minute period of time.*

By now you may be thinking, "Come on, let's not overdo it." Perhaps the example is overstated, perhaps not. Just how detailed should you be in writing specific objectives? Mager (1962) answered the question when stating the following.

You should be detailed enough to be sure the target behavior would be recognized by another competent person, and detailed enough so that other possible behaviors would not be mistaken for the desired behavior. You should be detailed enough, in other words, so that others understand your intent as you *understand it (p. 26).*

WHAT ARE SOURCES OF INFORMATION ON STATING OBJECTIVES?

Mager's (1962) *Preparing Instructional Objectives* is perhaps the best-known source for writing behavioral objectives. The book uses an easy-to-follow programmed learning format. It is an excellent basic reference to aid in the forming of specific objectives. Gronlund (1970) offers a well-written explanation of general and specific objectives. His chapter on a three-part taxonomy covering the cognitive, affective, and psychomotor domains clearly explains a useful classification system and offers examples of verbs that may be employed in writing objectives. For those with particular interest in the psychomotor domain, Harrow's (1972) book, *A Taxonomy of the Psychomotor Domain*, should prove helpful.

DETERMINING STRATEGIES AND ACTIONS: INDIVIDUAL, PERSONALIZED PROGRAM PLANS FROM GOALS

The individual program plan is a written document stating what the client and therapeutic recreation specialist intend to accomplish. The plan flows from the client's previously established goals set. This goals set must fit, of course, into any overall client plan and should coincide with the general objectives of the agency or institution. Furthermore, the goals should be realistic and attainable so that the client is not destined to failure. Goals may be classed as immediate or long range in order to direct the goal achievement process and more aptly assure feelings of success on the part of both the client and staff.

Many settings employ goal-directed planning, but the terms used to describe the individual program plan vary. In clinical facilities the individual program plan is usually referred to as a "treatment plan." The term "care plan" is often applied in long-range care facilities such as nursing homes and continued care centers (Avedon, 1974). With the advent of Public Law 94-142, The Education of All Handicapped Children Act, the term "Individualized Educational Program" (IEP) has come to be commonly employed in educational settings such as public schools and residential schools for special populations.

The exact nature of individual program plans will necessarily differ from setting to setting. Common elements that are likely to transcend all plans regardless of setting are:

1. An indication of the client's problems and needs.
2. A prioritized goals set appropriate to guide the delivery of therapeutic recreation services.
3. A listing of specific objectives for each goal.
4. A plan of activities or programs indicated for participation by the client, approaches to be utilized by staff, and the proper environment in which to facilitate change.
5. A brief description of methods by which client progress will be periodically evaluated.

By constructing a plan containing these elements, the client will have a personalized program plan based on sought behavioral changes, the strengths and weaknesses of the client, and the anticipated impact of the client, environment, and staff on behavioral change. The strategies formulated for the plan should meet the established goals and consider each client's unique background, psychological makeup, and personal needs and expectations. By so doing, each properly prepared plan will be distinctive or personalized.

The Case of Miller L. Bush

An example of a personalized program plan appears in Figure 3-2. It is based loosely on a case study that appeared in Lamson (1978). This case involved a single male in his midtwenties who became severely depressed after his girlfriend broke up with him. This psychologically threatening

Figure 3-2 Individual program plan.

Date Line:
   Who: Miller L. Bush
   Why admitted: Complaints of severe depression
   Subjective: States he lacks motivation to participate in leisure activity or work. Feels tired. Wishes to have friends but doesn't know how. Says no one would want him for a friend. Claims he can't sustain a conversation. Doesn't feel adequate in traditional male roles—"failure" in relationship with girlfriend, he says, confirms inadequacy. Likes sports, especially tennis and swimming. Wishes to continue them when he leaves the hospital.
   Objective: Extreme withdrawl from family and friends. Became depressed when he and girlfriend broke up. Observed on the admitting ward to gain satisfaction from watching tennis on TV. Until recently, very active person. On college tennis and swim teams. Likes unit TR specialist.
   Assessment: Very reserved. Appears to want to talk with others but isn't comfortable in doing so. Isn't confident. Lacks positive self-esteem. Is bright as evidenced in several brief conversations with the TR specialist, but holds back information as if frightened to reveal too much of himself.

Needs:
   1. To interact with others through verbal and nonverbal means.
   2. To take part in some type of gratifying physical activity with others in order to begin working toward meeting esteem needs.

DETERMINING STRATEGIES AND ACTIONS

Goals:
1. Increases interaction with others.
2. Participates in physical activity.

Specific Objectives:
1.A. Greets the TR specialist.
1.B. Answers questions posed by others.
1.C. Uses nonverbal means of responding to others.
1.D. Initiates conversations with others.
2.A. Takes walks around grounds in free time.
2.B. Rallys tennis balls with the TR specialist.
2.C. Works out at gym with TR specialist.
2.D. Swims at the hospital pool during ward swim.
2.E. Plays co-rec vollyball on ward unit when encouraged by the TR specialist.

Plan:
- Do not place on full activity schedule at this time.
- To participate in regular ward activities (swimming, volleyball) and in daily tennis or gym workout with the TR specialist.
- Don't demand the patient to interact with you but be pleasant; allow opportunities for interactions and encourage him when he does interact.
- Strive to gradually increase the length of interactions.
- Give approval for active participation in physical activity, praising his successes in an appropriate manner.

Evaluation:
- To discuss and reevaluate in team meeting at the end of the week.
- Keep daily progress notes of behavior on ward and in one-to-one activities.

October 16, 1981   David R. Austin
   (date)   (signature)

- How much recall (i.e., memory) is involved? For example, are there many rules to remember?
- What level of concentration is needed?
- What levels of analysis (i.e., breaking down material) and synthesis (i.e., putting parts together) is required?
- What level of verbal skill is needed?
- Are participants called on to think quickly and make rapid decisions?
- Is abstract thinking called for?

event was taken by the client as proof of his worthlessness and his inadequacy as a male. For those who might wonder, Lamson (1978) reported that the patient was able to overcome his depression, feel good about himself, and ultimately terminate treatment.

Activity Analysis

Once goals and objectives have been specified in the individual program plan, the therapeutic recreation specialist must select activities to apply in the intervention process. The activities utilized in intervention must be thoroughly understood in order to help assure optimal therapeutic benefit for the client. The name given the procedure for systematically achieving a precise and complete understanding of activities is *activity analysis*.

Peterson (1976) has defined activity analysis as follows.

> *Activity analysis is a process which involves the systematic application of selected sets of constructs and variables to breakdown and examine a given activity to determine the behavioral requirements inherent for successful participation.*

Activity analysis permits the practitioner to break down activities into their component parts. Thus a total comprehension of a given activity is acquired so that the activity may be properly utilized to meet the goals and objectives of the individual program plan.

In some instances the activity will be employed "as is." That is, no alterations will be required in order for clients to gain maximum benefit from participation. For example, a dance for clients would be planned and conducted in much the same way as a dance for any group. At other times, the therapeutic recreation specialist may manipulate the activity to bring about therapeutic intents. In so doing opportunities are created for the activity to contribute directly toward sought behavioral objectives. For example, cooperation might be emphasized in a particular sports activity in order to reinforce cooperative behaviors on the part of a certain client or clients. In still other cases, activities will need to be adapted or modified to accommodate clients with limitations. Adaptative equipment may be utilized, such as audible softballs for visually impaired clients or a handle grip bowling ball for those who have difficulty gripping. Games may be modified by reducing the dimensions of the playing area, simplifying rules, or through other similar means. Whatever the modification, it is important that the therapeutic recreation specialist have a detailed understanding of the activity so that artificial or unnecessary modifications are not made. As a general principle, the best modification is the least modification.

Gunn and Peterson (1978) and Kraus (1978) have suggested that activity analysis should include the three behavioral domains (i.e., psychomotor, cognitive, affective) as well as social or interactional skills. It is the task of the TR specialist to examine the demands placed on participants by the activity in regard to specificities. Each of the four components must be appraised to determine what behaviors and skills are required by those who take part in the activity. Examples of aspects for possible consideration follow under each of the four major components.

PSYCHOMOTOR (PHYSICAL) DOMAIN

- Is the full body involved or only part of the body?
- What types of manipulative movement is required (throwing, hitting, catching, kicking, bouncing, pulling, pushing, grasping, lifting)?
- What types of locomotor movements are required (crawling, walking, running, climbing, jumping, hopping, rolling, skipping)?
- What kinds of nonlocomotor movements are required (twisting, turning, stretching, extending, bending, swinging, hanging, landing)?
- What level of exertion is required?
- What degree of fitness is necessary?
- Is a high level of skill development required (e.g., hand-eye coordination, balance)?
- Is rhythm required?
- How much endurance is necessary?
- How much repetitiveness in movement is required?
- What sensory demands are made?

COGNITIVE (INTELLECTUAL) DOMAIN

- Is the level of complexity appropriate for the clients?
- Is there a high degree of repetitiveness in the activity?
- Are academic skills required (e.g., spelling, reading, or math)?

AFFECTIVE (PSYCHOLOGICAL) DOMAIN

- Does the activity release tension (stress)?
- Does the activity allow the client to communicate feelings?
- Does the activity generally lead to fun?
- To what degree is it possible to display creativity?
- Does frustration commonly arise from participation?
- How much control (over the environment) can the client experience?
- Does the activity have potential for enhancement of self-esteem?
- Is teamwork emphasized? Sharing? Helping others?
- Is self-discipline necessary? Listening skills?

- Are democratic processes followed?
- Is the activity stimulating? Exciting?
- Are values apparent in the activity? If so, what values?

SOCIAL (INTERACTIONAL) SKILLS

- Is cooperation emphasized? Competition?
- Do structures (rules) reinforce prosocial behavior?
- Is the activity individual? Small group oriented?
- How many persons may participate?
- How much leadership must be provided?
- How structured is the activity?
- May all ages take part? All sizes?
- Are traditional sex roles emphasized?
- What types of interaction patterns occur?
- What amount of initiative is required?
- Is a high level of interaction called for?
- Is verbal communication necessary?
- Does the space dictate being close to others? Physically touching?

The therapeutic recreation specialist will also necessarily need to analyze activities for other aspects in addition to social skills and the psychomotor, cognitive, and affective domains. Elements for consideration, drawn primarily from the work of Fidler and Fidler (1954), include the following.

ADAPTABILITY AND VARIABILITY OF ACTIVITIES

- How much time is required for participation?
- Is the activity adaptable to various chronological and mental age levels?
- How much is speed emphasized in completing tasks within the activity and to what degree can this be controlled?
- How much variety is possible in selection of tasks or projects within the activity (e.g., how many types and levels of leather-tooling projects would be available)?

USEFULNESS TO CLIENTS

- Does the activity have any carry-over value in terms of participating in it outside of the agency setting?
- Is the cost of the activity within the means of clients?
- Do products made have any useful value to clients (i.e., to use themselves or give as gifts)?

PRACTICABILITY

- Is the activity practical for bed patients when factors such as noise and equipment are considered?
- What are the space and environmental requirements for the activity (e.g., size of room or outdoor space needed, requirements for light, equipment readily adjusted to the needs of clients)?
- Is the activity too expensive for the agency in terms of equipment and supplies?
- How much staffing is required to conduct the activity?
- When would the activity be contraindicated (for particular types of clients)?

A word of caution is in order here. The therapeutic recreation specialist must remember that, for the individual client, an activity is *not* an activity, is *not* an activity. It is the individual's particular approach to the activity that defines his or her experience. *How* the client takes part in the activity has a primary impact on the experience. For example, those who are hard driven and competitive will approach an activity very differently from persons who have more relaxed dispositions.

Therefore it is not entirely the activity itself but also the way someone approaches the activity that affects the experience. The therapeutic recreation specialist must be aware that although understanding behavioral requirements of the activity is important, employing activities with clients is a complex task that should not be started on a simplistic level in which prescribed outcomes are expected by having clients participate in a given activity.

Assessing Progress

It was previously mentioned that the last step in the planning process is to determine methods of assessing client progress. In the case of Mr. Bush (Figure 3-2), assessment took the form of progress notes and discussion of his progress after a week.

The attentive reader may have noticed that Mr. Bush's program plan was an initial, preliminary effort to direct early stages of the helping process. As Burgess and Lazare (1976) have pointed out, there are likely to be three actual stages in planning: (1) the *initial plan* to deal with essential interventions while full assessment is being completed; (2) the *total assessment plan* based on a complete assessment utilizing the techniques mentioned earlier in this chapter and from which the major intervention strategies are evolved; and (3) the *revised plan* based on new data, which leads to altered actions either to bring about revisions in unproductive change strategies or meet newly identified needs. Therefore each client is apt to have several program plans developed as a result of the ongoing assessment process.

WHAT IS THE IMPLEMENTATION PHASE?

Implementation is the actual provision of the program. In implementation the strategies developed in the planning phase are employed. Perhaps the most important item to be considered in the implementation of the individual program plan is consistency. A well-formed plan allows all involved to strive for similar goals following agreed on approaches. Such planning also contributes to the continuity of care provided by establishing short-term, intermediate, and long-term goals.

Often an interdisciplinary team effort will be utilized in implementing the plan. In other instances the plan will be carried out by one or more TR specialists. The setting and needs of the client dictate the particular procedures to be pursued. In any case, it is necessary to determine who has the authority and responsibility for coordinating the client's activities. Without clear delineation as to who is in control of the plan, problems will likely arise, since much coordination is necessary in maintaining client plans.

Usually some type of written communication is sent to all appropriate staff members informing them of the individual program plan to be implemented. Additionally, in settings such as hospitals and residential centers where clients are in various types of activities throughout the day (therapeutic recreation, psychotherapy, physical therapy, etc.), an activity schedule is often provided for each client. This schedule usually lists the days of the week and the hours of each day so that the activities planned for the client may be recorded. Written communications, such as the individual program plan and activity schedule, provide sources of reference and serve as reminders of the client's program for all staff. By following a systematic routine and using written communication, misunderstandings are avoided and consistency is promoted in the carrying out of the program plan.

In some modern facilities client information is placed on a computer so that a clerk can call up data desired by staff on a particular client. This technological innovation allows changes to be made easily in the client's day-to-day activity schedule. The problem of retrieving and reissuing typewritten copies of client schedules is eradicated, thus eliminating a major practical difficulty in making revisions in schedules. It is anticipated that the computer will continue to play a growing role in the implementation phase as time goes on. *No — think?*

82

WHAT IS THE EVALUATION PHASE?

Evaluation is the final step in the therapeutic recreation process. Through evaluation, the effectiveness of the client's program is examined.

In therapeutic recreation we are concerned with individual client evaluation and program evaluation. Both are important, and each is difficult to separate from the other, since programs are the vehicles by which we in therapeutic recreation help individual clients to meet problems or needs. In individual client evaluation the client is central to our purpose. In program evaluation we target our concern on the program itself. In either case, distinctions may be conceived to be somewhat arbitrary and difficult to maintain.

For the purpose of this chapter, however, the focus will remain with the individual client (program evaluation is covered in Chapter 6). Therefore discussion will center on completing client evaluation.

Individual client evaluation is closely tied to the planning process because part of the planning process is determining methods to assess client progress. The actual carrying out of these methods is client evaluation. In the case of Mr. Bush, progress notes and staff discussion served as means to evaluation.

The approach taken in Mr. Bush's case is very representative of the general approach taken to client evaluation. Although some readers may be concerned about the lack of "rigor" provided by this general approach, they should not be. Staff should not limit their analysis only to "measurable" items. Staff can and should utilize naturalistic observations, observations of behaviors related to specific objectives (i.e., specific goal observation), and subjective feelings. Nevertheless, the emerging therapeutic recreation specialist will be more apt to rely on more quanitative means, such as norm-referenced tests and time-interval observations, since it requires some experience to develop observational skills and to learn to place trust in feelings.

In addition to the observational methods that have been mentioned, other methods used in initial client assessment are appropriate for evaluation. For example, the interview method offers an opportunity for clients to respond retrospectively as to how they perceive themselves after participation in perscribed activities compared to their perceptions prior to beginning the program. Secondary sources of information offer another means for client evaluation. For instance, pretest and posttest scores on standardized tests given by a psychologist may be contrasted to measure gains in a variable such as self-esteem, family and friends may be interviewed following a home visit by a hospitalized client, information may be gained from other staff at a team meeting, or progress notes may be reviewed.

If several different sources of information agree on the progress of the client, it can be said that congruence exists among them. Generally, the TR specialist should attempt to structure evaluation procedures to retrieve data from several independent sources to see if the data stand up to the test of congruence (i.e., the information is consistent).

Of course, all methods of client evaluation exist to determine if the hypothesized results transpired as a consequence of whatever therapeutic recreation intervention was applied. In other words, evaluation answers the question, "Were sought outcomes achieved as a result of the program?" If evaluation is not completed, the TR specialist has no basis on which to judge the effectiveness of the program in bringing about the objectives stated in the client's individual program plan.

It is essential to involve clients in the process of evaluation. Just as clients should be involved in the prior phases of the therapeutic recreation process, they should be involved to the fullest extent of their capabilities in evaluation. By engaging in evaluation, clients can help staff to judge the effectiveness of the program in reaching sought outcomes.

A FINAL COMMENT

The therapeutic recreation process has commonly been associated with highly clinical programs; however, its application goes far beyond the bounds of the clinical setting. The therapeutic recreation process of (1) assessment, (2) planning, (3) implementation, and (4) evaluation can be applied in any setting in which goal-directed programs are desired. Thus the therapeutic recreation process is not restricted to hospitals or rehabilitation or treatment centers. The systematic process outlined in this chapter can guide therapeutic recreation specialists who practice professionally in community-based programs, corrections facilities, nursing homes, and all other facilities where recreation is used with therapeutic intent. Conversely, if this process is not followed therapeutic recreation service is not being provided, no matter what group is being served. The simple provision of recreation service for individuals from special population groups does not constitute in itself the delivery of therapeutic recreation service. Recreation programs for special populations that do not utilize the therapeutic recreation process should make no claims on the term "therapeutic recreation." They are better called "recreation for special populations."

KEY WORDS

Humanistic Perspective. The humanistic perspective views the delivery of therapeutic recreation services as a human enterprise in which the dignity and rights of the client are fully recognized. Each of us is seen as a whole person striving to realize our individual potentials, yet capable of growing beyond ourselves in order to care about others.

High-Level Wellness. An approach that centers around the wholeness of the individual, calling for wellness or health enhancement in contrast to the illness orientation often found in the medical community.

Therapeutic Recreation Process. A systematic method of problem solving employed in therapeutic recreation. The process contains four phases: assessment, planning, implementation, and evaluation.

Assessment. The first phase of the therapeutic recreation process. It is concerned with collecting and analyzing information in order to determine the status of the client.

Goals. In this book the term goals is used interchangeably with the term general objectives. Goals or general objectives are statements of sought outcomes directed toward meeting the client's needs. They are written at a level of specificity aimed at directing action but not being overly restrictive.

Specific Objectives. "Mager-like" objectives written at a level to designate specific, or explicit, client behaviors.

Individual Program Plan. A plan flowing out of an established goals set that considers each client's unique background, psychological makeup, and personal needs and expectations. A properly prepared plan will reflect a personalized approach.

Reading Comprehension Questions

1 What is the humanistic perspective? Is it reflected in therapeutic recreation?
2 Describe the concept of high-level wellness.
3 Construct and interpret a continuum of service for TR.
4 Outline and describe briefly the phases in the TR process.
5 What is the purpose of therapeutic recreation assessment?
6 List methods the TR specialist might use in completing client assessment.
7 Would you approach an interview with a child in the same way as with an adult? If not, how might these interviews differ?
8 What secondary sources are used in assessment?
9 What basic general information might the TR specialist wish to gain on the client as soon as possible?
10 What is objective assessment data? Subjective data?
11 What are four steps in the planning phase?

12 How may Maslow's needs hierarchy be used to assist in setting priorities?
13 How do goals, or general objectives, differ from specific objectives?
14 Why formulate goals? Specific objectives?
15 Outline rules useful in stating objectives.
16 Clarify what Mager means by conditions and criteria as applied to specific objectives.
17 What common elements are likely to be found in individual (personalized) program plans?
18 Why is it important that each client's individual program plan is personalized?
19 Do you agree with the personalized program plan developed for Mr. Bush? Why or why not?
20 Can you apply activity analysis to a recreation activity of your choosing?
21 What are the three stages of planning described by Burgess and Lazare?
22 Outline considerations for the implementation phase.
23 With what types of evaluation are we concerned in TR?
24 What is formative evaluation? Summative evaluation?
25 Should the client be involved in decision making during the TR process? Why or why not?
26 Do you agree with the distinction made between "therapeutic recreation" and "recreation for special populations?"

REFERENCES

Ardell, B. 1977. *High level wellness: An alternative to doctors, drugs, and disease.* Emmaus, Pa.: Rodale Press.

Avedon, E. M. 1974. *Therapeutic recreation service: An applied behavioral science approach.* Englewood Cliffs, N.J.: Prentice-Hall, Inc.

Burgess, W., & Lazare, A. 1976. *Pscyhiatric nursing in the hospital and the community* (2nd edition). Englewood Cliffs, N.J.: Prentice-Hall, Inc.

Chapman, J. E., & Chapman, H. H. 1975. *Behavior and health care: A humanistic helping process.* Saint Louis: The C. V. Mosby Company.

Dunn, H. L. 1961. *High level wellness.* Arlington, Va.: R. W. Beatty.

Fidler, G. S., & Fidler, J. W. 1954. *Introduction to psychiatric occupational therapy.* New York: The MacMillan Company.

Gray, D. E. 1975. The future of American society. In J. F. Murphy, the epilogue to *Recreation and leisure services*. Dubuque, Iowa: Wm. C. Brown Company, Publishers.

Gronlund, N. E. 1970. *Stating behavioral objectives for classroom instruction*. London: The Macmillian Company.

Gunn, S. L., & Peterson, C. A. 1978. *Therapeutic recreation program design: Principles and procedures*. Englewood Cliffs, N.J.: Prentice-Hall, Inc.

Gunn, S. L., & Peterson, C. A. 1977. Therapy and leisure education. *Parks & Recreation*. *12* (11), 22–25+.

Harrow, A. J. 1972. *A taxonomy of the psychomotor domain*. New York: David McKay Company, Inc.

Kraus, R. 1978. *Therapeutic recreation service: Principles and practices* (2nd edition). Philadelphia: W. B. Saunders Company.

Lamson, A. 1978. *Guide for the beginning therapist*. New York: Human Sciences Press.

Mager, F. 1962. *Preparing instructional objectives*. Belmont, Calif.: Fearson Publishers.

Marriner, A. 1975. *The nursing process: A scientific approach to nursing care*. Saint Louis: The C. V. Mosby Company.

McDowell, C. F. 1974. Toward a healthy leisure mode: Leisure counseling. *Therapeutic Recreation Journal*. *8*(3), 96–104.

McKechnie, G. E. n.d. *Manual for the leisure activities blank*. Palo Alto, Calif.: Consulting Psychology Press, Inc.

McKechnie, G. E. 1974. Psychological foundations of leisure counseling: An empirical strategy. *Therapeutic Recreation Journal*. *8*(1), 4–16.

Mirenda, J. J. 1973. Mirenda leisure interest finder. In A. Epperson, J. Mirenda, R. Overs, & G. T. Wilson, eds., *Leisure Counseling Kit*. Washington, D.C.: American Alliance for Health, Physical Education, and Recreation.

Murphy, J. F. 1975. *Recreation and leisure services*. Dubuque, Ia.: Wm. C. Brown Company, Publishers.

Murphy, J. F., Williams, J. G., Niepoth, E. W., & Brown, P. D. 1973. *Leisure service delivery system: A modern perspective*. Philadelphia: Lea & Febiger.

O'Morrow, G. S. 1980. *Therapeutic recreation: A helping profession* (2nd edition). Reston, Va.: Reston Publishing Company, Inc.

Overs, R. P. 1970. A model for avocational counseling. *Journal of Health, Physical Education and Recreation. 41*(2), 28–36.

Peterson, C. A. 1976. Activity analysis. In *Leisure activity participation and handicapped populations: Assessment of research needs.* Arlington, Va.: National Recreation and Park Association.

Ringness, T. A. 1975.. *The affective domain in education.* Boston: Little, Brown and Company.

Schulman, E. D. 1978. *Intervention in human services* (2nd edition). Saint Louis: The C. V. Mosby Company.

Stanley, J., & Kasson, I. n.d. Guidelines for interviewing applicants and parents. Office on Community Recreation for Handicapped Persons, State of New Jersey Department of Community Affairs, Trenton, N. J.

Stephens, T. M. 1976. *Directive teaching of children with learning and behavioral handicaps* (2nd edition). Columbus, Ohio: Charles E. Merrill Publishing Company.

Sundeen, J., Stuart, G. W., Rankin, Ed, & Cohen, S. P. 1976. *Nurse-client interaction implementing the nursing process.* Saint Louis: The C. V. Mosby Company.

Takata, N. 1974. Play as a prescription, In Mary Reilly (ed.), *Play As Exploratory Learning: Studies of Curiosity Behavior.* Beverly Hills, Calif.: Sage Publications, pp. 209–246.

4

HELPING
OTHERS

PURPOSE OF THE CHAPTER

Professional helping relationships have much in common with social relationships. Nonetheless, there are distinctions between helping as a professional and helping as a friend. To be an effective helping professional requires certain characteristics. One of these is possessing self-awareness. This chapter will clarify the role of the professional helper and will discuss characteristics of professional helpers with particular attention to the development of self-awareness.

OBJECTIVES

- Comprehend the nature of a professional helping relationship.
- Appreciate the qualities or characteristics necessary for those who desire to be effective professional helpers.
- Recognize characteristics that should be possessed by therapeutic recreation specialists in order to practice as helping professionals.
- Appreciate the necessity for therapeutic recreation specialists to increase and refine their level of self-awareness.
- Analyze self-conceptualizations.
- Analyze fundamental personal needs.
- Recognize how values help to define behaviors.
- Recognize some of one's own values.
- Evaluate basic philosophical beliefs for practice as a therapeutic recreation specialist.

WHAT IS PROFESSIONAL HELPING?

One of the most widely read books within the clinical psychology and psychiatric communities has been Schofield's (1964) *Psychotherapy: The Purchase of Friendship.* In this book the author likened the role of some clinical psychologists, psychiatrists, and psychiatric social workers to that of a "professional friend." Schofield stated that the long-term relationships often provided to clients by these professionals were simply substitute friendships for those in need of someone with whom to talk about problems and concerns.

Helping relationships do share similarities with friendships. However, even though they have a great deal in common, professional helping relationships and social relationships do differ. With friends we are regularly giving of ourselves to assist them. In turn, we are helped by our friends. There is mutuality in the relationship. There is a norm of reciprocity at work. If we find ourselves constantly giving and never receiving, in all likelihood we will end the friendship. In such cases we may even claim we have been "taken advantage of."

Professional helping relationships differ from social relationships in that the primary focus is always on one person, the client. The client has come for professional help with no intent of reciprocating. The mutuality existing in friendships is not present in the professional helping relationship, since those involved have different roles; one is to give help (the helper), and the other is to receive help (the client). The fundamental reality that the relationship exists to meet the needs of the client, not the helper, is basic to maintaining a healthy helping relationship (Brill, 1978).

This, of course, is not to say professional helpers, including therapeutic recreation specialists, are not human. Helping others certainly does meet very real human needs. Through helping we gain satisfaction in seeing others succeed and experience a sense of feeling needed. Perhaps helping professionals need clients as much as clients need them. But help is given by the helping professional without the expectation of personal gain. Mayeroff (1971) has presented the concept of helping in an insightful work titled *On Caring* in which Mayeroff states: "To care for another person, in the most significant sense, is to help him grow and actualize himself. . . . Caring is the antithesis of simply using the other person to satisfy one's own needs" (p. 1). Through helping others we help ourselves. We fulfill ourselves, or actualize ourselves, through caring for others.

WHAT IS THE AIM OF THE HELPING RELATIONSHIP?

The helping relationship is, as stated in Chapter 1, directed toward maximizing the client's growth potential and preventing or relieving problems. Helping is *not resolving* problems *for* the client or handling crises *for* the client. Instead, in a helping relationship we *assist* the client to meet pressing needs and to go beyond current needs to prepare for the future. Therefore the ultimate goal of the helping relationship is to facilitate growth leading to independence and self-sufficiency.

WHAT CHARACTERISTICS ARE NEEDED?

What characteristics should the effective helper possess? Many answers have been given to this question.

Eubanks (1976, pp. 187–189) has listed the following as core elements in the helping relationship.

1. *Awareness.* Helpers should understand their own strengths, limitations, and needs as well as those of their clients.

2. *Honesty.* There should be no front or facade put up by the helper.
3. *Acceptance.* Helpers should show willing acceptance of the client by expressing trust and a caring attitude.
4. *Freedom.* Freedom deals with the helper's ability to allow the client to grow.

Brammer (1979, pp. 26–34) has presented the following characteristics of the effective helper.

1. *Awareness of Self and Values.* Helpers need to develop a sense of self and what is important to them.
2. *Ability to Analyze the Helper's Own Feelings.* Helpers need to be able to examine their feelings and how they may influence the helping relationship.
3. *Ability to Serve as a Model and Influence.* Helpers should realize their function as models and social influences for clients. The client sees the helper as an "expert" possessing a great deal of influence.
4. *Altruism.* The effective helper is extremely interested in others. He or she is interested in helping others rather than meeting their own needs.
5. *Strong Sense of Ethics.* Helpers subscribe to professional ethics in conducting helping relationships.
6. *Responsibility.* Helpers define their relationship with clients so that a common understanding concerning responsible helper behavior is made clear.

Carkhuff (1969, p. 216) lists four facilitative dimensions necessary in the initial stages of the relationship. They are:

1. *Empathetic Response.* Helpers use responses that reflect the feelings and meanings of the client.
2. *Open Unconditionality and Warmth.* Helpers accept the client without reservations and portray an accepting attitude.
3. *Concreteness.* Helpers are specific and immediate in their responses to client statements as they attempt to facilitate problem exploration.
4. *Genuineness.* The actions of the helper should be congruent with their thoughts. Helpers are honest with themselves and the clients.

Carl Rogers has had a significant impact on the helping professionals who have followed him. In fact, the triad of elements originally stipulated by Rogers (1961, pp. 61–62) are reflected in all subsequent lists. His three elements are:

1. *Congruence (Genuineness).* Helpers are themselves. They do not put up a false front or facade.

WHAT CHARACTERISTICS ARE NEEDED?

2. *Unconditional Positive Regard.* A warm, positive, accepting attitude is displayed by the helper. The helper prizes the client as a person.
3. *Empathetic Understanding.* Helpers experience an accurate understanding of the client's private world.

Okun (1976, pp. 31–35) has provided a practical list of helping characteristics. Her list includes the following qualities.

1. *Self-Awareness.* Helpers who possess self-awareness have a basis for helping others in the development of self-awareness.
2. *Honesty.* A crucial quality for helpers is to express themselves honestly and to develop trust.
3. *Congruence.* Helpers who have congruence between their values and beliefs and their style of communication are seen as more credible and as more potent models.
4. *Communication Skills.* Helpers' behaviors involve the ability to communicate observations, feelings, and beliefs.
5. *Knowledge.* Helpers know and interpret theories on which effective helping is based.

An extensive list of characteristics of the effective helper has been outlined by Eisenberg and Delaney (1977, pp. 5–10). The characteristics are as follows.

1. *Reach Out.* Helpers know how to reach out to others through skillful listening and responding, which avoids defensiveness and communication blocks.
2. *Inspire Trust, Credibility, and Confidence.* Helpers foster honest communications by acting in a straightforward and nonmanipulative fashion.
3. *Reach In.* Helpers are self-aware. They have looked inward and, therefore, can ask the same of their clients.
4. *Communicate Caring and Respect.* Showing clients that they are perceived to be worthy of receiving the helpers' respect is important.
5. *Respect Themselves and Do Not Use Others.* Helpers need to have an adequate concept of self so that they are not preoccupied with meeting their own needs rather than their client's.
6. *Special Knowledge.* Helpers need expertise in an area of value to the person seeking help.
7. *Nonjudgmental.* Helpers understand, rather than apply judgments, to client.
8. *Reason Systematically and Think in Systems Terms.* Helpers view clients in a holistic manner, realize that many complex variables affect behavior, and are aware of the social system of which the client is a part.

HELPING CHARACTERISTICS FOR THERAPEUTIC RECREATION SPECIALISTS

It can be seen from the lists of characteristics that the helper's *self-awareness* and *ability to communicate* are overriding themes. Effective helpers are also certainly seen to need to possess more than good intentions. I would agree with Okun (1976) and Eisenberg and Delaney (1977) that a *knowledge base* is a prime quality for a helping professional. Finally, I would submit that therapeutic recreation specialists additionally need to project a *strong belief in recreation and leisure experiences* and the values inherent in these experiences.

Therefore, in outline form, the following are proposed as characteristics of the effective therapeutic recreation specialist.

1. *Self-Awareness.* Therapeutic recreation specialists must know themselves or develop a sense of self.
2. *Ability to Communicate.* The ability to communicate effectively is basic to the helping process.
3. *Knowledge Base.* Therapeutic recreation specialists must possess special knowledge in therapeutic recreation in order to be effective.
4. *Strong Belief in Recreation and Leisure Experiences.* Therapeutic recreation specialists prize the positive consequences to be gained through meaningful recreation and leisure experiences.

These characteristics are a working list, and are not intended to be complete. However, these elements are, I believe, the *sin qua non* of the therapeutic recreation helping relationship.

SELF-AWARENESS

Therapeutic recreation specialists should pursue self-awareness from a personal viewpoint and from a professional one. Therapeutic recreation specialists must know themselves and feel reasonably satisfied with themselves as persons before entering into fully effective helping relationships.

In a curriculum study completed at Indiana University (Austin & Binkley, 1977) practitioners were asked to rate competencies needed for practice as a master's degree-prepared TR specialist. The competency "To increase and refine self-knowledge" was one of the highest-rated competencies. It would seem logical that practitioners would rate this competency high, since we must learn to know ourselves in order to help others. If we are overly concerned about ourselves and our personal needs, we are apt to have a difficult time helping others. Chapman and Chapman (1975) have reported that beginning helping professionals are often concerned first about themselves and second about the client. Such preoccupation with the self is a part of the natural evolution in becoming an effective helping professional.

Knowing ourselves helps us to understand the client more quickly. Having a personal experience with any problem enables us to identify and relate more readily to similar problems in clients. This, in part, is the logic behind having those who have had drinking problems work with individuals diagnosed with alcoholism. By being aware of our personal value system, we can also monitor ourselves to make a conscious attempt not to force our values on our clients. Finally, professionals are also people and, like clients, have strengths and weaknesses. Knowing ourselves helps us to realize when we reach the limits of our helping abilities (Chapman & Chapman, 1975).

Within the therapeutic recreation literature little mention has been made of the need to know ourselves or how to go about the critical task of gaining self-awareness. There are various ways to achieve self-knowledge. Brill (1978) has suggested we can get to know ourselves in two general ways: (1) introspection (looking within ourselves), and (2) interpersonal communication (interacting with others). In the remainder of the chapter specific techniques employing these two methods will be discussed. Admittedly, the coverage given to the specific self-exploration techniques is somewhat cursory considering the significance of self-awareness. Students should consult the selected sources cited later in the chapter to increase self-awareness further.

A word of warning should accompany this section That is, it is often an anxious experience to learn or relearn things about ourselves. It may even be a painful experience when we discover things that we dislike. Although learning about ourselves is not an easy process, it should be kept in mind that none of us is perfect. Even the best helpers possess limitations in addition to strengths.

Some questions to be pondered by the reader as a means to fostering self-learning follow. They were inspired by a similar list constructed by Brill (1978).

1. What is my sense of self?
2. How do I deal with my personal needs?
3. What values do I hold?
4. What basic philosophy do I hold?

WHAT IS MY SENSE OF SELF?

Perhaps no other question is as central to knowing ourselves as this one: "What is my sense of self?" Our concept of self is composed of all of the information, perceptions, beliefs, and attitudes we have about ourselves. Our self-conception is viewed by many social scientists (e.g., Cooper-smith, 1967; Gordon & Gergen, 1968; Gergen, 1971; Samuels, 1977) as a vital factor in determining what we do and what we become. For example, Eisenberg and Patterson (1979) propose that persons who feel inadequate and insecure see outside forces to be in control of their lives. In contrast, secure individuals preceive themselves to maintain the locus of control.

However, we do not have to be social scientists to understand how the images we have of ourselves can have considerable impact on our thinking and behavior. Can you remember days in which you have felt really good about yourself and imagined that you could tackle the whole world? You could "do anything." On the other hand, have you ever felt, as my daughter would say, "lower than a snake?" When we do not feel good about ourselves, we avoid setting high goals and may literally stay in bed instead of facing what we conceive to be a dismal world.

We can see that our self-concept is perhaps more accurately referred to as our self-concepts. Our self-conceptions are relatively stable, but we do hold differing opinions of ourselves at different times and in various situations. Likewise, self-concepts are not carved in stone. It is possible to change them.

Different authors hold varying views on exactly what core elements compose our self-concepts. Samuels (1977) states that the critical dimensions of self-concept are body image (feelings about your body), social self (your racial, ethnic, cultural, and religious self) your cognitive self (your perceptions about self), and self-esteem (your self-evaluation of self-worth). Eisenberg and Patterson (1979) propose the central elements of self-concept to be personal adequacy and worth ("I'm O.K."), appraisal of one's abilities or competencies ("I can't do anythng with my hands"), and interests and activities ("I like the solitude of walking in the woods"), along with self-attributions or explanations people provide for their own behavior ("I work hard to achieve, since success means a lot to me").

How do you see yourself? Are you obese, slim, weak, strong, young, old, handsome, pretty, or sexy? Are you able to reach personal goals? Do you meet personal standards or ideals you have set for yourself? What are your preferences for specific interests or activities? Do you like youself? Do you feel worthy of being loved?

Some of the suggested exercises that follow in this section on sense of self and in the ensuing sections covering personal needs, values, and basic philosophy may be completed as they are read. Others may be used as classroom exercises or may be participated in informally within small

96   SELF-AWARENESS

groups outside the classroom. The first two exercises, "Who Am I?" and "Collage" follow.

Who Am I?

Eisenberg and Patterson (1979) suggest that most of us are not fully aware of our beliefs about self. They submit that the "Who Am I" exercise, often used to bring about self-learning, causes difficulty for all but a few people. This activity requires two people. One simply repeats the question, "Who are you?" To each inquiry the other person must respond by providing a new description of self. Eisenberg and Patterson claim most people do not go beyond their roles (e.g., wife, husband) and cannot respond to more than 10 inquiries.

Collage

A self-awareness exercise that many students enjoy is completing a two-sided collage. [This exercise was adapted from Borden & Stone (1976)]. On one side of a piece of poster paper, a collage is prepared to represent how you think people see you. On the reverse side a collage is constructed representing the way you see yourself (the "real you"). The collages can be made out of pictures, advertisements, cartoons, or words from headlines from old newspapers and magazines. These can be cut out and pasted or taped to the paper. Or, you may draw or write things which represent you. The poster paper should be covered with collages on both sides in about an hour's time. Once completed, you may get together with another person to describe your artwork and have the other person describe their's to you. Following this, you may wish to display your collage for all to see. If done as a part of a class, you may desire to share information about your collages with your classmates and instructor.

The college exercise may be combined with a review, or class discussion, of the Johari Window (Luft, 1969), which diagrams four quadrants representing the total person in relation to others (see Figure 4-1). The four quadrants refer to the things (behaviors, feelings, motivation) (1) known to both self and others, (2) known to others but not known to self, (3) known to self but not known to others, and (4) known neither to self nor to others. Reviewing the Johari Window will provide further insights into how we are known to ourselves and others.

HOW DO I DEAL WITH MY PERSONAL NEEDS?

One of the first steps to success as a helping professional is to gain an understanding of one's own needs. The helper who is aware of the existence of his or her personal needs can then examine the ways in which he

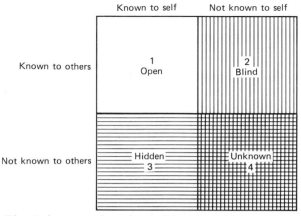

Figure 4-1 *The Johari window from* Of Human Interaction *by Joseph Luft by permission of Mayfield Publishing Company. Copyright © 1969 by the National Press.*

or she meets them. By doing so, the helping professional can: (1) gain personally from this knowledge, (2) better understand similar needs and expressions in clients, and (3) avoid using helping relationships to meet personal needs rather than those of clients.

Like most things, saying we should become aware of our personal needs is easier than doing it. A scheme useful in client assessment may prove helpful to self-assessment as well. Maslow's (1970) hierarchy of needs can serve as a means to self-understanding.

According to Maslow (1970), all people possess an innate tendency to become self-actualized, or to become what they have the potential to become. This need is the fifth, and highest, of the needs found on the hierarchy. Four other needs exist below that of self-actualization: (1) physiological needs, (2) safety needs, (3) belonging or love needs, and (4) self-esteem needs. Once a need has been met, it no longer evokes behavior; therefore we know that a need has been at least partially satisfied before a higher need appears.

Let us review briefly the five needs in the hierarchy. We will begin with the lowest, physiological needs, and proceed to the highest need, self-actualization.

Physiological needs are basic for survival. Included are physical needs for food, water, air, and sleep for self-preservation and sex for reproduction. Few helping professionals have to be concerned about the satisfaction of survival needs.

The second set of needs are *safety needs*. Safety needs have to do with

SELF-AWARENESS

psychological safety and security. Stability is needed in all of our lives, but so is some amount of risk-taking. In meeting our safety needs we keep tension resulting from uncertainty in a range that is comfortable for us as individuals.

The third level of need is *love and belonging.* This social need has to do with feeling wanted and accepted by others and with the giving and receiving of friendship and love. This need may be met through belonging to clubs or organizations, family relations, friendships, and intimate relationships. If we feel lonely or isolated from others we may resort to unproductive or attention-getting behaviors ranging from pouting and disruptive acts to severe depression and aggression. Scarf (1980) has suggested recently that promiscuous sexual behavior may result from depression brought on by feeling unloved and uncared for. Empirical evidence presented by Henderson (1980) strongly suggests that experiencing deficiencies in social relationships causes neurosis.

The fourth level of need is *self-esteem.* High self-esteem means having self-confidence, self-assurance, and a general feeling of adequacy and worth as a person. It means feeling good about ourselves. In order to achieve a genuine sense of self-esteem we must be able to conduct valid self-evaluation. We have to know our own strengths and weaknesses. One of the paramount outcomes of our work as helping professionals is to assist our clients to develop positive self-esteem. A lack in our esteem or our clients' might be reflected by *having to* drive the latest model car or live in the "right neighborhood" in order to prove to others that we are persons of worth.

The highest-level need is *self-actualization.* This represents the growth drive that moves us toward meeting our highest potentials. In self-actualization we have continued self-development leading us to a rich, full, and meaningful life.

Schultz (1977) has provided an excellent interpretation of Maslow's theory. In it he discusses the concept that those who have reached the level of satisfaction of the self-actualization need are no longer in a state of *becoming* but, instead, are in a state of *being.* They are no longer attempting to remove deficiencies (the lower-level needs). Instead, these extremely healthy persons experience *metamotivation* (otherwise known as growth motivation, or being, or B-motivation). *Metaneeds* (also known as B-values) represent a state of growth for self-actualizers. Among the metaneeds are concepts such as truth, beauty, unity, aliveness, uniqueness, justice, order, simplicity, meaningfulness, and playfulness. For most of us, metaneeds remain in the realm of ideals for which we strive.

In a moment you will be asked to think about yourself. First, read the remainder of this paragraph, which will invite you to engage in specific types of self-reflection. Close your eyes and reflect on yourself for a few minutes, thinking about your personal needs. Which have been past concerns? Which are most pressing now? How are these expressed in your actions and thoughts? Stop at this point in your reading and, for the next few minutes, engage in self-reflection.

Now that you have thought about yourself for a few minutes, what did you discover or rediscover? Are your adjustments to meeting your needs satisfactory to you? Are you engaging in any attention-getting or self-defeating behaviors? What things made you feel good about yourself?

If, through your self-anlysis, you find that you are not perfect, welcome to the club! Schultz (1977) states that Maslow found that even his self-actualizers could occasionally be irritating, temperamental, vain, stubborn, and thoughtless. Neither were they totally free from anxiety, guilt, and worry. Also, if you are young it would be anticipated that you would be still evolving as a person and would not yet be expected to be self-actualizing. A general characteristic of self-actualizers, reported by Schultz (1977), was that they were middle aged or older. According to Schultz, Maslow assumed that younger persons had not yet had the necessary life experiences to enable them to develop a powerful sense of identity and independence. It follows that you, if you are a young person, are in a natural state of becoming and should be optimistic about your ability for future growth. In fact, we all should remain optimistic about our abilities to change, since all of us possess the potential to grow and expand throughout our lives.

In order to stimulate further self-examination, I have constructed the list of questions that follows. It is not to be taken as an inclusive list, but the questions will reveal areas for exploration for you as an emerging, or even established, therapeutic recreation specialist.

ON PHYSICAL CONTACT

- Do you enjoy being touched?
- Do you feel comfortable in touching others?
- Do you feel touching has sexual connotations?

ON GIVING AND RECEIVING COMPLIMENTS

- Can you receive compliments without discounting them?
- Are you comfortable with issuing compliments?

ON SELF-ESTEEM

- Do you have a feeling of being esteemed by others?
- Do you continually seek support or reassurance from others?
- Do you have a need to boast about exploits?

100

ON BEING ASSERTIVE

- Are you able to reveal what you think or feel within a group?
- Do you attempt to make things happen instead of waiting for someone else to do it?

ON SOCIAL RELATIONSHIPS

- Are you free to let friends expand themselves or are you possessive or jealous when close friends make new acquaintances?
- Can you enter into intimate, honest relationships with others?

ON LEADERSHIP STYLE

- Are you people oriented?
- Are you task oriented?

ON PLAY

- Are you playful?
- Are you competitive, placing a priority on winning?

ON SHARING YOURSELF

- Are you willing to transcend your own needs in order to facilitate growth in others?

On Becoming a Helping Professional

One serious question that all therapeutic recreation specialists must address at some point is if they truly desire to become helping professionals. When students actually begin to gain field experience, they sometimes find that the helping relationship does not meet their personal needs. For example, they may learn that while they like being with other people, they do not enjoy participating in actual helping relationships. It is therefore critical that students gain experiences in the real world of the helping professional in order to confirm, or disconfirm, their suppositions. It is also important that students gain exposure to several different client groups. Some people work well with children who are mentally retarded. Others find enjoyment in serving adults with problems in mental health, individuals undergoing physical rehabilitation, old people, or members of some other special populations group. Professional exploration is essential for the helping professional. There is nothing wrong with students making alternative career choices. In fact, it reflects the development of self-awareness on their part.

WHAT VALUES DO I HOLD?

When I began my professional career in therapeutic recreation, two myths existed. One was that professionals were value-free. That is, their personal values were not allowed to enter into their professional lives. The second was that even beginning helping professionals held the highest of professional values. Young professionals assumably gained these through some unknown means since, to my knowledge, no college instructors ever helped us to develop them as students.

The myth of the value-free professional has passed. Professionals today are allowed personal values (i.e., values we hold as individuals). We have also come to understand that there is a place in professional preparation programs for examination of both personal and professional values (i.e., values accepted by our profession).

What Exactly Are Values?

Before proceeding further, it may be wise to make explicit exactly what is meant by values. To value something is to attribute worth to it. Beliefs that we prize form our value system and are one basis for determining our behavior. Reilly (1978) has defined a value as "an operational belief which an individual accepts as his own and serves as a determinant of behavior" (p. 37). Values are critically important to us. They are the principles by which we live our lives (Simon & Olds, 1977).

Ways of Knowing Values

Simon and Olds (1977) have discussed the ways by which we learn values. Included are "The Three Misleading M's." These are moralizing, manipulating, and modeling. These authors recommend none of the three methods. Few readers need convincing regarding the problems with moralizing. Manipulation limits choices and does not teach us how to think through conflicts. And, although modeling can be a potent force, learning by example does not afford the opportunity to make personal choices or wrestle with issues. Instead, Simon and Olds recommend the values clarification process developed by Raths. Through analysis of our choosing, accepting, and acting on values, the values clarification process helps us to determine our values for ourselves.

Values Clarification

Perhaps the most noted book on values clarification and values clarification strategies is *Values Clarification: A Handbook of Practical Strategies*

102

for Teachers and Students (Simon et al., 1972). Since Simon and his collegues have prepared this book and several others, values clarification will not be discussed in detail in this section. Instead, the reader is encouraged to seek out works on values clarification. The exercises, or strategies, found in these books offer enjoyment and insights to those who complete them. They are highly recommended. Among the topics covered are work, sex, friendship, family, ethics, authority, material possessions, self, culture, and leisure. (See Chapter 2 for a listing of specific values clarification exercises on leisure.)

Other ways of clarifying our values have been proposed by Reilly (1978). Among them are reading and discussing values found in good literature, such as Shakespeare's sonnets. A second method is listening to popular music and analyzing it to determine the values it reflects. Role playing value-laden situations is a third method. Another is taking field trips to unfamiliar environments in order to broaden understandings of values represented in other life-styles, cultures, and socioeconomic strata.

Through the process of examining your own values, you will learn to aid clients in clarifying their value systems, since exercises and experiences useful to you may be equally valuable to clients. A note of caution should, however, be sounded if you do deal with client values. Clients have the right not to have your values imposed on them. Avoid placing on them your personal values toward achievement, sexual behavior, conformity, work, leisure, and other issues (Brill, 1978).

WHAT BASIC PHILOSOPHY DO I HOLD?

The final self-examination question inquires about basic philosophy. It is important that we become aware of our basic philosophical beliefs, since these influence our theoretical notions which, in turn, affect the principles by which we operate. Or, as Frye and Peters (1972) said, "philosophy is the rudder that gives guidance and direction" (p. 32).

Brill (1978, p. 20) has listed seven beliefs that form her overall philosophical base for human service. As directly taken from Brill, these are:

1. Man is a social animal.
2. He exists in interrelationship with others of his own kind and with all other life forms. This relationship may be defined as one of mutual rights and responsibilities.
3. The welfare of the individual and of the group cannot be considered apart from each other.
4. Man and all living matter possess intrinsic worth.
5. Man and all living matter are characterized by a need to grow and develop toward the realization of a unique potential.

6. Man and his society can be understood by use of the scientific method.

7. Man and his society possess the capacity for change as a part of their intrinsic nature.

Do you subscribe to Brill's philosophical beliefs? If not, with which ones do you disagree? It might be anticipated that beliefs such as the necessity for play in the developmental process, the importance of recreation and leisure as means to attainment of basic human needs, and the fundamental right of all people to engage in the pursuit of happiness might be added by therapeutic recreation specialists. Do you agree with these? Can you add others?

Obviously, philosophical beliefs are required to direct our practice. For some time, we in therapeutic recreation struggled with the development of a philosophical statement to represent our field. It is important for the evolution of therapeutic recreation that such a process occurred, but it is more critical that budding therapeutic recreation specialists develop personal philosophies. The emergence of newer, creative philosophies will cause us to examine continually past beliefs and will ultimately strengthen the profession.

RESOURCES FOR SELF-EXAMINATION

There are many resources from which to draw in order to facilitate development of self-awareness. Some have been mentioned previously. Others are listed here.

- *Tape Recordings.* You may listen to tape recordings of interactions you have had with friends or actual clients. My students complete an interview tape with a person with whom they are not in a close relationship. Then they critique it with a classmate, discussing needs, values, and behaviors that reveal themselves. The information on communications in Chapter 5 may be helpful to such an evaluation.
- *Videotapes.* You may videotape the role playing of various situations typical of practice in therapeutic recreation and then review them. Students in my classes have videotaped role-playing situations of interviews and recreational groups and then reviewed and discussed them to gain insights.
- *Diaries.* Keeping a diary in which you express feelings about your self-concepts, values, and beliefs may be helpful. Students completing internships may find this technique particularly valuable to gaining self-awareness.
- *Small Group Discussions.* Self-disclosure in small groups offers the opportunity to share information and insights. It is important to foster an

104

open atmosphere conducive to such dialogue. Of course, confidentiality should be maintained.

Various books may also be helpful to developing self-awareness. In the list that follows I have cited several that have been beneficial to me and my students. One of the strengths of these publications is that they offer a multitude of useful self-awareness exercises.

- Borden, G. A., & Stone, J. D. 1970. *Human communication: The process of relating.* Menlo Park, Calif.: Cummings Publishing Company. (Contains many paper-and-pencil exercises and other individual and group human relationship activities.)
- James, M., & Jongeward, D. 1971. *Born to win: Transactional analysis with gestalt experiments.* Reading, Mass.: Addison-Wesley Publishing Company. (A best-seller containing many experiments and exercises drawn from TA and gestalt therapy.)
- Sax, S., & Hollander, S. 1972. *Reality games.* New York: Popular Library. (A book full of games to help us communicate our real feelings and understand others and ourselves.)
- Stevens, J. O. 1971. *Awareness: Exploring, experimenting, experiencing.* New York: Bantam Books. (Contains exercises to help us become aware of our sensory contacts, inner feelings, and fantasies.)
- Satir, V. 1972. *Peoplemaking.* Palo Alto, Calif.: Science and Behavioral Books, Inc. (A very readable book on communications in families. Experiments and exercises are found throughout.)
- Simon, S. B., Howe, L. W., & Kirschenbaum, H. 1972. *Values clarification: A handbook of practical strategies for teachers and students.* New York: Hart Publishing Company, Inc. (Contains 79 values clarification strategies.)
- Simon, S. B., & Olds, S. W. 1977. *Helping your child learn right from wrong: A guide to values clarification.* New York: McGraw-Hill Book Company. (Contains many values clarification exercises.)

OTHER CHARACTERISTICS OF THE THERAPEUTIC RECREATION SPECIALIST

Other helping characteristics previously listed for therapeutic recreation specialists included the ability to communicate, possession of a knowledge base, and a strong belief in recreation and leisure experiences. So important are communications that a separate chapter (Chapter 5) has been devoted to this topic. Hopefully, a knowledge base for practice will be built from many sources. Throughout this book specific information on theoretical approaches and practical techniques utilized in therapeutic recreation will be found. The therapeutic recreation specialist, in developing a personal and professional philosophy, will arrive at a belief in the values to be found in recreation and leisure.

A SUMMING UP

Helping others is a very human enterprise aimed toward the development of independence and self-reliance on the part of our clients. Certain characteristics are required of therapeutic recreation specialists in order to function as effective helping professionals. The characteristic receiving primary attention in this chapter was self-awareness. It is clear that we, as helping professionals, have a responsibility to know ourselves so we know what we bring to the helping relationship and what we have to offer clients.

KEY WORDS

Professional Helping. A process whereby assistance is given by a professional person, working from a knowledge base, in which client needs are paramount and the ultimate aim is to facilitate the highest possible level of independence in the client.

Values. Cherished beliefs, learned throughout our lifetimes, that are prime determinants of our behaviors.

Reading Comprehension Questions

1 How do professional helping relationships differ from social relationships?
2 Explain how helping others is a very human enterprise that meets the helper's needs.
3 What is the ultimate goal of the helping relationship?
4 Analyze the lists of characteristics of effective helpers. With which do you most fully agree?
5 Do you concur with the list of primary helping characteristics for the TR specialist? If not, how would your list differ?
6 Explain why we need to know ourselves in order to serve effectively as helping professionals.
7 Do you agree that gaining self-awareness may be a painful experience?
8 Review the list of questions posed for self-examination. Are there others that you might add? If so, think about yourself in regard to these questions.
9 Does self-concept influence our behavior and expectations? How?

10 Do you agree with Eisenberg and Patterson that those with high self-esteem are more likely to feel they have control over their lives?

11 Did you participate in the "Who Are You?" activity? Did it help you to examine yourself? How do you see yourself?

12 Why might it be important to become aware of your needs?

13 Can you outline Maslow's hierarchy? Do you recognize any of these needs in yourself?

14 Why might it be assumed that the majority of students are in a state of becoming?

15 Have you had firsthand experiences in helping relationships in therapeutic recreation? Were they what you thought they would be?

16 Why are values important? Can you recognize some of the values you hold in regard to work? Leisure? Other areas?

17 Do you agree with Brill's list of philosophical beliefs? Would you add or subtract any beliefs to form your own list of beliefs as a philosophical base for practice in therapeutic recreation?

18 Have you tried any of the resources suggested for self-examination? Have you read any of the books listed as useful to gaining self-awareness?

REFERENCES

Austin, D. R., & Binkley, A. L. 1977. *A summary of the curriculum plan for the master of science in recreation: Option in therapeutic recreation.* Unpublished report, Department of Recreation and Park Administration, Indiana University, Bloomington.

Brammer, L. M. 1979. *The helping relationship: Process and Skills* (2nd edition). Englewood Cliffs, N. J.: Prentice-Hall, Inc.

Brill, N. I. 1978. *Working with people: The helping process* (2nd edition) Philadelphia: J. B. Lippincott Company.

Borden, G. A., & Stone, J. D. 1976. *Human communication: The process of relating.* Menlo Park, Calif.: Cummings Publishing Company.

Carkhuff, R. R. 1969. *Helping & human relations: A primer for lay and professional helpers. Volume I: Selection and training.* New York: Holt, Rinehart and Winston, Inc.

Chapman, J. E., & Chapman, H. H. 1975. *Behavior and health care: A humanistic helping process.* Saint Louis: The C. V. Mosby Company.

Coopersmith, S. 1967. *The antecedents of self-esteem.* San Francisco: W. H. Freeman and Company.

Eisenberg, S., & Patterson, L. E. 1977. *Helping clients with special concerns.* Chicago: Rand McNally College Publishing Company.

Eubanks, R. E. 1976. Relationships: The manifestations of humanness. In G. A. Borden & J. D. Stone (eds.), *Human communication: The process of relating.* Menlo Park, Calif.: Cummings Publishing Company, pp. 185–191.

Frye, V., & Peters, M. 1972. *Therapeutic recreation: Its theory, philosophy, and practice.* Harrisburg, Pa.: Stackpole Books.

Gergen, K. J. 1971. *The concept of self.* New York: Holt, Rinehart and Winston, Inc.

Gordon, C., & Gergen, K. J. 1968. *The self in social interaction.* New York: John Wiley & Sons, Inc.

Henderson, S. 1980. A development in social psychiatry: The systematic study of social bonds. *The Journal of Nervous and Mental Disease.* *168*(2), 63–69.

James, M., & Jongward, D. 1971. *Born to win: Transactional analysis with gestalt experiments.* Reading, Mass.: Addison-Wesley Publishing Company.

Luft, J. 1969. *On human interaction.* Palo Alto, Calif.: National Press Books.

Maslow, A. H. 1970. *Motivation and personality* (2nd edition). New York: Harper & Row, Publishers.

Mayeroff, M. 1971. *On caring.* New York: Harper & Row, Publishers.

Okun, B. F. 1976. *Effective helping: Interviewing & counseling techniques.* North Scituate, Mass.: Duxbury Press.

Reilly, D. E. 1978. *Teaching and evaluating the affective domain in nursing programs.* Thorofare, N. J.: Charles B. Slack, Inc.

Rogers, C. R. 1961. *On becoming a person: A therapist's view of psychotherapy.* Boston: Houghton Mifflin Company.

Samuels, S. C. 1977. *Enhancing self-concept in early childhood.* New York: Human Sciences Press.

Satir, V. 1972. *Peoplemaking.* Palo Alto, Calif.: Science and Behavioral Books, Inc.

Sax, S., & Hollander, S. 1972. *Reality games.* New York: Popular Library.

Scarf, M. 1980. The promiscuous woman. *Psychology Today.* *14*(2), 78–87.

Schofield, W. 1964. *Psychotherapy: The purchase of friendship.* Englewood Cliffs, N. J.: Prentice-Hall, Inc.

Schultz, D. 1977. *Growth psychology: Models of the healthy personality.* New York: D. Van Nostrand Company.

Simon, S. B., Howe, L. W., & Kirschenbaum, H. 1972. *Values clarification: A handbook of practical strategies for teachers and students.* New York: Hart Publishing Company, Inc.

Simon, S. B., & Olds, S. W. 1977. *Helping children learn right from wrong: A guide to values clarification.* New York: McGraw-Hill Book Company.

Stevens, J. O. 1971. *Awareness: Exploring, experimenting, experiencing.* New York: Bantam Books.

5

COMMUNICATION
SKILLS

PURPOSE OF THE CHAPTER

OBJECTIVES

WHAT IS COMMUNICATION?

WHAT ARE SOME GUIDELINES FOR IMPROVEMENT IN
COMMUNICATIONS?

Presentation of Material
Attitudes
Voice Tone and Volume
Effective Listening

WHAT SPECIFIC LISTENING SKILLS SHOULD BE DEVELOPED?

Attending
Paraphrasing
Clarifying
Perception Checking
Listening Exercises

WHAT ADDITIONAL VERBAL RESPONSES ARE AVAILABLE?

Probing
Reflecting
Interpreting
Confronting
Informing

PURPOSE OF THE CHAPTER

Therapeutic recreation is action oriented, not talk oriented. Even though TR specialists do regularly interview clients and may engage in leisure counseling, the thrust of therapeutic recreation is toward active participation instead of the discussion of client problems and concerns. Nevertheless, the ability to maintain effective interpersonal communications is important and is a basic competency needed by the therapeutic recreation specialist in order to perform as a viable helping professional. If the therapeutic recreation specialist cannot communicate with his or her clients, the therapeutic recreation process is almost certainly doomed to failure. This chapter will help the student to develop a fundamental understanding of communication processes and refine specific communication skills.

OBJECTIVES

- Comprehend the pragmatic approach (i.e., practical approach) to communication taken in this chapter.
- Know determinants of successful verbal communication.
- Translate theoretical knowledge of effective listening into practice.
- Demonstrate knowledge of verbal responses that may be used to facilitate client self-understanding.
- Use feedback principles appropriate in learning and performance situations.
- Appreciate the importance of studying nonverbal communication.
- Analyze specific cues in nonverbal communication.
- Recognize the importance of a proper setting for interviews.
- Apply basic interview skills.

One day a student of mine excitedly exclaimed as she entered the classroom, "I used some of those verbal responses we've been practicing in class with my friends and they really worked!" Students are often surprised when they initially find that the interpersonal communication skills taught in their therapeutic recreation classes are useful in their everyday lives. Such skills have application because the things we do to be effective in our everyday encounters with others are the same skills we need to be capable helping professionals.

It is important to recognize that there is nothing particularly esoteric about the interpersonal communication skills employed in our relationships with clients. They are the skills used practically every day of our lives and are not the exclusive domain of therapeutic recreators or any other group of helping professionals. As difficult as it may be to admit, therapeutic recreation specialists possess no magical means by which to relate to clients.

All of this is not to detract from the communication process, but it does underscore the fact that the business of helping is a very human enterprise that employs communication skills used in our day-to-day lives. It follows that the higher our level of personal communication skills, the higher our potentials will be to perform successfully as helping professionals. This chapter emphasizes the communication skills necessary for effective listening, interviewing, counseling, and activity leadership.

WHAT IS COMMUNICATION?

There are several frames of reference from which to view communications, including syntactics (information theory), semantics (dealing with meanings), and pragmatics (behavior) (Watzlawick, 1967). In this chapter

112

we will deal with all three, but our primary concern will be with the pragmatics, or the behavioral effects of interpersonal communication. This practical approach will concentrate on basic communication processes in interacting with clients.

Because there are several perspectives from which to approach communication, there is no one single definition of communications that is appropriate to all. For the purpose of our pragmatic approach, communications may be defined as the verbal and nonverbal transmission of ideas, feelings, beliefs, and attitudes that permits a common understanding between the sender of the message and the receiver.

Thus communications implies the exchange of information and ideas between at least two people, resulting in a common understanding. The word communication is derived from a Latin word meaning "common," or "shared by all alike," (Gibson et al., 1976; Killen, 1977). If, through verbal and nonverbal symbols, people are able to achieve a common or shared understanding, communication has taken place.

The communication process has five elements: the *communicator* (Who. . .), *the message* (says what. . .), *the medium* (in what way. . .), *the receiver* (to whom. . .) and *feedback* (. . .with what effect) (Gibson et al., 1976). Therefore communication is clearly a two-way sharing of meaning in which a message is both sent and received. Feedback provides assurance that the intended message has been received. Through feedback the receiver either verifies that the message was understood or discovers that the message was misunderstood. Since feedback may be subtle, it is important that the sender be alert and sensitive to those with whom he or she is communicating. Okun (1976) has stipulated that effective helpers utilize verbal messages (containing cognitive and affective content) *and* nonverbal messages (including affective and behavioral content) and respond verbally *and* nonverbally to feedback.

To say that communication skills are important is an understatement. Satir (1972) has stated in regard to the human being that "communication is the largest single factor determining what kinds of relationships he makes with others and what happens to him in the world about him" (p. 4, italics removed).

Therapeutic recreation presents an environment conducive to the development of positive interpersonal communication. In the open, non-threatening atmosphere of the recreation situation clients often feel free to communicate with the therapeutic recreation specialist. This openness is, however, only one element in client-therapist interpersonal communications. Also critical is the appropriateness of the TR specialist's responses. Unless the therapeutic recreation specialist is prepared to respond appropriately, communications may break down. It follows that the therapeutic recreation specialist must learn to develop effective communication skills.

WHAT ARE SOME GUIDELINES FOR IMPROVEMENT IN COMMUNICATIONS?

Four factors influencing successful verbal communication are (1) the way in which material is presented, (2) the speaker's attitude or feeling toward the client, (3) the voice tone and volume, and (4) the speaker's and receiver's abilities to listen (Purtilo, 1978). The information that follows is based largely on Purtilo's (1978) discussion of these four influences.

PRESENTATION OF MATERIAL

Presentation of material has to do with the vocabulary used, the clarity of the speaker's voice, and the manner in which the message is organized.

Vocabulary

Failure to choose the right words will produce an unclear message. Acquiring an adequate professional vocabulary will allow the therapeutic recreation specialist to avoid using inappropriate words or giving rambling descriptions to clients or other staff. This does not mean, of course, using big, technical words in conversations with clients. Although a certain amount of professional jargon is necessary in staff communication, problems arise when highly technical terms are used when speaking with clients.

Once a colleague of mine jokingly remarked, "I never use a two-syllable word when an eight-syllable one will do as well." This man was noted across campus for his eloquent utterances. In the academic community, where a command of language is valued, my colleague succeeded as a communicator because he knew how to gear his message to that particular audience. He knew that presenting material that was too simple would fail (and throwing in a few eight-syllable words here and there might earn him some amount of credibility!). But being a good communicator, he also knew that presenting a message that was too complex would be equally bad. As all effective communicators know, failure to assess properly the receiver's ability to comprehend will severely hinder communication.

A good rule to follow is to state your ideas in simple terms in as few words as possible (Chartier, 1976). Although my colleague was an apparent exception to this rule, most of us are better off using everyday words, even when communicating with highly intelligent and well-schooled persons. In short, each of us should "be ourselves" and use our regular vocabulary.

Voice Clarity

Articulation is important in getting a message across. A clearly spoken sentence is not spoken too softly, nor is it rushed. Professionals who are regularly asked by clients to repeat instructions are likely speaking too softly or too fast. The rate of speaking must always keep pace with the listener's ability to comprehend. Therefore we should monitor ourselves to make certain that we are communicating with our clients. For example, we may find we are speaking too softly to be understood by older people who may have difficulty hearing, or we may be speaking too rapidly to get our message across to children effectively.

Organization

Chartier (1976) has presented several communication guidelines, some of which may be used to help avoid rambling communications.

- Good organization begins by having a clear picture of what the sender wants the other person to understand. It is particularly imperative that the communicator hold a clear conception of what he or she wishes to say when dealing with complex or ambiguous topics.
- Define terms before discussing them and explain concepts before amplifying on them. New terms and concepts cause problems for those not acquainted with them and, thus, require explanation before they are utilized.
- Organize messages into a series of sequential stages so that only one idea is developed at a time and it leads to the next idea.
- Redundancy leads to clarity. Repetition as a good form of learning, is helpful in communication. Summarizing at the end of the message is an example of a common form of repetition. As Chartier (1976) says, "repetition is important. Very important" (p. 153).
- Relate new concepts and ideas to old ones. Here the rationale is that an individual can better understand a new idea if he or she has been able to relate it to a previously held one.
- Determine which ideas in the message need special emphasis. Underscored ideas have increased impact. For example, Chartier (1976) has stated, *"this last principle is an important one—remember it and use it"* (p. 153, italics his.)

ATTITUDES

The second of Purtilo's (1978) determinants of successful verbal communication deals with the communicator's attitudes or feelings toward the client. When the sender and receiver have high regard for one another, the effectiveness of communication is aided. Displaying genuine concern for the client through a warm, caring attitude enhances the prospect for successful communication.

On the other hand, the therapeutic recreation specialist who is not honest with clients will run into difficulties with interpersonal transactions. Confronting a client about his or her behavior may be difficult. However, displaying an accepting attitude toward what is seen to be inappropriate behavior is not an honest or helpful response; in the long run, the nonconfronting professional is running the risk of destroying the helping relationship. Neither is it wise not to admit anger on the rare occasions when the professional is obviously feeling anger toward a client. Providing the client with an understanding of why the anger arose displays an open, honest attitude.

VOICE TONE AND VOLUME

Have you ever had persons remark to you, "You didn't say it like you meant it?" They were probably indicating that they detected a lack of commitment in the tone of your voice. Voice inflection can be more important to projecting understandings than the actual choice of words. For instance, uncertainty reflected in the voice may communicate "yes," even though the speaker says "no."

The tone of voice can express a variety of attitudes and emotions, ranging from pleasure and exuberance to dejection and depression. When clinical psychologists refer to the client as having a "flat affect," they are no doubt basing this observation at least partly on the client's tone of voice. Occasionally, a speaker will not realize the emotion accompanying his or her speech until another person makes an observation regarding it. When leading activities, the therapeutic recreation specialist needs to monitor his or her voice to make certain that it is projecting excitement, enthusiasm, or whatever the appropriate feeling.

Closely related to voice inflection is volume. Volume can be used to control others. Speaking loudly will keep people at a distance, while a whisper may be used to draw others closer. In therapeutic recreation leadership the attention of a group is usually better gained by speaking at a relatively moderate volume instead of using a loud voice. By doing so, the group must become quiet in order to understand you. This technique also has an added advantage in that clients feel irritated if you shout at them. As with tone of voice, it behooves the TR specialist to be constantly aware of implications of the volume of the voice. *How* you say things does make a difference.

EFFECTIVE LISTENING

To improve communication, therapeutic recreation specialists must seek not only to be understood but also to understand. The final, and perhaps most critical, of Purtilo's (1978) determinants of successful verbal communication is the ability to understand, or the ability to be an effective listener.

All of us who have ever had fun playing the gossip game know that listening can be difficult. This is a game where everyone sits in a circle. The leader whispers a tidbit of information to the next person in the circle, who in turn passes on the gossip. The gossip continues to be passed from person to person until it gets back to the leader. Rarely, if ever, are the original and final versions of the gossip even slightly related.

One author has stated that distortion may occur with the sender, the message itself, or with the receiver (Simmons, 1976). Primary factors influencing the sender are the physical ability to produce sound and motivation. Disease processes affecting the client's teeth, mouth, nose, or throat may impair speech, as may diseases such as aphasia. Motives such as fear or embarrassment may also cause the sender to distort or conceal information. For example, negative information may be "forgotten" for fear it might be upsetting to someone, or information may be slightly altered to give a more positive picture of an event.

The message itself may also become distorted. Words or phrases may be interpreted in several ways, causing semantic difficulties. For example, the phrase "Go jump in the lake," may be taken as either a helpful suggestion to beat the heat on a hot day, or as a derogatory remark.

Finally, communication may break down with the receiver. As with the sender, physical problems may be a factor in message distortion. A hearing problem can drastically alter the message's meaning. Additionally, there are several other ways in which the listener may distort what he or she hears. Chief among these are the listener's mental set, perceptual defenses, problems with directiveness, and sensory overloading.

Mental Set

The listener's mental set, or frame of reference resulting from previous experience, often brings about unintentional distortions of communication. One author has listed stereotypes, fixed beliefs, negative attitude, lack of interest, and lack of facts as pitfalls that may lead to distorted messages (Killen, 1977).

• *Stereotypes* are widely held generalizations about people or things. Although stereotypes may contain a grain of truth, they rarely hold when applied to a particular person or thing. Thus it is a pitfall to engage in close-minded stereotyped thinking instead of being open to new perceptions.

- *Fixed beliefs* are barriers to listening somewhat akin to stereotypes. The accurate listener does not filter out or automatically dismiss information just because it is not congruent with his or her own beliefs. *Important*
- A *negative attitude* toward the sender may interfere with listening. If the sender is not liked or trusted, the result will be a lack of credibility that will negatively effect how the receiver perceives the message.
- A *lack of interest* in the communication will cause the receiver to tune out the sender. The attention of others is aroused when people see how the message relates to them.
- A *lack of facts* causes people to complete information gaps with their own ideas, since people do not like incomplete information. Thus the listener must be aware of information gaps and seek to obtain all necessary facts rather than fill them in as he or she wishes them to be.

Perceptual Defenses

Another barrier to communication is to ignore aspects of a message or to distort material so it is congruent with the self-conceptions of the receiver. It may be expected that the client whose self-concept is threatened by an illness or disorder will experience difficulty in accepting information that might further threaten self-image.

Problems of Directives

Directives are phrases that instruct people to do certain things. For example, instructions given to clients or other staff are directives. A problem with directives is that sometimes clients can take them more literally than they are intended.

I can recall an experience during my first summer of working in therapeutic recreation at a state hospital in Indiana. At the time I conducted an afternoon program for a group of older male patients at a park on the hospital grounds. Each day I would scurry around beginning one activity and then another in an effort to get as many of the men active as possible. I began one afternoon program by tossing a playground ball with two of the men. As soon as I was sure that they were thoroughly engaged in tossing and catching the ball, I withdrew to try to interest others in activities. When I returned a full half-hour later, much to my dismay I found the two men (who were now obviously tired and totally bored) still dutifully tossing the ball to one another! Of course, I did not wish for them to keep up the activity to the point of exhaustion. I had no idea that they would interpret my communications to mean that they should continue until I instructed them to stop.

Professionals in clinical settings must be particularly alert to problems with interpretation of directives; clients may place a great deal of credence in instructions given by staff, perhaps feeling that they will become well if they do exactly what they are told. In such settings miscommunication can lead to false expectations, disappointment, and loss of trust.

Sensory Overloading

Sometimes people cannot absorb or adequately respond to all of the information directed toward them. At such times they are experiencing sensory overload. Limitations in the receiver's capacity to hear and comprehend all incoming stimuli cause barriers to communication. It was mentioned previously that talking too fast may cause problems for the receiver. The presentation of too many ideas or too much complexity may also cause difficulties. To prevent sensory overloading, the therapeutic recreation specialist must attempt to speak at a rate that the client can follow and use terms that the client can understand.

WHAT SPECIFIC LISTENING SKILLS SHOULD BE DEVELOPED?

Effective listening transcends structured interviews or leisure counseling sessions. Effective listening can be employed in any interpersonal transactions in which the therapeutic recreation specialist engages. It is an active process involving four major skills. These are attending, paraphrasing, clarifying, and perception checking (Brammer, 1979). Brammer's (1979) discussion of effective listening is the base from which the following materials spring.

ATTENDING

Attending behaviors let the client know you are interested in him or her and are paying attention to what he or she has to say. In my years of going to the inevitable receptions found at conferences and meetings, I have had the opportunity to view a number of humans behaving. One type of behavior I have regularly observed at these events is that of the person who I initially think wishes to speak with me, but who turns out to be more interested in looking past me to see if he or she can spot anyone they would rather be talking with. They do not attend to me or my conversation because they are much too preoccupied with their own hunting expedition. I usually feel as though I am being used as nothing more than a prop, and start looking around myself for a more stimulating or, at least, more attentive person with whom to share a conversation.

Having others pay attention to us is something most of us appreciate. Clients are no different. If anything, attending behaviors have even greater impact with clients, particularly those who are insecure and easily experience feelings of rejection. Attending skills are basic to our interpersonal transactions if we hope to develop and maintain positive helping relationships. Attending is accomplished through four primary means: eye contact, posture, gestures, and verbal behavior.

Eye Contact

All of us have heard the expression "He (or she) gave her (or him) the eye," meaning that one person was indicating a particularly high level of interest in another person. Our eyes offer an expressive mode of communication. Frequent eye contact is one way by which we indicate we are attending to clients.

Eye contact with clients should occur on a regular basis when communicating. This, of course, does not mean staring at the client. You do not continually fix your eyes on friends during social interactions. Clients also dislike being stared at, but they find frequent eye contact reinforcing.

Posture

As with eye contact, extremes should be avoided in posture. Neither appearing too tense nor too relaxed is good. You should not sit or stand in a rigid or stiff position with arms crossed, nor should you present yourself in a slouching fashion. Instead, sitting or standing in a relaxed and open body position, in which you lean forward slightly, should help the client feel comfortable while indicating that you are interested in what he or she is saying.

Gestures

When speaking with friends, you may, from time to time, nod your head as if to say nonverbally, "Yes, I see." This is a type of body movement that indicates interest in what the other person is saying. Other bodily movements, such as hand gesturing, can also be used to suggest that attention is being extended to the client.

Verbal Behavior

The fourth attending channel is verbal behavior. What you say as well as what you do indicates how attentive you are. Refraining from interruptions, questions, and topic jumping displays that you are interested in listening to what the client has to say. Hackney and Cormier (1979) have suggested that minimum verbal responses such as "ah," "I see," "mm-hmm," and "mm-mm" can be effective in indicating you are listening while not interfering with the client's verbal expressions. These authors also have stated that using animation in facial expression, such as an occasional smile, can create the feeling that you are attending to the client's communication.

PARAPHRASING

A second listening skill discussed by Brammer (1979) is paraphrasing. In paraphrasing the client's basic communication is restated in similar, but ordinarily fewer, words. This tells the client that you are listening. It also gives feedback to confirm your understanding of the client's central message.

A three-step process for paraphrasing is outlined by Brammer (1979): (1) listen for the basic idea or ideas expressed; (2) restate these in a brief way, summarizing what the client said; and (3) note the client's response to your restatement to determine the accuracy and helpfulness of your paraphrasing.

An example of paraphrasing follows.

Client: I really think it's neat to go out to the beach; it's so nice with all the sand and all. It's fun. I could spend days there.
Helper: You really do enjoy going to the beach.
Client: Yes, I like it a whole lot.

CLARIFYING

The clarifying response is admitting to the client that you are confused about what was said and wish to clarify its meaning. When you are confused by an ambiguous or cryptic message, you can simply request the client to rephrase what was said, or you can ask the client to respond to your interpretation of what he or she said.

In the first instance you might say, "I'm confused. Would you go over that again for me," or "I'm afraid I don't follow you. Could you describe your feeling in another way." When using the second clarifying technique, you are actually using a form of paraphrasing. This response might begin, "I think I got lost there. Let me try to restate what I thought you said."

PERCEPTION CHECKING

Perception checking, sometimes referred to as checking out, is very similar to clarifying. Here you are checking on the accuracy of your perceptions of what the client said. You are validating your understanding of the client's communication. You might say, "You seem to be happy—is that right?" Another example would be, "You really seem to care about attending the dance. Did I understand you correctly?"

A three-step process for perception checking has been provided by Brammer (1979): (1) paraphrasing what you think you heard, (2) asking for the client to confirm or disconfirm your understanding, and (3) permitting the client to correct inaccurate misperceptions.

LISTENING EXERCISES

The exercises that follow provide an opportunity to try out the four major listening skills: attending, paraphrasing, clarifying, and perception checking.

Attending Exercises

Eye contact, posture, gestures, and verbal behavior can have a powerful reinforcing affect on clients' communication. Although attending seems like a simple process to grasp and an easy thing to do, lack of attending in interpersonal relations is very common (Egan, 1975a).

One simple attending exercise you might try is nonresponse. Get a partner and decide who will be A and who will be B. For 2 or 3 minutes, A should talk about any topic of his or her choosing. B should not attend to A (e.g., avoid eye contact, look around the room). Discuss how this felt. Did A feel frustrated? What sort of attending behaviors would A have appreciated receiving? Did B wish he or she could have responded? How? When?

Now switch roles. A should assume the B role and vice versa. *At first,* B should not attend to A as this person talks about something he or she likes very much. But after 2 minutes, B should try out his or her best attending skills. For the next 2 or 3 minutes B should use eye contact, gestures, posture, and verbal responses to encourage A to talk. Stop after a total of 4 or 5 minutes and discuss the differences between minimal and appropriate attending behaviors.

Egan (1975) has suggested an exercise that involves four persons. In this group of four, decide who is A, B, C, and D. A and B should spend 5 or 6 minutes discussing what they like or do not like about their styles of interpersonal communication. C and D should act as observers, with particular attention paid to nonverbal behavior, voice tone, pitch, volume, pacing, and so on (sometimes referred to as paralinguistic behavior). C and D should give feedback to A and B regarding their observations. Then roles should be exchanged and the exercise repeated.

Paraphrasing Exercises

Following this paragraph are found some client statements. Practice restating these by writing your restatement either in the space that follows each or on a separate piece of paper.

Client: I really have an awful time with trying to remember everyone's names.

Response: _____

Client: Probably the worst thing I have to do is to see Dr. Smith.

Response: _____

Then, with a partner, practice using paraphrasing while a third person observes. After you have used this technique for 3 or 4 minutes, the observer should report his or her observations, and these should be discussed among the three of you. Following this discussion, you may wish to change roles and repeat the exercise.

In completing the exercise keep in mind that trite phrases prefacing your remarks such as, "I hear you saying . . . ," should generally be avoided (Brammer, 1979). It has also been warned that the overuse of paraphrasing can lead to a "parrotlike" effect (Hackney & Cormier, 1979), so attempt to interfuse other types of responses with the paraphrase. You may, for instance, try out some of the attending techniques.

Clarifying Exercise

College students have been exposed many times to clarifying in their classes as other students have attempted to clarify what instructors were saying. Within a small group of students, discuss occasions when you or other students have sought clarification in class. Do you remember any particularly well-stated clarification responses? Have any sounded like criticisms of the instructor instead of requests for clarification? For example, a student seeking clarification may, instead, sound critical by saying, "I haven't understood one word you've said all day. What in the world are you talking about!"

Listening Exercise

To listen effectively, the four major types of responses must become a natural part of your behavior repertory. Again, with a partner, try out perception checking, clarifying, paraphrasing, and attending listening skills. Discuss the importance of developing effective listening skills (or any other topic of your choosing) while being observed by a third person. After 5 minutes, this person should present feedback to you and your partner on the use of listening skills. The observer may wish to jot down behaviors to aid the discussion.

WHAT ADDITIONAL VERBAL RESPONSES ARE AVAILABLE?

Ten major verbal responses for helping professionals to employ in promoting the understanding of self and others have been presented by Okun (1976). They are minimal verbal responses, paraphrasing, checking out, clarifying, probing, reflecting, interpreting, confronting, informing, and summarizing.

A review of Okun's list of verbal responses may bring to mind visions of formal interviews or counseling sessions in which a therapeutic recreation specialist helps a client to gain self-understandings. Therapeutic recreation specialists do conduct interviews and engage in leisure counseling, but these structures account for only one segment of the total delivery of therapeutic recreation services. As with listening skills, it is more likely that these verbal responses will be a part of day-to-day contacts with clients. Thus, while particularly helpful to facilitating client self-understanding during interviews and leisure counseling, the effective use of these verbal responses has much wider application.

Neither is Okun's list as mysterious and foreboding as it might seem initially. As a matter of fact, 4 of the 10 responses have already been reviewed in the last section on listening skills. Thus the reader is referred back to the listening skills material for information on minimal verbal responses, paraphrasing, checking out (perception checking), and clarifying.

One final comment is necessary before reviewing specific verbal responses. That is, that these do not by any means constitute the universe of verbal responses that the therapeutic recreation specialist can employ. These particular responses are designed to facilitate self-knowledge in contrast to developing client skills or attitudes.

PROBING

A probe is a question that is directed toward yielding information in order to gain empathetic understanding. Probes are open-ended questions requiring more than a "yes" or "no" reply. Okun (1976) suggests probes such as "Tell me more," "Let's talk about that," and "I'm wondering about . . ." (p. 52). A brief example of a probe in a client-helper interaction follows.

Client: There are lots of things I like about hiking.
Helper: Tell me some of them.

REFLECTING

The reflection response is a statement to reflect feelings received from the client through verbal or nonverbal means. Its aim is to mirror the feelings or emotions of the client. An example is: "It sounds as if you were really pleased to learn the outcome." An example of a client-helper exchange follows.

Client: I was mad as hell that they didn't ask me to join the team.
Helper: It seems you were feeling *very* angry about not being chosen.

INTERPRETING

Through interpretation something is added to the statement of the client. Here the helper is trying to help the client understand his or her underlying feelings. These responses are based on direct observation of what the client does and says, not on deep psychology. After the interpretation has been given, immediate feedback is sought from the client in order to see if they collaborate. For example:

Client: I just can't seem to get my act together to join the club. I tend to put it off even though I really want to do it.
Helper: You seem to be frightened to take the first step in joining.

CONFRONTING

The purpose of the confronting response is to assist the client to achieve congruency in what he or she says and does, or to help him or her be fully aware and honest in gaining self-understanding. Confrontation involves "telling it like it is," without being accusatory or judgmental. If the client does not seem to be genuine in his or her communications, this is pointed out. Okun (1976) has given these examples: "I feel you really don't want to talk about this," "It seems to me you're playing games with her," and "I'm wondering why you feel you always have to take the blame. What do you get out of it?" (p. 53). In raising discrepancies [e.g., "You say you're angry, yet you're smiling," or "On the one hand, you seem to be hurt by not getting that job but on the other hand you seem sort of relieved, too" (Okun, 1976, p. 53)], the helper expresses what seem to be contradictions in the client's comments or behavior.

It has been suggested that confrontation should not be used until rapport has been fully established and a positive helping relationship has developed (Egan, 1975a). Another author has mentioned that the wise helper will limit confrontations to strengths instead of picking on the client's imperfections (Schulman, 1978).

An example of a confronting verbal response follows.

Client: I don't want to be around any girls.

Helper: You say you don't want to associate with girls, yet I saw you dancing with both Nancy and Joyce last night and you seemed to be having a very good time.

INFORMING

Informing is the providing of factual information to the client. In therapeutic recreation this might be describing types of programs available to the client. Informing is *not* telling the client what to do. For example:

Client: I don't know what to get into.

Helper: Let me describe the choices you have here at the center.

SUMMARIZING

Summarizing brings together the client's central ideas, feelings, or both. The summary synthesizes what has been communicated so the client can see significant patterns. It is normally applied at the conclusion of a counseling session or after several sessions. An example of a summarizing response follows.

Client: A lot of time I'd rather stay home and watch a game on TV, or read the paper, or something like that. My wife always wants to go out and I don't think I should have to go just because she wants to.

Helper: You would prefer to stay home, while your wife wishes for you to go out with her.

In closing this section it should be mentioned that the verbal responses presented here may seem at first to be very similar in nature. They are actually distinctive types of responses that the emerging helping professional should learn to discriminate among. Once familiar with them, their use will become more natural. Just as typists differentiate among the keys on a typewriter without having to think about striking a particular letter, helping professionals learn to use the verbal responses without consciously defining the type of response before employing it.

It should also be reiterated that the verbal responses outlined by Okun (1976) bring about an expanded understanding of self and others. Although these responses are generally employed in formal interviewing and counseling sessions, they may also be appropriately applied in less structured interpersonal communications that typify therapeutic recreation. With the knowledge of these responses also comes the responsibility to resist any temptation to become a pseudo-psychotherapist.

VERBAL RESPONDING EXERCISE

Okun (1976) has presented an exercise on identification and recognition of the 10 major verbal responses. This exercise is adapted from that of Okun. Each of the helper statements uses one of the 10 responses. Read the helper's response, then identify it as one of the following: minimal verbal response, paraphrasing, checking out, clarifying, probing, reflecting, interpreting, confronting, informing, or summarizing. Record the responses you identify on a piece of paper. Then check them with the answers provided.

1. *Client:* I really felt good about being at the dance last night.
   Helper: You were glad to be there.
2. *Client:* I don't even want to think about the swim team, let alone join it.
   Helper: I saw you at the pool yesterday and you are an excellent swimmer, yet you always back off when the swim team is mentioned.
3. *Client:* I used to be really involved but during the last term I haven't done anything for recreation. I guess I've been too busy . . . but that's not it either. . . . I just don't know exactly why I've gotten into this rut.
   Helper: You have been active in recreation in the past but you have been inactive for the last few months, and you are unsure as to the cause for this.
4. *Client:* I can't really get with it.
   Helper: I see.
5. *Client:* I really like being in a group.
   Helper: Let's talk about that.
6. *Client:* Which program is the best for me?
   Helper: I would advise you to look at three of the programs offered here at the center. Let me tell you about them.
7. *Client:* As I've said before, I just don't like it.
   Helper: I want to check out with you what I'm hearing. You said that you really didn't enjoy. . . .
8. *Client:* At any rate, I just can't do it because it's too far away and in addition they aren't interested in helping me anyway.
   Helper: I'm not sure I follow you. Could you tell me some more about it.

9. *Client:* I just don't know what to do. One time he tells me do this. The next time he says just the opposite.
Helper: He seems to confuse you.

10. *Client:* All they care about is themselves and not what happens to me.
Helper: It is tough when you don't feel people care about you.

ANSWERS

1. Reflecting.	6. Informing.
2. Confronting.	7. Checking out.
3. Summarizing.	8. Clarifying.
4. Minimum verbal response.	9. Paraphrasing.
5. Probing.	10. Interpreting.

Now you may wish to get together with others who have independently completed the exercise so you can discuss the responses. Did all of you agree with the "book answers?" Did members of the group feel any of the helper's responses were inappropriate or poorly phrased? If you have time, half of the group should rewrite the helper's statements 1 to 5; the other half should rewrite 6 to 10. Share your statements and discuss which were most difficult to write.

COMMUNICATION PATTERNS IN SUCCESS-FAILURE SITUATIONS

Therapeutic recreation specialists spend a great deal of time interacting with clients while the clients take part in recreation activities. It is important, therefore, to explore communications between leaders and clients so that an understanding of effective feedback patterns can be gained. In the following paragraphs feedback patterns and their effects are discussed.

Recent research strongly suggests that therapeutic recreation specialists need to develop both an awareness of the messages given their clients during recreation participation and a working knowledge of the types of effective feedback that may be applied in leader-client communications. In a study completed at a camp for handicapped children, researchers (Bullock et al., 1980) examined the nature of feedback counselors provided to campers. Prior findings (Panada & Lynch, 1972) had indicated the importance of proper feedback, but Bullock and his colleagues found that no feedback at all was supplied in more than 20 percent of the interactions where campers experienced success on a task. As pointed out by these researchers, lack of feedback may be interpreted by the child as an indication of failure.

Furthermore, these researchers commented that for feedback to be most useful in failure situations, it should be specifically related to the task at hand (i.e., contingent), should give the participant information to make corrections in performance (i.e., informational), and should give some amount of encouragement (i.e., motivational). In situations where the campers did not succeed, the researchers found that less than 50 percent were furnished this type of feedback. In another approximately 16 percent of the failure situations, no feedback at all was provided.

The Bullock team also considered the attributional nature of counselor feedback. The theoretical basis for this portion of the study was Weiner's (1974) attribution theory, which theorizes that people formulate explanations for their own and others' successes and failures. Basically, these explanations involve two dimensions, stability (stable, unstable) and locus of control (internal, external), and four determinants of success or failure, ability (a stable internal factor), effort (an unstable internal factor), task difficulty (a stable external factor), and luck (an unstable external factor). Therefore the camp counselor might judge a camper was successful because he or she had a high level of ability (a stable-internal attribution), because he or she tried hard (an unstable-internal attribution), because it was an easy task (a stable-external attribution), or because of chance (an unstable-external attribution). On the other hand, the counselor could stereotype the handicapped child and therefore reason that any failure was due to a low ability ascribed to the handicap. This would result in the expectation that the child could not succeed unless the task were made easier. If, instead, the failure was judged to be because of an unstable factor (low effort or bad luck), a more optimistic expectation would follow.

The possible effects of voicing these judgments in feedback statements seems obvious. Naturally, the child could be given certain concepts of his or her abilities (or lack of abilities) through communication from significant others. Thus, in addition to possibly establishing a "self-fulfilling prophecy," a child's self-concept could be seriously affected as a result of feedback. Much to the distress of Bullock and the other researchers, observations of counselor-camper interactions revealed relatively few explicit attributional statements by counselors that either attributed unsuccessful performance to unstable determinants (effort or luck) or offered praise directly tied to the camper's ability.

All in all, the study by Bullock and his colleagues revealed that staff generally seemed unaware of their feedback patterns or of the possible effects their feedback might have on the children. The results have obvious implications for leader-client feedback patterns in all therapeutic recreation settings.

GUIDELINES FOR FEEDBACK

Bullock and his colleagues (1980, pp. 147–148) presented several explicit guidelines for providing feedback in therapeutic recreation leadership situations. These are:

- Feedback should be given in nearly all if not all performance situations.
- In successful outcomes, the feedback should be contingent, motivational, and positive.
- In unsuccessful situations, feedback should be contingent, informational, and positive and/or motivational.
- Attributional statements should be made more frequently.
- Attributional information must be explicitly stated in order for a clear understanding to (be given) the client.
- Reinforce success with internal stable attributional statements such as "Nice shot, I knew you could do it!"
- Encourage the child with unstable attributional statements following unsuccessful attempts. For example, "You'll have to try harder."

FEEDBACK EXERCISE

This exercise takes three people. A should take the role of the leader and B the role of the client. The third person should serve as an observer. A and B should complete a 3- to 5-minute role play in which the client is learning or performing a task. This might be making a leather belt or taking part in archery. As B takes part in the activity, A should attempt to offer helpful feedback. The observer should review the guidelines for feedback stated in the previous section. He or she should then take notes regarding the feedback of A. At the conclusion of the role play, these observations should be discussed by all three members of the group. If time is available, change roles and repeat the exercise.

WHAT IS THE IMPORTANCE OF STUDYING NONVERBAL COMMUNICATION?

Although we usually think of communication as involving verbal behavior, words represent only a small part of our total interpersonal communication patterns. The vast majority of our communicating is done on a nonverbal level (Sundeen et al., 1976). One author has stated that in face-to-face communication, only one-third of our communicating takes place on a verbal level, while two-thirds is nonverbal (Brill, 1978). Additionally, nonverbal communication is important in therapeutic recreation, since it can be particularly effective as an outlet for expressing feelings and attitudes that clients cannot express or do not wish to express verbally. Expressive recreation pursuits such as music, physical movement, and creative writing allow for the manifestation of feelings and attitudes through nonverbal means.

Nonverbal communications are, of course, the messages passing between a sender and receiver that do not rely on the spoken word. It has been specified that nonverbal communication is expressed continuously in human interactions. With or without accompanying verbal behavior, nonverbal communication is continuous in the presence of others, since all nonverbal behavior has potential message value (Brill, 1978). From this perspective " . . . it follows that no matter how one may try, one cannot *not* communicate. Activity or inactivity, words or silence all have message value: they influence others and these others, in turn, cannot *not* respond to these communications and are thus themselves communicating" (Watzlawick et al., 1967, p. 49). Thus, for example, even silence or inactivity in the company of others may carry a message that a person is sad, bored, or perhaps depressed. Nonverbal communication is going on all the time, making it impossible not to communicate.

Nonverbal communication is obviously of great importance in interpersonal transactions. Therapeutic recreation specialists must become aware of nonverbal communication to (1) pick up nonverbal cues from clients and staff, and (2) be aware of possible effects of their own nonverbal communication on others.

WHAT ARE SPECIFIC EXAMPLES OF NONVERBAL BEHAVIORS?

Tubbs and Moss (1978) have classified nonverbal into three categories: visual cues, vocal cues, and spacial and temperal cues. The information about these cues that follows has been drawn primarily from the work of Tubbs and Moss (1978).

VISUAL CUES

Some visual cues to nonverbal communication have been mentioned as a part of the discussion on listening skills. Nevertheless, information on eye contact, body movement, and gestures is important and is therefore repeated in the list of visual cues that follows. Visual cues in nonverbal communication are:

• *Facial Expression.* Our faces express numerous feelings and emotions. A friendly smile invites further interaction. A frown may indicate sadness. Grimaces may be a sign of anger. Blushing often indicates embarrassment. An animated face may show excitement and vigor, while a "poker face" may project the image of a bland person.

- *Eye Contact.* It is reinforcing to receive eye contact. When someone does not look us in the eye, we may feel they are shifty or that they are hiding something.
- *Body Movements.* Our bodies are used to signal others in various ways. Biting our nails may indicate nervousness. Physical touch may be used to demonstrate caring and support. Women may signal sexual interest by crossing the legs or exposing a thigh. Fidgeting, however, may distract from other messages.
- *Hand Gestures.* The peace sign and the hitchhiker's raised thumb are two gestures we all recognize. Most people would also recognize the drumming of someone's fingers on a table as a sign of impatience. Hand gestures may substitute substantially for verbal behavior, as in the case of sign language for those who are deaf.
- *Physical Appearance and the Use of Objects.* Rightly or wrongly, as documented by the classic social psychology study of Kelley (1950), first impressions have a potent affect. Therefore it becomes important to realize that we may project a negative impression through extremes in clothing or jewelry. Equally important is that therapeutic recreation specialists guard against the pitfall of stereotyping that may result from generalizations made about clients after only brief contact. The term "object language" is used by authors to denote the message value in physical objects. How people dress, decorate their homes and offices, their choices of magazines, the car they drive, and many other physical objects communicate nonverbal messages about them. Bumper stickers and T-shirts are popular means today for passing along nonverbal messages about ourselves. When we see a bumper sticker stating "I'm a Leisure Lover" or a T-shirt reading "Let's Park and Recreate," these bring certain connotations to mind.

VOCAL CUES

Earlier in this chapter vocal cues such as tone of voice and volume and rate of speech were discussed. These, and voice pitch and quality, constitute vocal phenomena that accompany speech and are sometimes termed paralinguistics. Various vocal cues are briefly reviewed here.

- *Volume.* Speaking too loudly is likely to offend others. Speaking too softly also can be irritating. However, what is an appropriate level of volume to one group of people may not be for another group coming from a different cultural background. Therefore it is best to test what volume works best in each situation.

- *Rate and fluency.* Our rate of speech may be taken by others as evidence of our mood. We often speak rapidly when we are excited and exhibit slower speech when depressed. Speaking too rapidly or too slowly may cause tension to be revealed in the listener. Fluency has to do with the continuity of speech. Pausing frequently and inserting "ah" or "er" distracts from the central message.
- *Pitch.* The unvarying use of one level of voice pitch can be monotonous. An expressive person will vary voice pitch to reflect attitude or mood naturally.
- *Quality.* Voice quality deals with how pleasant we perceive a voice to be. For example, a harsh, piercing voice may be distracting.

SPATIAL AND TEMPERAL CUES

To be effective in our interpersonal communications, we should be aware of the factors of time and space and the possible effects they may each have on communications.

- *Time.* The concept of time varies from culture to culture. Americans generally seem to be very aware of time and may react when normal customs regarding time are violated. For instance, arriving late for a social invitation or a business appointment may offend those who are expecting you. This behavior may say to them that you do not hold them in high regard.
- *Space.* Human communication may be affected significantly by the way people position themselves in relation to others. We might stand or sit very close to someone with whom we are in an intimate relationship. On the other hand, we normally attempt to maintain some social distance with clients so as not to infringe on their sense of personal space. As Sommer's (1969) work has shown, interaction patterns can be affected by something as simple as how furniture is placed. Certain seating arrangements foster interpersonal transactions, while others have the opposite effect. Unfortunately, many times this variable has not been considered by those in helping relationships.

To summarize this section, it seems clear that nonverbal communication processes are extensive. In face-to-face communication with clients we must take advantage of all the cues available to us. Therefore the development of skills in interpreting nonverbal communications is essential. The exercises that follow provide one vehicle to improve understanding of the often subtle but pervasive visual, vocal, and spatial and temporal cues available in nonverbal communication.

NONVERBAL COMMUNICATION EXERCISES

Several excellent exercises related to perceiving and giving nonverbal cues are available. The following are drawn and adapted from Hackney and Cormier (1979), Okun (1976), and Stevens (1971).

Portraying Feelings (Hackney & Cormier, 1979)

This exercise is done with a partner. A is the speaker and B assumes the role of the respondent. The idea of the exercise is to portray feelings exclusively through nonverbal means. A selects a feeling from the following list without identifying it to B. A then portrays it, and B should attempt so identify the feeling. After a feeling has been identified, choose another feeling and repeat the process. Then reverse roles so B may portray the feelings. Choose feelings from the following:

Contented.
Puzzled and confused.
Angry.
Discouraged.

Magazine Pictures (Okun, 1976)

From magazines, cut out pictures of people but leave out any captions. First, ask a partner what he or she believes to be the message in each picture. Then ask for the responses in a group of four to six people. After you have looked at several pictures, see if your group can identify any common patterns for the group members' identification of feelings expressed in the pictures. The exercise is designed to examine different responses to the same nonverbal stimuli. Was there agreement on rationale behind the identifications? Was there disagreement? If so, what was the basis for them? Can you explain the diversity in perceptions?

Identifying Feelings (Okun, 1976)

This is similar to the portraying-feelings exercise but involves three or more people. In this exercise A identifies a specific feeling or emotion and informs an observer of what it is. A then attempts to communicate the feeling or emotion nonverbally to a partner or to members of a small group. When it has been identified, another person should take the place of A, and the exercise should continue until all in the group who wish to participate have had an opportunity. When you have finished, process on your experience to determine reasons for agreements and disagreements in identifications.

Self-Analysis (Okun, 1976)
Self-awareness is the purpose of this exercise, which asks you to list nonverbal behaviors used with each of the four major emotions: anger, fear, happiness, and sadness. For example, list what nonverbal behaviors you engage in when angry (such as frowning or clenching your fist). After recording these behaviors for each emotion, share your list in a small group, noting similarities and differences. As an alternative, you may share your list with a close friend. See if the friend agrees with how you express yourself in the ways you have listed. If your friend disagrees, what is the basis for this?

Nonverbal Canceling (Stevens, 1971)
The object of this exercise is to become aware of possible nonverbal messages you or others provide. A should purposefully cancel out everything stated to B with an accompanying nonverbal cue. Whatever the spoken message, cancel it out with an opposite gesture, facial expression, body movement, eye contact, or any other nonverbal means of communication. A and B should switch the sender-receiver roles back and forth for 5 minutes. At the end of this time, each should sit quietly and reflect on the exercise before processing on it. Begin the processing by telling each other what you experienced during the exercise. How did you feel when canceling verbal messages? Did you recognize any of the canceling behaviors from previous personal experience? As an alternative, you might complete this exercise in a small group, allowing all members to take both the sender and receiver roles.

Shoulder Massage (Stevens, 1971)
This is a group exercise in which a circle is formed by standing behind someone to whom you would like to give something. Once you are in a circle, you should face clockwise, sit down, and silently begin to massage or rub the shoulders, neck, and back of the person in front of you. Everyone should close their eyes and refrain from speaking. The only communication is with your hands. After several minutes, you may make noises (but do not use formal language) to let the person giving the massage know how it feels. Your noises should tell the person behind you what kind of things you like best. After 5 minutes, silently turn around in the other direction and give a massage to the person who has been massaging you. Again, communicate with noises to inform the person what feels good to you. Do

this for 3 to 5 minutes more. Before you begin, tell those in the group that the exercise may make them slightly uncomfortable and, if this happens, not to laugh and talk but to follow the directions. After you have finished, share your ideas on the experience with the person in front of you and the person behind you. How did you communicate? Was this nonverbal expression natural? Did you feel uncomfortable in touching others of the opposite sex or others of the same sex?

INTERVIEWING: A FORM OF COMMUNICATION

The interview is a structured, face-to-face method of communication directed toward a particular end. Intents for interviews in therapeutic recreation will vary, but probably the most common type is the initial assessment interview discussed in Chapter 3. TR specialists may additionally conduct interviews with clients' families and friends, during new client orientation programs, during leisure counseling, and for other purposes.

THE SETTING

Ideally, the interview setting should offer a quiet, relaxed atmosphere where privacy is assured. Too often, it seems, therapeutic recreation specialists are expected to conduct interviews on busy admissions wards or in active recreation areas. Do not trap yourself, or the client, into approaching the interview too casually because it concerns "only recreation." There is a great deal of difference between being "relaxed" and being "careless" in your approach.

Interviews can be structured to be formal or informal. Formal interviews are often conducted in an office or in a special room designed for interviewing. An informally structured interview might be conducted in a recreation area. In fact, some clients (and interviewers) feel most comfortable in an informal recreation setting. If this is the case, interviews might be conducted while shooting baskets in a gym, playing a table game, or having a soft drink in a quiet area of a snack bar. Psychological privacy, or feeling that you have a place to yourselves, is perhaps as important as the actual physical setting that is chosen.

Whatever the area selected to conduct the interview, it should be free from interruptions. There is nothing more distracting than to have clients called away in order to take medication, see the social worker, or participate in some seemingly "more important" activity. Protect yourself by scheduling your interviews at times when competition for the client's time is minimum and clearly inform other personnel of the need for an uninterrupted interview.

PHASES

Most authorities agree that interviews have three phases, the beginning phase, the working phase, and the termination phase.

In any interview the first step is to help the client feel as comfortable as possible (Bernstein et al., 1974). The therapeutic recreation specialist should strive to create an atmosphere displaying openness, warmth, and respect for the client.

Just how the client should be greeted varies from interview to interview and person to person. It would be inappropriate to approach a small child with a strong handshake or to provide a depressed individual with a vigorous welcome (Schulman, 1978). It has been suggested that a good beginning may be simply welcoming the client with a smile, introducing yourself, and inviting the person to sit down. Early in the initial interview you may indicate the length of time available for the session, your role, and the purpose of the interview. You may wish to inform the interviewee how you prefer to be addressed and also inquire as to how he or she would like to be addressed. Finally, you may want to talk with new clients about the confidentiality of the situation. Will you share the information with anyone? If you are taking notes or tape-recording, who will have access to these? Depending on your agency and situation, particular questions on confidentiality may or may not be important. You will have to determine which specific confidentiality issues are seen as important at your agency or institution (Hackney & Cormier, 1979).

Next comes the working phase. During this stage, both you and the client have settled into comfortable positions and are ready to begin work. At this time, you direct the interview toward the primary goal for the session. This might involve any number of general objectives, such as gaining information regarding a client's leisure interests or allowing the client to express how he or she would expect to profit from therapeutic recreation programming.

Toward the conclusion of the session, the TR specialist should indicate that it is almost time to stop. This may be done with a short, clear statement ("It seems our time is almost up for today"), summarization, or mutual feedback. By briefly summarizing the information and/or feelings expressed, the therapeutic recreation specialist and the client leave the interview with similar ideas about what has been communicated. Mutual feedback involves both the client and helper. This termination strategy is recommended if a plan has been formed or specific decisions made. Both participants can clarify and verify what has been decided and what future steps are to be taken (Hackney & Cormier, 1979). Of course, it is appropriate to use the last few seconds of the session to make arrangement for the time and place of the next session if additional interviews are necessary.

INTERVIEWING EXERCISE

Hackney and Cormier (1979) have outlined an exercise that involves videotaping two persons in an interview situation. The exercise that follows has been based on that of Hackney and Cormier.

In this exercise A is the interviewer and B is the client. Their communications are videotaped for 4 or 5 minutes. During this time, A should try to accomplish the following:

1. Welcome B appropriately.
2. Set B at ease (less bodily tension, voice not tense).
3. Project being at ease (relaxed, open posture).
4. Use reinforcing attending behaviors (e.g., eye contact, gestures).
5. Get B to start talking about anything.
6. Get B to identify a current concern or problem in regard to his or her leisure.

After this, A and B should reverse roles and repeat the exercise. Again, this segment should be videotaped. Once all pairs have been videotaped, the tapes should be replayed and critiqued for strengths and weaknesses displayed in the interviewers' skills.

SUMMARY STATEMENT

Success in helping relationships depends to a large degree on the ability of the therapeutic recreation specialist to communicate effectively with clients. The interpersonal communication skills employed in client transactions are basically the same skills used in everyday encounters. In social relationships, however, they may be casually employed. In contrast, in professional helping relationships where our primary focus is always on the client, our communications are consciously directed toward client needs in order to facilitate growth leading to independence and self-sufficiency.

KEY WORDS

Communications. Verbal and nonverbal transmission of ideas, feelings, beliefs, and attitudes that permits a common understanding between the sender of the message and the receiver.

Effective Listening. An active process that can be used in any interper-

138

sonal transactions. It involves four major skills: attending, paraphrasing, clarifying, and perception checking.

Nonverbal Communications. Messages passing between the sender and receiver that do not use the spoken word are nonverbal communications. These may be categorized as visual cues, vocal cues, and spatial and temporal cues.

Reading Comprehension Questions

1 Define the term communication in your own words.

2 Why are communication skills important to therapeutic recreation specialists?

3 Is professional jargon appropriate in client communications?

4 What are some guidelines to help avoid rambling communication?

5 How may attitudes enter into interpersonal comunication?

6 How may voice tone and volume affect communication?

7 What things may cause the receiver to distort a message?

8 Explain why listening may be termed an active process.

9 What behaviors let the client know you are attending to what he or she is saying?

10 Explain the four major listening skills discussed in the chapter.

11 Briefly explain each of the verbal responses outlined in the chapter.

12 Do you understand the rationale behind each of the guidelines for feedback?

13 How much of our face-to-face communication is transmitted through nonverbal means?

14 What is the importance of studying nonverbal communication?

15 Why might it be said that one cannot not communicate?

16 Give some specific examples of nonverbal cues.

17 What does an "I'm a Leisure Lover" bumper sticker have to do with nonverbal communication?

18 Can you make any suggestions as to the setting for interviews?

19 What may be stipulated as the initial step in any interview?

20. Outline the phases of an interview.

REFERENCES

Bernstein, L., Bernstein, R. S., & Dana, R. H. 1974. *Interviewing: A guide for health professionals* (2nd edition). New York: Appleton-Century-Crofts.

Brammer, L. M. 1979. *The helping relationship: Process and Skills* (2nd edition). Englewood Cliffs, N. J.: Prentice-Hall, Inc.

Brill, N. I. 1978. *Working with people: The helping process* (2nd edition). Philadelphia: J. B. Lippincott Company.

Bullock, C. C., Austin, D. R., & Lewko, J. H. 1980. Leadership behavior in therapeutic recreation settings. In G. Hitzhusen, J. Elliott, D. J. Szmanski, & M. G. Thompson (eds.), *Expanding horizons in therapeutic recreation* (Vol. 7). Columbia, Mo.: University of Missouri.

Chartier, M. R. 1976. Clarity of expression in interpersonal communication. In J. W. Pfeiffer & J. E. Jones (eds.), *The 1976 annual handbook for group facilitators*. Iowa City, Iowa: University Associates.

Egan, G. 1975. *Exercises in helping skills: A training manual to accompany the skilled helper*. Monterey, Calif.: Brooks/Cole Publishing Company.

Egan, G. 1975a. *The skilled helper: A model for systematic helping and interpersonal relating*. Monterey, Calif.: Brooks/Cole Publishing Company.

Gibson, J. L., Ivancevich, J. M., & Donnelly, J. H. 1976. *Organizations: Behavior, structure, processes*. Dallas: Business Publications, Inc.

Hackney, H., & Cormier, L. S. 1979. *Counseling strategies and objectives* (2nd edition). Englewood Cliffs, N. J.: Prentice-Hall, Inc.

Kelley, H. H. 1950. The warm-cold variable in first impressions of persons. *Journal of Personality. 18*, 431–439.

Killen, K. H. 1977. *Management: A middle-management approach*. Boston: Houghton Mifflin Company.

Okun, B. F. 1976. *Effective helping: Interviewing & counseling techniques*. North Scituate, Mass.: Duxbury Press.

Panada, K. C., & Lynch, W. W. 1972. Affects of social reinforcement on the retarded child: A review of interpretation for classroom instruction. Education and Training of the mentally retarded. *7*, 115.

Purtilo, R. 1978. *Health professional/patient interaction* (2nd edition). Philadelphia: W. B. Saunders Company.

Satir, V. 1972. *Peoplemaking*. Palo Alto, Calif.: Science and Behavioral Books, Inc.

Schulman, E. D. 1978. *Intervention in human services* (2nd edition). Saint Louis: The C. V. Mosby Company.

Simmons, J. A. 1976. *The nurse-client relationship in mental health nursing: Workbook guides to understanding and management* (2nd edition). Philadelphia: W. B. Saunders Company.

Sommer, R. 1969. *Personal space: The behavioral basis for design.* Englewood Cliffs, N. J.: Prentice-Hall, Inc.

Stevens, J. O. 1971. *Awareness: Exploring, experimenting, experiencing.* New York: Bantam Books.

Sundeen, J., Stuart, G. W., Rankin, E., & Cohen, S. P. 1976. *Nurse-client interaction: Implementing the nursing process.* Saint Louis: The C. V. Mosby Company.

Tubbs, S. L., & Moss, S. 1978. *Interpersonal communication.* New York: Random House.

Watzlawick, P., Beavin, J. H., & Jackson, D. D. 1967. *Pragmatics of human communication: A study of interactional patterns and paradoxes.* New York: W. W. Norton & Company, Inc.

Weiner, B. (Ed.), 1974. *Achievement and Motivation and Attribution Theory.* Morristown, N. J. General Press.

6

BEING
A
LEADER

PURPOSE OF THE CHAPTER

Leadership is vital to therapeutic recreation. Even so, leadership has remained a relatively neglected area in therapeutic recreation literature. Few researchers have carefully examined the dynamics of leadership processes in therapeutic recreation. Neither have professionals in the field taken on the cause of writing extensively of their leadership experiences.

Nevertheless, all would probably agree that there is no substitute for effective leadership. In fact, many therapeutic recreation specialists would propose that the effectiveness of the leader is the single most important factor affecting therapeutic outcomes with clients. This chapter will help the student to develop a general understanding of leadership and to gain exposure to specific information applicable to leadership in therapeutic recreation.

OBJECTIVES

- Understand leadership, its levels, and its basis.
- Comprehend major leadership styles.

- Recognize factors influencing choice of leadership style.
- Identify possible leadership roles.
- Know ways to deal with dependency.
- Evaluate principles listed for the TR leader.
- Explain the function of the group leader.
- Distinguish between various structures for therapeutic recreation.
- Show awareness of what constitutes a sense of "groupness."
- Interpret stages of group development.
- Recognize leader concerns in group development.
- Distinguish between functional and nonfunctional behaviors in groups.
- Understand various group phenomena, including social facilitation, conformity, and risky shift.
- Interpret principles for group leadership.
- Justify writing progress notes.
- Analyze a progress note.
- Know categories of behavior for progress-note writing.
- Understand major principles in the teaching/learning process.
- Distinguish between Tylerian and naturalistic approaches to evaluation.
- Appreciate the usefulness of logical steps to program evaluation.
- Define the term counseling.
- Recognize the state of the art of leisure counseling.
- Appreciate topics of concern in understanding leader transactions.

WHAT IS LEADERSHIP?

Authors of early books in recreation (e.g., Stone & Stone, 1952) often wrote of the personal characteristics of the recreation leader. Now we realize that leadership involves much more than the personality traits of the leader. The myth of the "born leader" has been dispelled.

Good leadership in therapeutic recreation involves the ability to influence the activities of clients toward accomplishing sought outcomes. Therefore, at a specific level, a leader's effectiveness may be primarily measured by how well clients do in achieving prescribed objectives. More generally, the therapeutic recreation specialist's success as a leader may be evaluated by his or her ability to facilitate the movement of clients toward an optimal level of independence and healthful living.

WHAT ARE THE LEVELS OF LEADERSHIP?

Kraus and Bates (1975) have listed four levels of recreation leadership: (1) administrative leadership; (2) supervisory leadership; (3) team leadership; and (4) direct program leadership.

144

Administrative Leadership

Administrative leadership is one task of the administrator who must also plan, organize, coordinate, evaluate, and generally control the operations of the agency. In heading an agency, the administrator provides overall direction and leadership for all subordinates within the organization.

Supervisory Leadership

Supervisory leadership involves providing supervision for other staff. On this level, the therapeutic recreator may supervise TR specialists and/or other agency staff, depending on the organizational structures of the agency.

Team Leadership

Team Leadership may involve teamwork with other therapeutic recreators or teamwork with an interdisciplinary team. In either case, the therapeutic recreator may be called on to exert leadership within a peer situation.

Direct Program Leadership

Direct program leadership deals with the actual delivery of therapeutic recreation programming to clients. Here the leader is directly involved in face-to-face leadership with individuals in recreation or leisure-related activities. It is with this last level of leadership that this chapter is concerned, although much of the information presented may have application at the other leadership levels as well.

WHAT IS THE BASIS FOR INFLUENCE?

It is useful for the therapeutic recreation specialist to understand the basis for the leader's influence and power. Five types of power have been proposed by French and Raven (1959). These are *expert power* (gained by being viewed as having knowledge or expertise), *referent power* (gained by the identification or closeness others feel for the leader), *legitimate power* (gained by being designated by those in control who bestow the right of the leader to be influential), *reward power* (gained by being viewed as having the ability to give rewards), and *coercive power* (gained by being perceived as being able to levy punishment).

The therapeutic recreation specialist is likely to have legitimate power, since he or she is designated for leadership by those in authority. Clients are also apt to bestow reward and coercive power on the TR specialist. Depending on the particular situation, the TR specialist may also be attributed expert power, since he or she may have a high degree of skill or knowledge in a certain activity. The leader who develops rapport with clients obtains referent power.

Schmuck and Schmuck (1975) have suggested it is important for teachers to attempt to gain expert and referent power to accompany the legitimate, reward, and coercive bases of power usually granted them so that they may be able to maintain control over the classroom. In doing so, teachers are able to meet occasions of conflict with high-power students, who usually gain their influence through being good at things (expert power) or who possess highly valued personal characteristics (referent power).

In order to understand the atmosphere within a TR group, it is important that those in leadership positions be able to analyze the power structures that are present. The leaders should know who has power and how it is being employed.

Schmuck and Schmuck (1975) have further stated that a positive group atmosphere generally exists when members see themselves as having some amount of power. Most persons want to feel they have influence in relation to important others (such as the leader) and, when they have some degree of influence, they feel more secure.

Therefore it is the wise therapeutic recreation specialist who (1) understands the issues of power within groups, and (2) uses his or her leadership position to create a positive social climate by encouraging feelings of influence among group members.

LEADERSHIP STYLES

Most discussions of leadership center around three leadership styles: autocratic, democratic, and laissez-faire. These styles are outlined next.

Autocratic Leadership. Autocratic leadership is a directive style of leadership. The autocratic leader has superior knowledge and expertise. He or she makes all decisions and expects obedience from others. All authority and all responsibility remain with the leader. Autocratic leaders allow minimal group participation. There is never any question as to who is in charge.

Democratic Leadership. The democratic leader involves others in decision making. He or she draws on group members for ideas, thus creating a feeling of participation and teamwork. Under democratic leadership, people sense that their participation is important.

Laissez-Faire Leadership. Laissez-faire leadership is an open and permissive approach. The leader does not exercise authority. Instead, minimum control is used so that participants may take on responsibility for decision making. Laissez-faire leadership is participative and client centered.

146

WHICH STYLE IS BEST?

There really is no one best leadership style in therapeutic recreation. A number of factors influence the best style for any given situation. These factors include: (1) the ability and personality of the leader, (2) the characteristics and needs of clients, and (3) the environment in which the leadership occurs (e.g., pediatrics unit, adult psychiatric unit, nursing home). Figure 6-1 illustrates the three major factors affecting leadership in therapeutic recreation.

Leader Abilities and Personality
As discussed in Chapter 4, it is very important that each therapeutic recreation specialist gains self-knowledge. This includes becoming aware of which leadership style best suits the abilities and personality of the individual. Good leaders choose a style with which they feel comfortable most of the time but remain flexible enough to deviate from it when clients or situations dictate another style.

Client Needs and Characteristics
The second factor to consider in selecting a leadership style is the type of client being served. For example, an autocratic style initially may be

Figure 6-1   Factors influencing choices of leadership style.

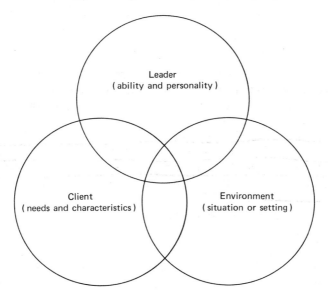

BEING A LEADER

appropriate for clients who have difficulty in making decisions or accepting responsibility, but such an approach would be inappropriate with most clients served in therapeutic recreation.

The Environment or Situation

The final factor to be considered is the environment or situation in which leadership transpires. Generally, the environment is closely tied to client needs and characteristics, since policies and practices or organizations are based largely on the type of clients being served. For example, confused psychiatric patients may be placed on a locked ward for their own safety and protection. The types of activities provided in such an environment might likely be highly structured, allowing for a minimum of control by the clients.

The type of clients discussed in the prior example (confused psychiatric patients), coupled with the environment (a locked ward with a highly structured program), might well dictate an autocratic style of leadership. If a therapeutic recreation specialist was not comfortable with this style, he or she would be better suited to another client population or setting. It is important for emerging TR specialists to realize that various types of leadership styles are needed because of the diversity of clients and variety of settings in therapeutic recreation. There is no one *best* leadership style. A wide variety of persons with varying abilities and personalities may become successful therapeutic recreation practitioners, each fitting into the type of leadership position for which he or she is most ideally suited.

CONTINUUM OF LEADERSHIP STYLES

The three major leadership styles—autocratic, democratic, and laissez-faire—may be conceptualized to exist along a continuum, with autocratic leadership on one end and laissez-faire leadership at the other extreme. This continuum is represented in Figure 6-2.

Even when therapeutic recreation specialists must initially be autocratic in leadership, it is important to remember that the ultimate goal is to help each client move away from dependency on the leader and thus gain greater self-dependence. Progressive movement along the continuum of

Figure 6-2 Continuum of leadership style.

Autocratic (leader centered)	Democratic	Laissez — faire (client centered)
Dependency		Independence

leadership style from a controlling, autocratic style toward the client-centered, participative leadership style is the goal of all leadership in therapeutic recreation. The therapeutic recreation specialist sincerely believes that all clients are first-class citizens who deserve the right to move toward the greatest possible level of independence.

The process of allowing clients to move past planned activities to choosing their own leisure pursuits requires a supportive atmosphere that provides for—and fosters—the growth of the individual. The leader moves toward ultimately reaching the role of an enabler who promotes the greatest possible level of independence and self-determination on the part of clients.

Leadership Roles

Avedon (1974) has listed eight diverse roles that the TR specialist may assume as clients move from dependence to independence: controller, director, instigator, stimulator, educator, advisor, observer, and enabler.

The *controller* exercises a high level of control over clients, making all decisions regarding the activities of the group. The *director* still holds most of the power and leads the activities of the group but does allow clients some latitude in decision making. The *instigator* incites action on the part of the group and then withdraws, leaving the group members in control. The *stimulator* begins activities by generating interest on the part of clients and then helps maintain this interest by encouraging participation. The *educator* instructs clients in activities and social skills. The *advisor* provides counseling and guidance to clients. The *observer* provides leadership by his or her presence and evaluates and reacts to clients' responses. The *enabler* role fits well into the laissez-faire style, where the leader simply provides opportunities for participation in activities determined by clients.

The leadership styles and roles discussed in this section exist only as means by which to help clients move toward their optimal level of independence and healthful living. During this process of moving away from dependency, the TR specialist will necessarily have to help clients with problems and feelings related to dependency.

WHAT IS DEPENDENCY AND HOW CAN IT BE DEALT WITH?

Dependent clients rely on staff for psychological and social support. They accept a subordinate status in which they depend on others instead of acting independently.

Dealing with dependency is a concern in almost every therapeutic recreation setting. In fact, Kutner (1971) has suggested that a certain amount of dependency is a natural part of successful rehabilitation, since clients must give their consent to be influenced by those directing the treatment or rehabilitation program. However, some individuals may use their role as client as a means to gain excessive attention and/or escape personal responsibilities. If reinforced, such behavior can produce clients who learn to be "helpless," relying on others instead of on their own initiative (Schmuck & Schmuck, 1975).

Haber and her colleagues (1978) have suggested various ways to deal with dependency on which the guidelines that follow are based.

1. Be conscious of demands for advice and answers to problems by clients who lack the confidence to make decisions for themselves.
2. Show acceptance of clients but do not give in to their demands if demands are excessive or irrational.
3. Help clients become aware of their feelings of dependency and develop new ways to seek gratification of their needs through more independent means.
4. Build the self-esteem of clients by making ability statements in which they are assured they have the ability to succeed.
5. Provide opportunities for clients to make decisions and accept responsibility.

WHAT IS THE FUNCTION OF THE GROUP LEADER?

Much of the therapeutic recreation specialist's time is apt to be spent in working with groups of various types. Knickerbocker (1969), Schul (1975), and Gordon (1977) have stated that human beings participate in groups because they believe that their needs will be satisfied as a result. People accept the influence and direction of leaders in order to meet their individual needs.

Gordon (1977) has provided a model as an explanation of group leadership. The model rests on the assumption that people are continually in the process of *satisfying needs or relieving tension*. In order to satisfy their needs some *means* is necessary. Most needs in our society are satisfied through *relationships with other individuals or groups*. Persons therefore take part in groups because they anticipate that this participation will result in meeting their individual needs. Individuals accept direction from a leader because this behavior is considered to be a means to needs satisfaction. The relationship with the leader is seen as an avenue through which they will get their needs met.

Our clients join therapeutic recreation groups in order to satisfy needs.

Consequently, it is the function of the TR specialist to organize the activities of client groups so that individuals may reach needs satisfaction.

WHAT ARE STRUCTURES FOR TR?

Avedon (1974) has outlined a number of structures for group participation in therapeutic recreation.

Informal Lounge Programs. An informal lounge program is a casual program of low organization in which a multipurpose area is made open to clients on a drop-in basis. Actvities vary from agency to agency but usually include pool or billiards, table shuffleboard, electronic games, card games, and table games. The choice of activity is left to each participant. Staff may provide some informal instruction and guidance, but their main roles are as observers and enablers.

Clubs. Clubs are made up of clients who meet regularly to pursue a common interest. They generally have officers who are elected by the club members. Examples are current events clubs, art clubs, and teen clubs. Clubs may be completely client run or may rely heavily on staff for leadership. Most would probably fall somewhere between these extremes.

Special Interest Groups. Special interest groups, like clubs, are scheduled on a regular basis. They are for clients who share a common interest in a particular recreation or leisure activity. For instance, a group of clients might get together regularly to pursue an interest in photography. In all likelihood, leadership would be shared, depending on the specific activity being engaged in at the time.

Classes. Classes are scheduled opportunities for instruction. They generally have a regular membership of clients who have sought the class or have been placed in the class as a part of their individual program plan. Classes range from instruction in bowling or swimming to sewing and flower arranging. Usually the instructor is the TR specialist, although volunteers with expertise in an area may be utilized as instructors.

Leagues, Tournaments, and Contests. Competitive structures are leagues, tournaments, and contests. These are organized by therapeutic recreation personnel. Examples would be bowling leagues and card tournaments. In some settings staff and clients participate together in team sports in public leagues and tournaments.

Special Events. Special events typically are large-scale affairs held by institutions at holiday times. Events such as Christmas dinner-dances and Independence Day carnivals were annual occurrences at most state psychiatric hospitals, state residential schools, and Veterens Administration hospitals. Similar activities are found at hospitals and other institutions today, but the concept of special events has been broadened to include many different types of occasions such as dining in restaurants, theater parties, and special tours.

Mass Activities. Mass activities are for large numbers of clients and perhaps their families and friends. Movies, concerts, and dances are examples. Staff organize and conduct these events.

WHAT MAKES A GROUP?

Do the clients involved in the types of program structures outlined by Avedon (1974) really constitute groups? Think for a moment of the groups of which you are a member. What makes each of them a group? Is there a difference between a collection of individuals and a group?

Most of us have a feeling about what constitutes a sense of "groupness." First, we want to be a part of the group. There is a conscious *identification* with the group, or a sense of belonging. We also have some sort of *interaction* with others in the group. We communicate with and react to others in our group. Finally, there is a sense of *shared purpose,* or group goals or ideals that are held by members (Knowles & Knowles, 1959; Cartwright & Zander, 1968).

Are therapeutic recreation "groups" really groups? It is perhaps best to not answer this question in absolute terms but to recognize that most TR groups can be described as ranging somewhere along the previously identified dimensions of identification, interaction, and shared purpose by which groups may be defined. In some TR situations a sense of groupness exists; in others a complete sense of group does not form because the members have not developed along one or more of the dimensions. This may occur in situations in which there is continual change in the composition of the membership, in instances where the program itself is structured in a way that discourages client interaction (such as an art class in which clients engage in separate projects), or in cases where members are not yet ready to interact with others. TR groups that do remain intact, enjoy structures condusive to group formation, and are constituted of members who feel comfortable interacting go through several stages of group development.

WHAT ARE STAGES OF GROUP DEVELOPMENT?

Different phases of group development have been proposed by various authors (e.g., Hansen et al., 1980; Longo & Williams, 1978; Tubbs &

Moss, 1978). Usually authors talk of four stages that groups encounter. They are the orientation or forming stage, the conflict stage, the group cohesion stage, and the performance or production stage. Some authors add a fifth stage, the termination stage, in which members may revert to old behaviors typical of the conflict stage. *A little bit Perl*

During the *orientation stage* or *forming stage*, the natural insecurity and apprehension about being in a new group is paramount. There is a great deal of reliance on the leader because group members still feel dependent on the leader for direction. Here we are likely to observe group members all looking at the person speaking and then shifting their focus to the leader for his or her reaction. At this time, the leader must help the group break the ice so that members get to know each other and become comfortable in the group. In the second phase a period of *conflict* is likely to occur. As people reveal more of themselves, their personalities, beliefs, or values may begin to clash. They may become hostile toward each other and toward the leader. This may be overt or covert. Generally, groups work through this phase. As they do, they resolve conflicts, develop sensitivity to one another, and begin to enter a stage of *group cohesion*. During this stage, individuals begin to identify with the leader and other group members. Longo and Williams (1978), who refer to this as the "we stage," suggest that members may find such pleasure in the cohesiveness of the group that they may even set aside their tasks just to enjoy being part of the group. In the fourth stage, *performance or productivity*, members become functional and devote themselves to achieving individual and group goals.

Although it is true that groups go through somewhat predictable stages, each individual group will be different from other groups. As various writers have discussed (Hansen et al., 1980; Longo & Williams, 1978), groups vary in the amount of time spent in any stage and may move through several stages in the space of one meeting of the group. Groups also may not move precisely from one stage to the next in a sequential fashion. Instead, they may bypass a stage or may move backward to a previous phase. Nevertheless, it is important for the leader to develop an understanding of the developmental stages so that he or she may better help members in their individual and group development.

SOME LEADER CONCERNS AND STRATEGIES

NEW CLIENTS

Many clients want to be a part of a TR group but, like most of us, they are likely to find new situations threatening. They will have a natural concern about how they will be accepted by the leader and other clients and whether or not they will be able to perform to the expectations of the group." With such uncertainty, it is not surprising that the defense mechanisms of new clients may cause blocks to group participation. Persons may approach new situations by simply repeating old behaviors (Hansen et al., 1980), even though these behaviors may not be functional. Fears of rejection or incompetence must be understood by the therapeutic recreation specialist. He or she must not ridicule the client who attempts to adjust to a new experience by employing some nonfunctional defense mechanism. Understanding potential client problems will allow the leader to assist clients to overcome fears that interfere with their adjustments. Instead of becoming angry at clients for their inappropriate behaviors, the TR specialist must learn to ask the important question of "Why?"

Thus the first task of the therapeutic recreation group leader is to reduce threat to new members by helping them to become comfortable. This involves expressing a warm, accepting attitude toward new clients, interacting with them in an open, nonjudgmental way, and helping them become acquainted with other members of the group. In doing so the leader creates a positive atmosphere for new members and functions as a model for the total membership of the group.

THE IMPORTANCE OF MODELING

One way for people to learn new behaviors or strengthen existing behaviors is to observe others who exhibit the desired behavior. Many of us can recall how our coaches and physical education teachers would model motor skills for us to imitate and then reinforce us for following their example. Or we can remember how we learned a new dance step or some social behavior by watching older brothers and sisters and their friends. Our clients also learn from imitation. Therefore it behooves the TR group leader to consider the potentially potent effect of modeling.

Because modeling can play a large role in shaping clients' behaviors, the emerging TR specialist particularly should engage in self-examination to become aware of the picture he or she is presenting to group members. This requires that he or she first think in advance about which social-recreational behaviors are desired and therefore should be demonstrated and, second, monitor his or her own behavior to assure that appropriate behaviors are displayed. Of course, once appropriate social-recreational behaviors are imitated, the TR specialist should reinforce clients for performing them.

154

DEALING WITH CONFLICT

Perhaps as critical as any understanding of group leadership is the realization that the leader is occasionally apt to encounter direct conflict and confrontation with group members. This may occur initially because the leader may not fit the preconceived stereotype of a leader formed in the mind of the client. As discussed by several authors (Knickerbocker, 1969; Hansen et al., 1980), people possess previously developed concepts of what a leader should be like based on prior experiences with significant others such as parents and teachers. If the leader refuses to fit this stereotype, conflict can arise and hostility may result. Another possible occasion for conflict is when the relationship between the group leader and members begins to change as a result of group members becoming less dependent on the leader. Conflict can develop if the members see the leader as being unwilling to play a reduced role in order for them to assume more leadership. If, in either case, conflict occurs the leader must handle any resulting personal attacks in a mature manner without retaliating against the attacking client or clients so that a positive example of dealing with aggression is provided for the group.

Obviously, there are many other concerns and strategies with which the therapeutic recreation group leader must deal. However, those covered in this section represent three areas that merit particular attention on the part of emerging therapeutic recreation specialists.

WHAT SHOULD THE LEADER LOOK FOR IN GROUPS?

The activities of members of groups can be analyzed in terms of the function performed by the members. Two major functions are generally discussed in group dynamics literature. These are *task functions* (or content functions) and *social-emotive functions* (or maintenance functions). Task functions promote the work or task of the group. They are activities that help group members to achieve their goals. Social-emotive functions have to do with group building or promoting group development. They include activities that produce a positive group atmosphere in which members can find satisfaction through their group participation. Longo and Williams (1978) have used the term *nonfunctional behavior* to describe a third class of activities in which group members may engage. These activities interfere with the processes of the group.

In the section that follows guidelines are offered to assist the group leader to analyze functional and nonfunctional behaviors in groups. These guidelines have been drawn from several sources (Knowles & Knowles,

1959; Jones & Pfeiffer, 1972; Beal, Bohlen, & Raudabaugh, 1976; Longo
& Williams, 1978).

PARTICIPATION

- What percent of the members actively take part?
- Which members are high participators? Low participators?
- Do participation patterns shift? Why?
- Do those who participate too much realize this?
- How are quiet group members treated?
- Do certain members regularly withdraw?
- Who speaks to one another? Why does this interaction take place?
- Are members included in goal setting and major decisions, or does the leader set goals and make decisions without involving group members?
- Does the leader consciously try to involve members in the activities of the group?
- Are activities analyzed to bring about the type of participation desired?

INFLUENCE AND CONTROL

- Which members have a high amount of influence?
- Which members have a low level of influence?
- Is there rivalry or competition for leadership in the group? If so, between whom? How does this affect the group?
- Do any members seek recognition by drawing attention to theselves by presenting extreme ideas, boasting, or other behaviors?
- Are rewards or incentives used to influence others? How?
- Are formal and informal controls used to maintain group standards?
- Are members ever involved in deciding the means to enforce group standards?
- Are standards enforced relatively uniformly?

STANDARDS OR NORMS

- Are members overly nice or polite? Do they agree too quickly? Do they express only positive feelings?
- Are norms of behavior made explicit to all?
- Are certain areas avoided (e.g., sex, feelings)?
- Does the leader reinforce avoidance of certain areas?
- Does the informal leader serve as a model by living up to group standards? What about informal leaders?

- Are members consulted regarding group standards?
- Are standards realistic and reviewed periodically?

ATMOSPHERE

- Is the physical setting condusive to the group atmosphere (e.g., size of meeting room, furniture arrangement, lighting, ventilation)?
- Are new members helped to feel a part of the group?
- Do members seem involved and interested? Do they seem to gain satisfaction?
- Is there much disruptive behavior such as clowning around or making fun of others?
- Which members seem to prefer and encourage a friendly atmosphere? Which prefer conflict and disagreement?
- Do members share and cooperate?
- Does the leader set a good example by projecting a warm, accepting attitude?

MEMBERSHIP

- Do any subgroups exist? Do some people almost always agree and others consistently oppose one another?
- Are some members "outsiders" in the group? How are they treated?
- Does the body language of some members (i.e., leaning forward or backward) indicate moving in or out of the group?
- Is the size of the group about right for group involvement and participation?

FEELINGS

- What signs of feelings of group members are observed (e.g., anger, frustration, warmth, boredom, defensiveness)?
- Do members attempt to block the expression of feelings?
- Do they stop discussion by blaming or insulting others?

SOCIAL-EMOTIVE FUNCTIONS

- Which members help others get involed? Which ones are friendly and encouraging?
- Which members cut off or interrupt others?

- Do members attempt to mediate conflict by bringing about compromise or reconciling divergent ideas?
- Do members encourage others to express ideas and feelings?
- How are ideas rejected?
- Are members supportive of others by recognizing others ideas and actions?
- Do members relieve tension through a healthy sense of humor?
- Do members assume follower positions by going along with the group and listening to others during discussions?
- How good are members about accepting new members?
- Do members really identify with the group?
- Is there really two-way communication with the leader?

TASK FUNCTIONS

- Do members initiate ideas and suggestions?
- Do members ask others for ideas and suggestions?
- Are there attempts to gain feedback and clarification?
- Are there attempts to elaborate on the thoughts of others?
- Does anyone attempt to summarize what has happened?
- Do members check out or evaluate the opinions of others in regard to making group decisions? Do they test for consensus?
- Who keeps the group on target?
- Does the leader underestimate or overestimate how much members really know and understand?

GROUP PHENOMENA

Various group phenomena have been studied by social psychologists. Several of these have application to the theory and practice of therapeutic recreation. Three areas of group dynamics discussed in this section are social facilitation, conformity, and the risky shift phenomenon.

SOCIAL FACILITATION

According to Martens (1975), Zajonc popularized the term *social facilitation* to indicate that the mere presence of others has a significant effect on individuals' intellectual and motor performance. This effect can either enhance or hinder performance. Performance is enhanced on simple tasks and hindered for complex and/or unlearned tasks.

The terms *audience effect* and *coaction effect* have been used to describe

158

the conditions under which the social facilitation effect may occur. Audience effect refers to the effect of a passive audience viewing the performance. The effect of several persons independently doing the same thing at the same time is the coaction effect.

Most of us have experienced being in top form in tennis, racketball, or some other sport until we noticed someone watching us—at which time our game fell apart! Conversely, many of us have experienced a peak performance when others viewed us taking part in an activity in which we have a high level of skill. These two extremes may be explained by the audience effect. Likewise, most of us have had personal experiences in attempting to learn new skills along with other people. We have all probably undergone occasions when we had to go to a place of solitude in order to work alone on a new task after failing to learn the task with others. This behavior can be attributed to the coaction effect.

Martens (1975) has presented research evidence to indicate that the explanation for the social facilitation phenomenon is more involved than originally conceptualized. It seems that audience or coactors must be perceived to possess the potential to evaluate the performance. Instead of the mere presence of others, it is apparently the apprehension experienced over the possibility of being evaluated positively or negatively by others that affects individuals' performances.

Another concept related to the social facilitation phenomenon is arousal. When we know how to perform a task (i.e., it is a well-learned task), the social facilitation hypothesis predicts that performance will increase as arousal increases. However, when arousal or anxiety gets too high, it hinders performance. The hypothesized relationship between arousal and performance is known as the *inverted-U hypothesis* (Martens, 1975). According to the inverted-U notion, performance increases as arousal increases up to the point of optimal arousal. After the point of optimal arousal, performance is hindered as a result of too high a level of arousal. In everyday terms we might say that individuals become "uptight" or "tense" when they exceed their optimal level of arousal. Many of us have experienced this phenomenon. When we do, we may say that we "tried too hard."

There are obvious implications of the social facilitation phenomenon for TR specialists. When clients are learning new skills, it would seem wise to minimize evaluation apprehension. Instructional situations should provide a supportive environment where clients see the leader as nonthreatening and accepting and where "outsiders" are not allowed to observe. However, once skills are mastered, the presence of others should aid performance—at least up through the point of optimal arousal.

CONFORMITY

In the small group social influence can have a potent effect on attitudes, beliefs, values, and perceptions. Festinger's *social comparison theory* has been offered as an explanation as to why the group has a potentially strong influence on individual judgment (Tubbs & Moss, 1978). According to Festinger, people evaluate their views, abilities, and emotions by comparing them with those of other people when they do not have access to objective means of evaluation. Therefore, when objective criteria are absent, individuals will rely on the judgment of others in order to evaluate the validity of their own opinions, judgments, or feelings. Individuals with discrepant opinions or emotions will supposedly change them to agree with others in their group, so that each individual's ideas tend to be in line with those of the group as a whole. Think about yourself for a moment. Have you ever conformed in your thinking to fit with the opinions of others in your group? Have you ever decided your abilities were of a certain level because of the opinions expressed about your skill by those in a group to which you belong? Have you ever compared your performance with others in your peer group? Have you ever observed the emotional reactions of others before expressing an emotion? We do seem to evaluate our opinions, abilities, and emotions by determining if they are possessed by others. If held by others, we are more confident that our views or emotions are correct (Worchel & Cooper, 1979).

RISKY SHIFT PHENOMENON

Another social psychology concept related to the small group is the *risky shift phenomenon*. This is the tendency for people to behave with greater risk as a result of being in a group. In other words, group members take greater risks as members of a group than they would as individuals. For instance, persons in a group are likely to shift toward a more risky position in making a decision than they would if making the same decision singly. Several explanations have been given for this phenomenon, but no single one has yet been generally accepted (Tubbs & Moss, 1978).

It is important that TR group leaders realize that their groups are subject to the social facilitation, social comparison, and risky shift phenomena. These phenomena most certainly occur in client groups and therefore influence the thinking and behavior of our clients.

SPECIFIC PRINCIPLES FOR GROUP LEADERSHIP

Hansen, Warner, and Smith (1980, pp. 563–569) have developed principles to guide the practice of leaders in groups. Although they were developed specifically for group counselors, many of their principles apply in therapeutic recreation group leadership. Selected principles of Hansen and his colleagues have been stated here, followed by implications for therapeutic recreation practice.

Group leaders have a responsibility to develop a theoretical rationale for group practice which will enable them to identify goals of their activity.

Therapeutic recreation group leaders need to recognize that their practice must rest on a philosophical base. They must know the "why" underlying the goals for their groups as well as the "how" of conducting the group. If the purpose of the TR group is not clearly articulated by the leader it will be extremely difficult to set directions for the group's activities.

Group leaders have a responsibility to limit their group practice to developed levels of competence and skills and to reveal these limits to clients.

The principle holds in any type of therapeutic recreation programming but has particular application to leisure counseling. Leaders of leisure counseling groups must have the level of competence called for to conduct the type of counseling in which they are engaged. Once that level has been determined, its limits should not be exceeded.

Group leaders have the responsibility to be familiar with the standards and codes of ethical behavior of their parent professional organization and apply them, where appropriate, to group practice.

Therapeutic recreation specialists must become familiar with the code of ethics of their national organization and follow those standards of conduct.

Group leaders should be relatively congruent and stable individuals, free from gross pathology and with developed insight into their own unique characteristics and needs.

Leaders of therapeutic recreation groups must know themselves and feel reasonably satisfied with themselves as persons before they can help others. If overly concerned about his or her own ego, the leader will have a difficult time helping others, since it takes ego strength to deal with the stresses of group leadership.

In general, professionally conducted groups should limit the process to those verbal and nonverbal techniques that do not have the potential to harm participants. Physical assaults, sexual behavior between participants, and excessive verbal abuse are unacceptable.

Leaders of TR groups should not permit any behavior they feel may do harm to a group member, whether in the form of physical attack, sexual behavior, or verbal abuse. When conflict results in physical assult, it is never acceptable and should not be tolerated. Handling sexual behaviors and verbal attacks will call for the leader to exercise a certain amount of judgment. For instance, some "sexual behavior" (e.g., holding hands or placing an arm around another's shoulder) may be acceptable in some TR groups. In regard to verbal attack, it may facilitate a client's growth to be "told off" by another client. Therefore the leader must decide when sexual behavior or verbal attacks are "excessive" and act accordingly.

Every effort should be made to ensure the maximum privacy of participants in the group process by appropriate discussion of the principles, needs, and implications of the concept of confidentialy. Leaders should frankly confront the fact that they are able to guarantee only their own commitment to the privacy of discussions.

Professional ethics dictate that therapeutic recreation specialists maintain confidentiality in helping relationships. In one-to-one situations this simply means that the therapeutic recreation specialist must maintain discretion in the use of client information. Group leaders face a different situation, since others are involved. Particularly when dealing with the discussion of potentially sensitive topics—as might be discussed in some types of leisure counseling—the issue of confidentiality should be discussed with group members.

Individuals and institutions that offer and support group activities have the obligation to evaluate those activities periodically. Furthermore, those professionals and institutions have an obligation to participate in research activities designed to reform and refine practice and to determine the effectiveness of variations in practice.

Ongoing evaluation is necessary for the improvement of services offered in therapeutic recreation groups. Additionally, therapeutic recreation specialists should feel an obligation to conduct research efforts themselves and/or cooperate with university faculty and others in carrying out research investigations.

TR LEADERSHIP TASKS AND CONCERNS

Several specific tasks and concerns of the therapeutic recreation specialist as a leader are discussed in the final section of this chapter. Included in this discussion are (1) writing progress notes, (2) the TR specialist as teacher, (3) program evaluation, (4) leisure counseling, and (5) understanding transactions.

WRITING PROGRESS NOTES

Why Progress Notes?
Most TR specialists would agree that observations of clients should be carefully documented in order to provide a written record of each client's progress. To begin, written records are far more reliable than memory. Progress notes also make it possible to review what each client has accomplished during a period of time and provide a basis for what should be done next. In short, the written documentation supplied by progress notes allows both staff and clients a basis for evaluation.

Guides to Effective Progress Note Writing
It is important that the TR specialist stick to observations of actual behavior in writing progress notes instead of attempting to interpret behavior. The following guidelines are provided to assist the therapeutic recreation leader in making specific behavioral observations and to offer other hints to successful progress-note writing.

1. *Use Simple Descriptive terms.* Avoid the use of jargon as much as possible. The use of "big words" does not make a person into an expert. For instance, in working with persons who have problems in mental health, avoid terms such as "psychotic," "schizophrenic," and "bizarre" to describe behavior. Instead, describe the specific event or activity that was seen and heard. If a particular professional term is used, define it or tell what you mean by it.
2. *Be Informative.* Ask yourself, "Does this note contain the information I intended it to?"
3. *Be Brief.* Eliminate unnecessary words. The term "client" or "patient" is not usually required and may be left out of notes. Incomplete sentences may be used, along with appropriate symbols or abbreviations.
4. *Be Precise.* Attempt to be as precise as possible. For example, state "six times in one hour," not "often."
5. *Write Legibly.* Use clear handwriting. If others cannot read the note it will not serve its intended purpose.
6. *Employ a Format.* Use a systematic format. For example, when recording observations about physical conditions, start with the head and go down to the body.
7. *Use Original Sources if Possible.* Attempt to obtain firsthand information from the client. Write only what you know is correct, always

verifying secondhand information. If you must report unsubstantiated information, label it as such and identify the source of the information.

8. *Consider Confidentiality.* Always preserve the dignity and privacy of every client. Progress notes should be used only as a means to improve client care and treatment.

9. *Reflect Accuracy and Truthfulness.* No erasures should appear in progress notes (since others would not know if you or someone else erased the information). Errors should be corrected by drawing a line through the error and writing the word "error" next to the mistake.

10. *Be familiar with Agency Policies.* Agencies may have policies as to who may place information in the client's record, or they may require different staff (e.g., nurses, social workers, therapeutic recreators) to use a particular color of ink when writing notes.

11. *Determine Frequency of Recordings.* It should be determined precisely how often observations are to be made (e.g., daily, weekly), and this system should be strictly followed. As a rule, it is usually best to record after each session with clients.

12. *Date and Initial Each Entry.* Be certain to date and initial (or sign) each progress note you make.

An Example

An example of what *not* to do in writing a progress note appears here. Following it is a brief analysis of this poorly prepared recording.

> *The client often becomes angry when he plays basketball and when he is not playing he is always pacing the sidelines. He is uncooperative and more psychotic than before.*

Obviously, the writer did not have access to the information provided previously in this section. Some apparent criticisms appear next. You may add others.

1. The phrase, "The client," is not necessary. It would have been fine to use an incomplete sentence.
2. The use of the word "often" is not precise. Does this mean every day, three times a week, or once every hour?
3. What is meant by the word "angry?" What behavior is the writer describing? Did the client hit, kick, get red in the face?
4. In what kind of basketball activity was the client engaged? Was this a scheduled game, a team practice, or an informal, pickup game?
5. The word "always" is not precise. Does this mean the client never stops?
6. The terms "pacing" and "uncooperative" are not defined. What exactly was the client doing?

164

7. The expression "more psychotic than before" employs jargon (i.e., psychotic) and lacks precision (i.e., more than before).
8. Finally, the writer failed to date and initial the entry.

What Should Appear

Just what sort of information should be contained in progress notes? O'Morrow (1980) has suggested that routine progress notes might properly include general progress (or lack thereof), specific symptoms or problems interfering with progress, alterations or modifications made in client plans, client proficiency in the use of any device or adaptive equipment employed, and various evaluations made by staff. Quattlebaum (1969) has proposed that progress notes in psychiatric facilities should include information on response deficits and excesses, deviant and inappropriate responses, and the people and situations causing these responses.

Different categories of behavior are utilized in various types of settings for the reference of those writing progress notes. Through my personal observation of materials prepared by agencies, it seems that there are several broad categories of behavior that therapeutic recreation specialists employ as guides to writing progress notes. Frequently used categories seem to be participation, performance, interpersonal relationships, personal habits, and state of consciousness and/or mental activity. These major categories follow along with items that relate to them.

PARTICIPATION

- Interest in activities.
- Extent and nature of involvement.
- Attention shown (attention span).
- Appropriateness of energy output.
- Initiative in choosing activities.
- Attitude expressed toward own participation.
- Attitude toward rules, winning, competition.

PERFORMANCE

- Level of performance.
- Quality of performance.
- Hindering factors.
- Ability to make decisions.
- Quality of judgment.
- Ability to express self adequately.
- Ability to express self appropriately.

- Physical movement (e.g., slow, rigid).
- Use of any device or adaptive equipment.
- Attitude expressed toward own performance.
- Ability to follow rules and directions.
- Special incidents.
- Summary of change in performance.

INTERPERSONAL RELATIONSHIPS

- Relationships with therapeutic recreation specialist and others (e.g., dependency, hostility).
- Acceptance of limits.
- Manipulative.
- Passive, aloof, or withdrawn.
- Reserved, insecure, timid, or shy.
- Outgoing, confident, or extroverted.
- Ability to make friends.
- Acceptance by others.
- Agreeable, cooperative, or helpful.
- Resistive or stubborn.
- Verbalizes appropriately.

PERSONAL HABITS AND APPEARANCES

- Appropriateness of dress.
- Grooming.
- Cleanliness and neatness.
- Concern with appearance.
- Walk or gait.
- Tics, rituals, habitual movements.

STATE OF CONSCIOUSNESS AND/OR MENTAL ACTIVITY

- Orientation to time.
- Orientation to place.
- Orientation to persons or objects.
- Preoccupied (responsiveness).
- Slow in answering or thinking.
- Distracted by others or events.
- Ability to remember (retention).
- Hallucinations or delusions.

166

- Intellectual functioning.
- Stability of mood.

THE TR SPECIALIST AS TEACHER—PRINCIPLES IN THE TEACHING/LEARNING PROCESS

Many situations require the therapeutic recreation specialist to instruct clients. There is not a set formula for learning, but there are basic principles that can be used to guide instruction. The principles that follow have been drawn primarily from those outlined by Mosey (1973). Other sources of information for this section include Kibler, Barker, and Miles (1970), Kraus and Bates (1975), and Marriner (1975).

1. *Start at the level of the client and move at a rate that is comfortable.* It is important to assess the client's ability so the leader will not place too much or too little demand on the client. The rate of learning will vary, so the therapeutic recreation specialist must be prepared to adjust instruction accordingly.

2. *Individual differences must be given consideration.* Each client is an individual and will learn in a unique way. Individuals differ in their abilities, backgrounds, interests, ages, and readiness for learning. Intellectual capacities, physical health, and energy levels are ability factors demanding consideration. Educational and cultural background also influence learning, as does the level of client interest in the particular activity. Additionally, the individual must perceive the activity being learned to be age appropriate or it will likely be rejected. Finally, readiness plays a large part in learning. If the client does not have the physical and cognitive development to cope with the learning situation, he or she will probably fail.

3. *Active participation is essential for learning.* Active participation in planning for and engaging in learning means the client has a thorough involvement in the total learning process. It may be said that the best teaching is the least teaching. People do learn by doing, so it is generally better to engage them actively in learning to the fullest possible degree. After all, it is what the learner does—not the instructor—that determines learning.

4. *Reinforcement strengthens learning.* People tend to repeat the things that they enjoy or find rewarding. Teaching new behaviors then depends on clients finding the behaviors rewarding. Therefore the TR specialist should strive to provide social reinforcement when clients perform appropriately. Usually social reinforcers take the form of attention, encouragement, and approval. Another reinforcer comes

in the form of the client feeling mastery or a sense of accomplishment. Extrinsic rewards, such as money or food, may also be used to reinforce behaviors.

The timing in delivering all types of reinforcers is critical to their success. Rewards have the most effect when administered immediately after the behavior. When new behaviors are initially being learned, a continuous schedule of reinforcement should be used. Once the behavior has been established, it does not need to be rewarded each time it is performed. It is possible to reward the client infrequently. (More detailed information on reinforcement as a technique is found in Chapter 2.)

5. *Opportunities for trial and error can enhance learning.* Trial-and-error learning allows the learner to use a variety of approaches until he or she finds one that works. Of course, trial-and-error learning works best in an atmosphere that allows the time and freedom for people to work things out for themselves. Errors are perceived as a natural part of the learning process, and clients are not told what they should do. The therapeutic recreation specialist must therefore remain flexible when using the trial-and-error approach in order to encourage inventive problem solving.

6. *Imitation and modeling can enhance learning.* When making projects, clients should be shown models or examples of what they are to produce at the end of the learning experience. For example, a completed arts-and-crafts project might be displayed so that clients have an idea of what the finished product will be like. In teaching sports activities the leader can demonstrate proprer form, or audiovisuals (films, film strips) can be used to show clients correct methods. Social behaviors for adults and play behaviors for children can be modeled by staff. New social and play behaviors can be gained more quickly if the learner can see a model demonstrate the desired behavior. As discussed in Chapter 2, modeling can also be combined with reinforcement to make it an even more potent means to learning.

7. *Practice facilitates learning.* The actual amount of practice needed to master a new skill or behavior will vary with the level of complexity of that skill or behavior. Therapeutic recreation specialists must remember that clients are sometimes taught new skills but are not given enough time to practice them. Therefore therapeutic recreation programs should offer many informal opportunities for clients to try out new recreational and social skills. It may be that the TR specialist will help the client to arrange for postdischarge opportunities to practice newly acquired skills that the client does not have time to practice while undergoing treatment.

168 TR LEADERSHIP TASKS AND CONCERNS

8. *Feedback facilitates learning.* Leaders should provide learners with feedback as they learn and practice new skills. This feedback can take the form of positive reinforcement for doing well, encouragement for trying hard, or corrective instruction that will allow the client to improve. The general thought of many clients is that "no news is bad news." Therefore it is critical to provide regular feedback to clients who are acquiring and practicing new skills.

9. *Clients should know what is to be learned and why they are learning it.* Our clients, as all learners, need to have prelearning preparation. They must be prepared for what is coming and the reasons for learning. Little learning will occur if clients do not understand what it is they are supposed to learn and why they are being taught something new.

10. *Move from simple to the complex.* A general rule of learning is to move the learner from the simple toward the complex, or from the familiar to the unfamiliar. However, Mosey (1973) stresses that the teacher should not fall into the trap of teaching meaningless parts that learners are somehow supposed to connect to a whole on their own. She gives the example of teaching clients how to use public transportation as a natural detail of a pleasurable outing instead of taking the client on a meaningless trip for the sake of leaning how to ride the city bus.

11. *Perception affects learning.* A client's perceptions come about as a result of the brain's processing of stimuli received through the sense organs. Maturation and learning both impact on the client's perceptions of the environment. Therefore a child may miss subtle cues or an older adult may perceive things much differently than a relatively young helping professional. Also, a person with sensory problems may experience difficulty in receiving stimuli. Therefore the therapeutic recreation specialist must become aware of possible client problems in receiving sensory impulses (e.g., sight, hearing) as well as differing perceptions on the part of individual clients.

12. *Anxiety affects learning.* Some anxiety, in the form of general arousal and interest, positively affects learning, but too much anxiety can interfere with the learning process. The TR specialist must attempt to identify the optimal level of anxiety for each client and gear the learning situation accordingly. Many clients require an accepting, nonjudgmental atmosphere in which to learn and try out new skills and behaviors. They learn best with individual instruction or in a small group where support and cooperation are emphasized. Once the skill is acquired, they may be ready to practice or perform gradually the skill in larger and larger groups. It is the role of the therapeu-

tic recreator to judge, with the client, what pace is appropriate for each individual. (The discussion on social facilitation found earlier in this chapter provides further information on learning and anxiety.)

Summary Statement on Teaching/Learning

The basic principles of teaching/learning have been presented to help therapeutic recreation specialists facilitate client learning. Remember, however, that every principle presented will take on a different level of emphasis or importance with each individual client and each new learning situation. Learning is obviously far more complex than is reflected by the traditional teacher-learner paradigm where the teacher's role is that of dispenser of information for eagerly waiting learners. Certainly the role of the TR specialist as a leader is far greater than this as he or she helps clients to find ways to learn.

PROGRAM EVALUATION

Therapeutic recreation is becoming more concerned with determining the overall quality of programs. Proper evaluation procedures allow the TR specialist to make decisions regarding the merit and worth of program offerings.

Ongoing program evaluation is sometimes referred to as *formative evaluation,* since it takes place at the formative stage of the program. Formative evaluation is used to make corrections in a program in progress. Through formative evaluation the program is modified or improved. The term *summative evaluation* is used to describe the procedure of summarizing evaluation data in order to critique a completed program.

The Traditional Tylerian Model

Traditionally, therapeutic recreation specialists have followed a Tylerian model in program evaluation. Tyler (1949) primarily defined evaluation as a process utilizing the scientific approach for determining the congruence between stated objectives and actual behavior during summative evalutaion. Under this model, the stated objectives for the program become the criteria for evaluation. Actual outcomes are compared with sought outcomes (i.e., objectives) to determine if any discrepancies exist and, if discrepancies are found, to explain why they occurred. Therefore a common design under this model is the pretest-treatment-posttest design in which clients are tested before taking part in an intervention and again after participation.

Although Tyler's model offers a systematic, logical approach to evaluation, there are some possible problems that may arise in its application.

One is that there may be a tendency for personnel only to establish program objectives that can be easily measured while ignoring important potential outcomes because of the difficulty in measuring them. For example, cognitive objectives might be emphasized at the expense of objectives from the affective domain simply because cognitive objectives are more easily measured. A second potential problem is that of establishing valid and comprehensive program objectives. If stated program objectives are not meritorious or if critical objectives have not been included, information regarding progress toward the objectives will be of little value, since the entire evaluation is a measurement of client progress toward *stated* objectives. For example, if a sports club did not include an objective dealing with a necessary outcome such as sportsmanship, any evaluation would be of questionable value, no matter what other objectives were appraised. A third problem area for the "evaluation-by-objectives" approach concerns unplanned outcomes. What about things that are not planned objectives but nevertheless occur during recreation programs? These Stake (1969) has termed "side effects" and "bonuses." As all seasoned TR specialists know, some of the most important outcomes are not planned but evolve naturally out of the recreation experience. Finally, Tyler's model fails to provide information related to patterns of participation (e.g., interaction between participants or between participants and leaders) or strengths and weaknesses of the program. For example, if a program was very poorly attended, the Tylerian model, with its focus on objectives, would not gather data relevant to the poor attendance.

Naturalistic Evaluation Model

Guba and Lincoln (1981) have suggested the use of a *naturalistic evaluation model* (in contrast to the scientific model), which is broader in scope than the Tylerian model. This model focuses more on program activities rather than intents, although it provides for the inclusion of measuring whether objectives are met. The naturalistic model does not, therefore, restrict evaluation only to examining objectives. Instead, it strives to go beyond stated objectives to describe the processes that transpire during the program and to identify unique characteristics that may have influenced the program. Furthermore, Guba and Lincoln (1981) have emphasized that behavior is never context-free. Behavior cannot be understood apart from the context in which it occurs. Therefore attention must be given to the intrapsychic, interpersonal, social, and cultural variables that surround behavior. Since therapeutic recreation attempts to take the context of the situation into account during assessment, planning, and implementation, it only seems reasonable that it be considered during the evaluation phase.

Qualitative Evaluation

Olson (1980) has suggested the employment of a qualitative approach to program evaluation emphasizing a broad description of the program in contrast to the collection of numerical data often found in traditional evaluation. The term *portrayal evaluation* has been used to depict this type of evaluation, which is conducted by staff members as a routine duty and relies on information gained chiefly by direct observation, informal discussion, and intuitive judgments of professionals. The exact nature of the data collected is determined by the types of skills and interests possessed by the staff completing the evaluation. Through this descriptive method, client and staff interactional patterns and the strengths and weaknesses of the program are identified.

Detailed explanations of the concepts of Guba and Lincoln (1981) and Olson (1980) are beyond the scope of this segment on program evaluation, but these authors do present an important message for TR specialists. That message is that program evaluation need not be narrowly conceptualized to be concerned only with quantitative data directly tied to stated objectives of the program being evaluated. Program evaluation can go beyond the mere measurement of objectives.

Steps in Program Evaluation

It should be useful for program evaluators to have a logical series of steps in order to approach evaluation systematically. The steps that follow have been modeled after those listed by Stufflebeam (1968) and Howe (1980), although all of the material presented under each of the steps has not necessarily been proposed by these authors. Instead, the steps represent an eclectic approach to program evaluation.

Step One—Focusing the Evaluation

The initial step begins with identification of the various audiences (i.e., persons interested in the program) for whom the evaluation is to be accomplished. Potential audiences might include persons such as parents and/or clients, administrators of the sponsoring agency, therapeutic recreation specialists, and other professionals who work with the clients or who refer clients into the program. From each appropriate audience concerns are drawn through qualitative measures such as unstructured interviews and discussions in order to seek differing views. This process determines the purposes for the evaluation, or what broad evaluation questions should be addressed. Examples of differing points of view would be represented by the administrators' concern over the level of client participation in the program, the patients' or clients' concern with the provision of an enjoyable experience, and the therapeutic recreation leaders' and supervisors' concern about whether the treatment of objectives of the program were being met.

Once identified, concerns can be categorized for review. Those reviewing the categories can determine if they feel each category is valid, partially valid, or invalid. Next the reviewers can prioritize the concerns, perhaps removing some low-ranked items. Agreed on concerns can then be turned into broad evaluation questions such as: What was the level of client participation? Did clients gain enjoyment from the program? What were the outcomes of the program? The various audiences may raise a variety of broad evaluation questions related to numerous concerns including the completeness and validity of program objectives, unplanned outcomes, resource utilization, participation patterns, and program strengths and weaknesses.

Step Two—Determining Subquestions

The next step is to decide what subquestions must be asked in order to answer the concerns raised in step one. The evaluator simply generates subquestions related to the previously developed broad evaluation questions. For instance, to the question of the level of participation, subquestions might be: What were the number of clients involved? What was the average attendance at each session? What percent of the clients actively participated during each session? Did clients interact with one another? Did the type of disability affect participation? Did the number of staff present affect the amount of client participation? Were clients more responsive to particular program structures or formats? Did any outside forces seem to enhance or hinder participation within the group?

You can perhaps add to or refine the subquestions stated in the previous paragraph. Any subquestions are appropriate as long as they address the primary evaluation concern expressed in the broad evaluation question.

Step Three—Determining Resources

Next the evaluator must determine what resources are available to aid in the data collection. Resources, of course, can be human or physical. In all probability therapeutic recreation specialists will be assigned the responsibility of evaluating their own programs as a routine assignment. Help in the form of outside evaluators is not commonly available to TR specialists. Physical resources may range from sophisticated devices such as videotape recording systems or computers to those very simple in nature. For instance, much TR program evaluation is accomplished by a single staff member utilizing paper and pencil.

Step Four—Collection of Information

In this step the evaluator must first decide what information to collect in order to answer the subquestions. Next the information sources have to be determined along with the actual ways to collect necessary information. Of course, the nature of the questions being investigated and the resources available to the evaluator will influence decisions made during step four.

Both quantitative and qualitative data can be collected, although the major portion of data in the evaluation of therapeutic recreation programs is likely to be qualitative. Among the methods that can be used to collect data are surveys of previous program participants and skilled observation and interview techniques (discussed in Chapter 3). Often forms are used to assist in observations and/or interviews. For example, a checklist might be used to record the frequency of client interactions, or a client interview form could be employed that has questions regarding what clients liked or disliked about a program.

Bullock and Coffey (1980) have claimed that evaluators too frequently use only one data collection method, thus ignoring other valuable means of data collection. These writers advocate the use of multiple methods and procedures in the collection of evaluation data, since they feel singular approaches are not as productive. The name given to the use of several methods together is *triangulation*.

Step Five—Organization and Analysis of Information

The fifth step concerns how data are arranged and treated. First, a format will have to be developed to classify and store information as it is gathered so it may be retrieved for later use. This might involve the development of a filing and storage system for forms that staff complete, narratives on programs, and similar materials. Depending on the nature of the information, organization of the data might also call for a procedure for coding and storing data for later analysis.

The second component in this step involves analysis of the information. Generally, highly sophisticated statistical analysis is unnecessary when dealing with program evaluation in therapeutic recreation. Information collected is likely to be descriptive in nature and will be used to answer the subquestions.

Step Six—Reporting Information

The purpose of the reporting of information is to insure that relevant audiences will have the information they require. Two approaches may be used. One is to provide a single report prepared for all audiences. A second approach is for different reports to be provided for various audiences (administrators, program supervisors, etc.). The reports may be written or verbal.

When separate reports are provided, they can be tailored for each audience. They may be written or given in the language of the audience receiving them. Additionally, the exact content of the report may be geared to the audience. One means to accomplish this is to address in depth the concerns of each audience and include only summaries of other findings. For example, the report to administrators might concentrate on concerns raised by the administrators, with only summaries provided of information related to concerns raised by parents, clients, and therapeutic recreation personnel.

Concluding Statement on Program Evaluation
It is an understatement to say that program evaluation is important. Without proper evaluation, therapeutic recreation specialists cannot know what outcomes a program produces or what aspects of the program need revision. Evaluation is then a fundamental part of the ongoing functions of all therapeutic recreation specialists who lead programs.

LEISURE COUNSELING

Leisure counseling is an area of interest to many therapeutic recreation specialists. In this section counseling is defined, factors distinguishing leisure counseling are presented, general orientations to leisure counseling are detailed, and conclusions are made regarding leisure counseling.

What Is Counseling?
Most TR specialists would probably agree that counseling is an interpersonal process involving communication between a skilled helper and a client, or clients, seeking help in attempting to discover and/or change feelings, thoughts, or behaviors. Counseling usually is entered into voluntarily with assurances that the counseling relationship is private and confidential, thus providing a condition in which clients freely express themselves (Blackham, 1977; Hackney & Cormier, 1979). The broad goal of counseling is to help clients enhance personal development.

Factors Distinguishing Leisure Counseling
Two primary factors distinguish leisure counseling from other types of counseling. First, the main intent of leisure counseling is to help the client in regard to his or her leisure well-being. Many variables impact on an individual, but they are of concern only to the extent that they affect leisure. The prime focus always remains on the client's leisure. Second,

because of the nature of leisure counseling, the counselor must be conversant with the dynamics of leisure participation and with concrete information related to leisure opportunities. This assures that the counselor will be knowledgeable of the leisure experience and with problems related to leisure participation. It is also assured that the counselor will be well versed on particular leisure programs or situations that may be valuable to clients.

What Are General Orientations to Leisure Counseling?

McDowell (1980) has provided what perhaps has become the most accepted formulation of major orientations to leisure counseling. These deal with (1) leisure-related behavior concerns, (2) leisure life-style awareness concerns, (3) leisure resource guidance concerns, and (4) leisure-related skills development concerns.

Leisure-Related Behavior Orientation

The goal of the leisure-related behavior orientation is to help clients resolve behavioral concerns. These concerns may exhibit themselves in the form of feelings such as obligation, anxiety, guilt, or boredom or through escape behaviors such as chronic television viewing or excessive drinking. During leisure counseling, the counselor attempts to assist clients express themselves so that their concerns may be clarified, understood, and resolved. Therefore the focus of facilitation is with clarifying and understanding leisure-related behaviors so that clients may make reasoned decisions regarding their leisure patterns. This orientation is the most complex one and perhaps most closely resembles traditional counseling. Because of the complexity of the orientation, well-developed listening and facilitation skills are demanded of the counselor.

Leisure Life-style Awareness Orientation

Leisure life-style awareness counseling is directed toward helping improve clients' self-knowledge and understandings pertaining to leisure values, beliefs, and attitudes. This orientation also encompasses counseling regarding personal leisure and life-style needs, particularly as they relate to felt difficulties surrounding life events such as retirement, career change, marriage, or divorce. Here the counselor's role is active in initiating awareness on the part of the clients through the employment of experiential exercises and self-help leisure learning exercises. Often leisure life-style awareness concerns are met through group counseling.

Leisure Resource Guidance Orientation

The leisure resource guidance orientation deals with matching clients' interests with community resources. The leisure counselor helps clients to identify past, present, and potential leisure interests, perhaps using one of the leisure inventories discussed in Chapter 3. Interests are then matched with opportunities available to clients. Thus this model of leisure counseling essentially is a referral service. The basic assumption underlying this approach is that clients can function adequately in the community and require concrete information in regard to their interests and resources available to meet those interests.

Leisure-Related Skills Development Orientation

Underlying the skills development orientation is the assumption that clients lack certain leisure-related skills or abilities. Under this model, personal, social, and recreational skills are appraised and remedial counseling is begun to help clients attain these skills. This counseling may be provided in coordination with client participation in therapeutic recreation programs that provide opportunities for mastery of skill deficiencies. The facilitating focus of the counselor is initially with identifying concerns of each client in regard to skills, prioritizing these concerns, and stipulating criteria for goal attainment. Once this has been accomplished, the counselor plays an active role in helping the client to establish means to move toward alleviation of the concerns. Evaluation of client progress is completed by the counselor while maintaining a supportive/confrontive role.

As McDowell (1980) has indicated, the four orientations discussed in this section are not mutually independent. Although each has a particular focus, in actual practice it is likely that the orientations will overlap.

Conclusions Regarding Leisure Counseling

Leisure counseling has been a much discussed topic since the 1960s; however, from several extensive reviews of the state of the art of leisure counseling (Fikes, 1976; Shank & Kennedy, 1976; Compton, et al., 1980), it can be concluded that leisure counseling is still in its infancy. Confusion regarding an agreed on set of goals or outcomes for leisure counseling and the related problem of the lack of a clear definition of leisure counseling have created a high level of ambiguity. Because of this ambiguity a wide span of diverse service has been rendered under the banner of leisure counseling. This has been positive in that the existing lack of clarity has allowed for experimentation in the past. However, it seems that those engaged in leisure counseling must more define their service precisely if they hope to see leisure counseling grow and gain widespread acceptance.

It would seem premature to attempt to suggest specific competencies that TR specialists should gain in order to do leisure counseling because of the present level of ambiguity. Such a list should probably await a generally accepted definition of leisure counseling and its outcomes. However, it seems that the basic characteristics outlined in Chapter 4 as being necessary for success as a therapeutic recreation specialist would provide a strong base for the leisure counselor.

UNDERSTANDING TRANSACTIONS

Self-concept, learned helplessness, the self-fulfilling prophecy, and labeling are topics of concern in understanding leader transactions with clients.

Self-Concept

One's concept of self plays a large role in influencing behavior. For instance, one's self-concept affects whether a particular situation is viewed as routine, challenging, or threatening. If we perceive ourselves to be highly competent we are apt to enter into new experiences and challenges. Conversely, perceiving oneself as inadequate can be debilitating (Borden & Stone, 1976; Iso-Ahola, 1980).

Our self-concept is the result of our life experiences, including the feedback received from those around us. Research reviewed in a major work on self-concept in early childhood by Samuels (1977) has substantiated that successful experiences can enhance self-concept. Furthermore, in Samuel's review she found that if significant others enhance self-concept through realistic evaluation of a person during the performance of a task, intrinsic satisfaction may eventually develop from the performance itself. Accordingly, less and less external feedback will be needed as time goes on and feelings of competency and control are instilled.

Samuels's (1977) work dealt with children, but the concepts reviewed here also seem valid for adults. The implications for the TR specialist should be obvious. The TR specialist must keep in mind that he or she can have a great impact on client self-concepts and regularly strive to provide positive feedback realistically.

Learned Helplessness

Repeated failure can produce feelings of inadequacy, leading to the conclusion that no matter how much energy is expended it is futile and the person is helpless to alter things. The state that results when events are perceived to be uncontrollable has been termed *learned helplessness*. The person experiencing feelings of helplessness may become passive, anxious, and depressed and may develop difficulty believing he or she can actually be successful in life (Iso-Ahola, 1980).

In order to avoid learned helplessness, individuals must be given opportunities to feel in control of their environment. This must involve experiences in both mastering challenges and learning to endure frustrations. In doing so, individuals can learn that they are able to affect the world and deal with the consequences. They learn to accept personal responsibility for their actions through these experiences, from which they develop healthy self-regard (Iso-Ahola, 1980). Therefore leaders who do not allow clients to be in control of their lives may foster learned helplessness.

The Self-Fulfilling Prophecy

The self-fulfilling prophecy also has the potential to affect client behavior. It is based on the idea that individuals will exhibit the behaviors others expect of them. Thus, if leaders have an invalid conception of clients (e.g., the clients are helpless), this may bring about behaviors to make the false concept come about (e.g., the clients would act helpless).

People learn to see themselves and behave as others treat them and expect them to behave according to the notion of the self-fulfilling prophecy. If leaders hold negative preconceptions about their clients' abilities, this can lead to lowered expectations and decreased demands, resulting in poor performance on the part of clients. Therefore the leader must become aware of his or her expectations for clients, must be flexible so that expectations and behaviors can be modified as new information is gained, and must remember the possible influence of the leader's expectation on client behavior (Schmuck & Schmuck, 1975; Samuels, 1977).

Labeling

Leaders' transactions with clients can be influenced by the application of labels to clients. We usually associate labeling with the act of assigning a negative categorical term to an individual, often causing stigmatization. For instance, to label a client as "mentally ill" could result in having him or her perceived as an inadequate person possessing negative traits.

Stereotyping a client by classifying him or her only on the basis of disorder or disability does not, of course, take the individual's uniqueness into account. It puts the focus on categorical differences instead of on the person. Thus the TR specialist must be on guard against the dangers of labeling clients. Each client needs to be treated as a unique human being with individual limitations and abilities.

This does not mean that diagnoses (a type of labeling) should be done away with. Well-grounded diagnoses may serve valid legal and administrative purposes, enabling clients to receive care and agencies to organize services. Nevertheless, factual information regarding each client's abilities, needs, and desires—instead of a general label or diagnostic category—should form the basis for individual program planning.

KEY WORDS

Therapeutic Recreation Leadership. The ability to influence the activities of clients in therapeutic recreation programs toward accomplishing sought outcomes.

Autocratic Leadership. A directive style of leadership in which the leader makes all decisions and expects obedience from others. All authority remains with the leader.

Democratic Leadership. A style of leadership in which the leader involves group members in decision making, creating feelings of participation and teamwork.

Laissez-Faire Leadership. An open and permissive style of leadership in which the leader exercises minimum control so that group members take all responsibility for decision making.

Dependency. Reliance on another (usually a helping professional) for psychological and social support.

Group. A collection of individuals who coordinate their activities toward a common goal or who cooperate to fulfill some purpose. Group members relate to one another and are interdependent.

Social Facilitation. A social psychology phenomenon in which the mere presence of others is seen to have a significant effect on individuals' intellectual and motor performance.

Labeling. The act of assigning a categorical term to an individual, often causing stigmatization.

Reading Comprehension Questions

1 Define leadership in your own words.
2 What are four levels of leadership?
3 What are the major types of power? In what ways may these be possessed by therapeutic recreation specialists?
4 How will the wise leader deal with power?
5 Explain autocratic, democratic, and laissez-faire leadership.
6 Is there one best leadership style for therapeutic recreation? Why or why not?
7 Describe the continuum of leadership styles outlined in this chapter.
8 Do you understand the eight leadership roles of Avedon?
9 What is dependency? Have you felt dependent? How can dependency be dealt with positively?

10 What is the function of the group leader?
11 Can you name and describe structures for group participation in therapeutic recreation?
12 What makes a collection of people into a group?
13 What are stages of group development? Can you describe each?
14 What are some things you might do as a leader to ease the entry of a new member into a TR group?
15 Why is the leader's example important to the group?
16 Do TR specialists ever have to face conflicts with clients? If so, how should they be handled?
17 Can you identify major types of functions performed by group members?
18 Can you successfully employ the guidelines for group leader observations?
19 What is social facilitation? How may it affect clients in TR groups?
20 How may conformity affect individuals in a group?
21 What is the risky shift phenomenon?
22 Do you agree with Hansen's principles to guide the practice of group leaders? Which do you feel have particular application to therapeutic recreation groups?
23 Why write progress notes?
24 Do you understand the guidelines for progress note writing? Can you apply them?
25 What categories of behavior might you use in making observations for progress notes?
26 Do you understand the principles for the teaching/learning process? Can you give examples of how you might apply one or more of these principles?
27 Define formative and summative evaluations.
28 Compare the Tylerian and naturalistic modes of evaluation.
29 Do you agree with the steps in program evaluation outlined in this chapter? What is good or bad about them?
30 Define counseling in your own words. What factors may be thought of as distinguishing leisure counseling from other types of counseling? Would you add any other factors of your own?
31 What are the four orientations to leisure counseling proposed by McDowell?
32 Explain why the TR specialist should consider self-concept in client transactions.
33 What is learned helplessness?
34 Explain the concept of the self-fulfilling prophecy.
35 What are concerns related to labeling?

REFERENCES

Avedon, E. M. 1974. *Therapeutic recreation service: An applied behavioral science approach.* Englewood Cliffs, N.J.: Prentice-Hall, Inc.

Beal, B. M., Bohlen, J. M., & Raudabaugh, J. N. 1976. *Leadership and dynamic group action.* Ames, Iowa: The Iowa State University Press.

Blackham, G. J. 1977. *Counseling: Theory, process, and practice.* Belmont, Calif.: Wadsworth Publishing Company, Inc.

Borden, G. A., & Stone, J. D. 1976. *Human communication: The process of relating.* Menlo Park, Calif.: Cummings Publishing Company.

Bullock, C. C., & Coffey, F. 1980. Triangulation as applied to the evaluative process. In C. Z. Howe (ed.), *Leisure Today. Journal of Physical Education and Recreation.* 51(8), 50–52.

Cartwright, D., & Zander, A. 1968. *Group dynamics* (3rd edition). New York: Harper & Row.

Compton, D., Witt, P. A., & Sanchez, B. 1980. Leisure counseling. *Parks & Recreation.* 15(8), 23–27.

Fikes, C. R. 1976. A description of leisure counseling services in Texas community mental health and mental retardation centers. Unpublished master's thesis, North Texas State University.

French, J., & Raven, B. 1959. The basis for social power. In D. Cartwright (ed.), *Studies in Social Power.* Ann Arbor, Mich.: Institute for Social Research.

Gordon, T. 1977. *Leader effectiveness training: L.E.T.* New York: Wyden Books.

Guba, E. G., & Lincoln, Y. S. 1981. *Effective Evaluation.* San Francisco: Jossey-Bass Publishers.

Haber, J., Leach, A. M., Schudy, S. M., & Sidelean, B. F. 1978. *Comprehensive Psychiatric Nursing.* New York: McGraw-Hill Book Company.

Hackney, H., & Cormier, L. S. 1979. *Counseling strategies and objectives* (2nd edition). Englewood Cliffs, N.J.: Prentice-Hall, Inc.

Hansen, J. C., Warner, R. W., & Smith, E. M. 1980. *Group counseling: Theory and process* (2nd edition). Chicago: Rand McNally College Publishing Company.

Howe, C. Z. 1980. Models for evaluating public recreation programs: What the literature shows. In C. Z. Howe (ed.), *Leisure Today. Journal of Physical Education and Recreation.* 51(8), 36–38.

KEY WORDS

Iso-Ahola, S. E. 1980. *The social psychology of leisure and recreation.* Dubuque, Iowa: Wm. C. Brown Company, Publishers.

Jones, J. J., & Pfeiffer, J. W. (Eds.) 1972. What to look for in groups. *The 1972 Annual Handbook for Group Facilitators.* Iowa City, Iowa: University Associates.

Kibler, R. J., Barker, L. L., & Miles, D. T. 1970. *Behavioral objectives and instruction.* Boston: Allyn and Bacon, Inc.

Knickerbocker, I. 1969. Leaderships: A conception and some implications. In C. A. Gibb (ed.), *Leadership.* Baltimore: Penguin Books, Inc.

Knowles, M., & Knowles, H. 1959. *Introduction to group dynamics.* New York: Associated Press.

Kraus, R., & Bates, B. 1975. *Recreation leadership and supervision: Guidelines for professional development.* Philadelphia: W. B. Saunders Company.

Kutner, B. 1971. The social psychology of disability. In W. S. Neff (ed.), *Rehabilitation psychology.* Washington, D.C.: American Psychological Association, Inc.

Longo, D. C., & Williams, R. A. 1978. *Clinical practice in psychosocial nursing: Assessment and intervention.* New York: Appleton-Century-Crofts.

Marriner, A. 1975. *The nursing process: A scientific approach to nursing care.* Saint Louis: The C. V. Mosby Company.

Martens, R. 1975. *Social psychology and physical activity.* New York: Harper & Row, Publishers.

McDowell, C. F. 1980. Leisure counseling issues: Reviews, overviews, & previews. In F. Humphrey, J. D. Kelley, & E. J. Hamilton (eds.), *Facilitating Leisure Development for the Disabled: A Status Report on Leisure Counseling.* College Park, Md.: University of Maryland.

Mosey, A. C. 1973. *Activities therapy.* New York: Raven Press, Publishers.

Olson, E. G. 1980. Program portrayal: A qualitative approach to recreation program evaluation. In C. Z. Howe (ed.), *Leisure Today. Journal of Physical Education and Recreation.* *51*(8), 41–42.

O'Morrow, G. S. 1980. *Therapeutic recreation: A helping profession* (2nd edition). Reston, Va.: Reston Publishing Company, Inc.

Quattlebaum, M. S. 1969. Analyzing patients' behavior as an aid to disposition. *Hospital and Community Psychiatry.* 20, 241–242.

Samuels, S. C. 1977. *Enhancing self-concept in early childhood.* New York: Human Sciences Press.

Schmuck, R. A., & Schmuck, P. A. 1975. *Group processes in the classroom* (2nd edition). Dubuque, Iowa: Wm. C. Brown Company, Publishers.

Schul, B. D. 1975. *How to be an effective group leader.* Chicago: Nelson-Hall.

Shank, J. W., & Kennedy, D. W. 1976. Recreation and leisure counseling: A review. *Rehabilitation Literature. 37*(9), 258–262.

Stake, R. E. 1969. Evaluation design, instrumentation, data collection, and analysis of data. *Educational Evaluation.* Columbus, Ohio: State Superintendent of Public Instruction.

Stone, W. L., & Stone, C. G. 1952. *Recreation leadership.* New York: The Williams Frederick Press.

Sufflebeam, D. L. 1968. *Evaluation as enlightenment for decision-making.* Columbus, Ohio: Evaluation Center, Ohio State University.

Tubbs, S. L., & Moss, S. 1978. *Interpersonal communication.* New York: Random House.

Tyler, R. W. 1949. *Basic principles of curriculum and instruction.* Chicago: The University of Chicago Press.

Worchel, S., & Cooper, J. 1979. *Understanding social psychology* (2nd edition). Homewood, Ill.: The Dorsey Press.

184

7

HEALTH
AND
SAFETY
CONSIDERATIONS

PURPOSE OF THE CHAPTER

OBJECTIVES

DIABETIC REACTIONS

What Causes Diabetic Reactions?
Do Diabetic Reactions Require First Aid Treatment?
What Are Other Safety Considerations for the Client with Diabetes?
What Are the Diet Restrictions that the TR Specialist Should Know
About?

SEIZURES

Is There More Than One Type of Seizure?
What Kind of First Aid Treatment Is Necessary for Seizures?
Should Activities Be Restricted?
Anticonvulsant Drug Therapy

PSYCHOTROPIC DRUGS

Antipsychotics
Antidepressants
Antimania
Antianxiety

PHYSICAL LIMITATIONS REQUIRING MECHANICAL AIDS

SUMMARY

PURPOSE OF THE CHAPTER

There are common physical occurrences or conditions that may threaten clients' health or physical safety. Intermittent episodes such as diabetic reactions or seizures can have serious consequences on the clients' physical health. Sometimes side effects from long-term drug therapy may affect the client's ability to participate safely in an activity. Other threats to client safety can occur when physical mobility or ability is reduced due to injury or physical conditions. This chapter presents health and safety information that will help the TR specialist when providing services for these clients.

One type of physical concern, diabetic reaction, requires careful attention to prevent possible physical injury to the client. Diabetic reactions occur in clients who suffer from a condition known as diabetes mellitus. Approximately 5 percent of the population suffers from diabetes (Krall, 1978). It is especially common in clients over age 50 and in those who have vascular problems (e.g., heart disease, stroke) and are blind. Basic information on diabetes mellitus is necessary for the TR specialist in order to understand the causes of diabetic reactions, their treatment, and possible prevention. The first section of this chapter presents information on diabetic reactions.

Another possible threat to clients' safety can occur during a seizure. Approximately 2 percent of the population suffers from seizures (Epilepsy Foundation of America, 1975). When clients have recurrent seizures, the condition is known as epilepsy. Epilepsy is often associated with other conditions affecting the brain such as mental retardation and cerebral palsy. In addition, about one-third of clients with epilepsy suffer from emotional problems that require psychiatric intervention (Scott, 1978). Thus the TR specialist needs basic information regarding seizures, their usual treatment, and first aid measures. Information regarding seizures is presented in the second section of the chapter.

Another section in the chapter is devoted to the client who takes psychotropic drugs for the treatment of emotional problems. Many therapeutic recreation specialists come into contract with these clients at mental

186

health facilities. However, clients from any of the special populations may receive psychotropic drugs. Consequently, TR specialists who work with a variety of special populations will come into contact with clients receiving psychotropic drugs. Clients who receive these drugs may experience side effects, that should be taken into consideration when recreational activities are planned and provided. Information on commonly prescribed psychotropic drugs includes desired effects, side effects, and possible implications for the practice of therapeutic recreation.

The final section of the chapter provides general guidelines for therapeutic recreation specialists to follow when working with clients who use mechanical aids such as braces, crutches, and wheelchairs. Clients who have common physical conditions such as arthritis, broken bones, spinal cord injuries, cerebral palsy, cancer, and muscular dystrophy often have physical limitations requiring mechanical aids, either temporarily or permanently. Therapeutic recreation specialists who work in hospital settings, nursing homes, rehabilitation centers, camps for physically handicapped children, and institutions for severely retarded persons regularly serve clients with physical limitations. Information regarding possible safety hazards and implications for providing services are given. In addition, step-by-step guides for transferring clients from a wheelchair to a bed and from a bed to a wheelchair are provided.

Throughout the chapter the emphasis is on providing information for the therapeutic recreation specialist that will facilitate client safety. Common physical disorders and limitations that could result in client injury have been selected for presentation. The information is practical in nature and builds on information presented in introductory courses in therapeutic recreation.

OBJECTIVES

- Appreciate the importance of client safety needs resulting from physical disorders, physical limitations, or effects of drugs.
- Know causes and first aid treatment of insulin reaction and diabetic coma.
- Know first aid treatment for different types of seizures.
- Describe desired effects and side effects of selected drugs (anticonvulsants, psychotropics, antidepressants, antimania agent, and antianxiety agents).
- Recognize safety considerations for clients who use mechanical aids during recreational activities.
- Recognize safety considerations for both the therapeutic recreation specialist and the client when transferring clients.

DIABETIC REACTIONS

WHAT CAUSES DIABETIC REACTIONS?

Diabetic reactions are caused by diabetes mellitus, which occurs when a person has insufficient insulin available for use by the body. If the body does not have enough insulin, the glucose (sugar) in the blood becomes too high. Causes for the insufficient insulin are as yet unknown. Fortunately, diabetes is treatable with dietary restrictions, daily insulin injections, and/or oral medications. There are two types of diabetes—juvenile and adult-onset. Juvenile diabetes usually begins before age 15 and is more severe in that it is more difficult to maintain the proper amount of glucose in the bloodstream. The instability of juvenile diabetes is reflected in its synonyms—labile diabetes and brittle diabetes. Insulin is almost always needed in the treatment of juvenile diabetes. On the other hand, adult-onset diabetes is usually mild and is referred to as maturity-onset diabetes or mild diabetes. It usually occurs between the ages of 40 and 60 years of age. If the person is also obese, susceptibility to diabetes increases (Luckmann & Sorensen, 1980).

DO DIABETIC REACTIONS REQUIRE FIRST AID TREATMENT?

Yes; if there is either too much or too little glucose in the bloodstream the client's physical safety is threatened. Both reactions need treatment, and the TR specialist should be aware of the causes, symptoms, and treatment of each reaction.

The most dangerous reaction occurs when the body has too little glucose or too much insulin. This is called hypoglycemia, or an *insulin reaction*. The body needs some glucose to function. The three main causes of an insulin reaction are: (1) too much insulin, (2) too little food, and (3) too much physical activity. Physical activity reduces the body's need for insulin. Consequently, a client beginning a new activity program may be more susceptible to an insulin reaction. The onset can occur in minutes; symptoms include shakiness, nervousness, sweating, hunger, weakness, and confusion. Treatment involves giving the client food that contains sugar such as orange juice, Coke, lumps of sugar, or Lifesavers. The food should be given immediately, since failure to treat an insulin reaction can sometimes lead to convulsions, brain damage, or even death. If a client is not conscious, do not force fluids because the client may get the liquid in the lungs (Krall, 1978; Luckmann & Sorensen, 1980).

Insulin reactions are more apt to occur when the diabetes is unstable; they are far more common in the more severe type, juvenile diabetes.

188

Therefore it is essential that the TR specialist individually assess each client regarding his or her experience with diabetes. Ask the client if he or she ever has insulin reactions and, if so, to describe what happens. The TR specialist should especially watch children with diabetes early in a camping or activity experience, since the increase in activity could result in an insulin reaction. Some clients have insulin reactions at the same time each day. Ask the client or the family if there is a common time for the reaction. For example, one child at a day camp had an insulin reaction at 11:00 each morning. An extra snack at 10:00 A.M. while at camp prevented the insulin reaction. Plan with the client and/or the client's family what provisions need to be made. It is best for the therapeutic recreator to attempt to avoid insulin reactions by making sure that meals are not delayed and that no meals are missed. In addition, sugar should be readily available (e.g., in orange juice) in case of an insulin reaction.

The second reaction that occurs when there is too much glucose in the blood is called a *diabetic coma*. For the person with diabetes it can be caused by an insufficient intake of insulin, excessive intake of food, illness, or too little physical activity. The onset of an diabetic coma is gradual and can take days. Symptoms include thirst, headache, drowsiness, nausea, vomiting, and dry skin. Treatment includes the administration of insulin to reduce the blood glucose level (Krall, 1978; Luckmann & Sorensen, 1980).

Krall (1978) points out that it can be difficult always to recognize reactions. Insulin reactions are the most dangerous. Therefore, when medical personnel are not immediately available and a client is having a reaction that could possibly be an insulin reaction, the therapeutic recreator should give extra sugar immediately and seek medical attention as soon as possible. It is better to give unneeded sugar than to risk unconsciousness from an insulin reaction. Medical personnel can give insulin later to cover the extra sugar in case it was not an insulin reaction.

WHAT ARE OTHER SAFETY CONSIDERATIONS FOR THE CLIENT WITH DIABETES?

Diabetes is a long-term disorder that over a period of years, can cause negative bodily effects. Chronic complications include damage to blood vessels and nerve tissue, bringing on a reduced blood supply to the extremities, visual problems, inability to feel pain, kidney disease, and an increased susceptibility to infection. Thus the therapeutic recreation specialist should be aware that the client with diabetes may be more susceptible to physical injury because of visual disturbances and an inability to feel pain. Furthermore, the reduced blood supply and increased suscept-ibility to infection causes physical injuries to heal more slowly (Luckmann & Sorensen, 1980).

Even the slightest injury, such as a scratch or a blister on the foot, can be a major problem for the client with diabetes. Any break in the skin can lead to ulcers or gangrene without immediate and proper medical care. Thus the therapeutic recreation specialist should make sure that precautions are taken to prevent injury, especially to the feet, of the client with diabetes during recreational activities. Before embarking on activities that require running or extended walking, such as basketball or hiking, the therapeutic recreation specialist should inspect the client's shoes to make sure they are appropriate for the activity and fit well. The client should wear thick, warm socks to protect the feet. In long-term camping situations where the therapeutic recreation specialist is responsi-ble for daily supervision of the client's hygiene, it is imperative that the client's feet be regularly cleaned and inspected for any minor skin breaks or irritation. If any blister, redness, swelling, pain, or break in the skin is found, the therapeutic recreation specialist should obtain immediate medical consultation.

WHAT ARE THE DIET RESTRICTIONS THAT THE TR SPECIALIST SHOULD KNOW ABOUT?

Diets are individualized for each person. However, carbohydrates are almost always restricted. Generally, people with diabetes must avoid add-ing sugar to foods such as coffee and cereal and avoid foods that contain large amounts of sugar such as ice cream, cookies, and jellies (Luckmann & Sorensen, 1980). Consequently, if a client is to participate in an activity that involves food, the TR specialist should talk with the client and/or family in advance and determine whether the client will be able to select proper foods from the menu. Some individuals may prefer to bring their own meals if they are unable to eat the food served at the activity. At other times, just making diet drinks available may be sufficient.

SEIZURES

Epilepsy is a disorder that is characterized by recurrent seizures. A sei-zure is believed to occur when a group of abnormal brain cells fire at the same time. Sometimes the abnormal firing or discharge spreads in the brain. Whatever the abnormal brain cells control in the body determines the nature of the seizure. For example, if the cells control movement of the right arm, the right arm could have repetitive movements.

190

IS THERE MORE THAN ONE TYPE OF SEIZURE?

There are many different types of seizures that can be classified into two large groups—partial and generalized. Partial seizures occur when the discharge from the abnormal brain cells remains in only one section of the brain. When the discharge spreads to most or all of the brain, a generalized seizure occurs.

Partial seizures can be broken down into two divisions—*elementary* and *complex*. Elementary partial seizures involve only one section of the brain and the person does not lose consciousness. Another term for a partial seizure is a focal seizure. An example would be the seizure described earlier where the client had repetitive jerking of one arm. Complex partial seizures involve parts of the brain that control thought processes. The person is not unconscious but experiences reduced consciousness. The person sometimes describes the seizure as being in a fog. One common complex partial seizure is called a psychomotor seizure. In a psychomotor seizure the person may make senseless movements such as walking around pulling at his or her clothes, smacking his or her lips repeatedly, or speaking in an unintelligible manner. Complex partial seizures may last from minutes to hours and are often followed by confusion and loss of memory during the seizure (Sands & Minters, 1977; Solomon & Plum, 1976).

In *generalized seizures* there is a loss of consciousness. If the loss is brief, the seizure is called a petit mal or absence seizure. The *petit mal seizure* generally lasts 5 to 20 seconds and usually consists of staring or rolling back of the eyes. To an observer, the seizure may be seen as a brief lapse in activity.

Another type of generalized seizure is the *grand mal seizure.* Typically, the person loses consciousness, stiffens all over, has jerking movements of the arms and legs, and has loss of urine. At the onset, the person temporarily stops breathing and the skin may become pale or bluish. The breathing resumes during the jerking (tonic and clonic) phase. Following the seizure the person is often sleepy and may have muscle soreness. The grand mal seizure may be frightening to watch and generally seems to last longer than it does. The usual time is 2 to 3 minutes (Sands & Minters, 1977).

WHAT KIND OF FIRST AID TREATMENT IS NECESSARY FOR SEIZURES?

Since there are different types of seizures and the same type may manifest itself differently in different people, first aid procedures vary. Some people have more than one type of seizure. It is necessary to find out what happens during the seizure, how long the seizures usually last, whether there is loss of consciousness, and whether there are any symptoms before the unconsciousness occurs.

The primary concern for the therapeutic recreation specialist is the safety of the client. Generally, no first aid is necessary for any seizure except the grand mal. The lapses in the petit mal seizures are so short they are generally not dangerous. Normal safety precautions for crossing streets and bicycling should be sufficient. During psychomotor seizures, it may be necessary to guide the person if his or her actions could result in danger. The Epilepsy Foundation of America, in its pamphlets for school-teachers, suggests that an explanation be given to observers in order to help them understand that the person with epilepsy does not have control over his or her actions (Epilepsy School Alert, 1974).

Grand mal seizures may be unpleasant to watch and will often precipitate a feeling of needing to do something in the observer. The most important thing for the therapeutic recreator is to keep calm. It is especially important if the seizure occurs around a large group of people, since anxiety and panic could spread among the group. If the client is sitting or standing, ease the person to the floor and loosen any constricting clothing. Do not try to stop the seizure or try to revive the client. Once the seizure has started, it cannot be stopped. Do *not* under any circumstances try to force anything between clenched teeth. People do not swallow their tongues during a seizure, and a great deal of damage can be done to the teeth and mouth (Sands & Minters, 1977). It is also helpful to clear the area around the person of any hard objects so he or she will not inadvertently inflict self-harm with the seizure movements. Turning the head to the side may help the release of saliva. It is not necessary to call the doctor unless the seizure lasts for more than 10 minutes or if the client passes from one seizure to another without gaining consciousness (status epilepticus). Status epilepticus is rare but does require immediate medical treatment (Sands & Minters, 1977). After the seizure, someone should stay with the client until he or she is awake and no longer is confused.

Medical attention is necessary for the client who is *not* known to have seizures, however, even if the seizure does not last very long and the client appears unharmed. The cause of the seizure may be an underlying medical problem that may require further attention. Thus the TR specialist should be knowledgeable of the client's medical history.

The therapeutic recreation specialist should be matter of fact about the seizure with both the person who had the seizure and those who watched it. It is important to get back to business as usual in order to decrease the possibility of embarrassment for the client who has had the seizure.

192

SHOULD ACTIVITIES BE RESTRICTED?

Since therapeutic recreation often involves physical activity, the question regarding activity restriction is often encountered. There are no firm rules for the therapeutic recreator to follow. Information from the client or the client's family regarding the nature and frequency of the seizures is an important consideration when deciding about the appropriateness of the activities. In addition, recommendations from the client's physician in regard to contact sports and swimming must be followed. It must be pointed out that there is risk in living, and the client should not be unduly restricted or overprotected. The TR specialist should weigh three factors—seizure control, seizure type, and the nature of the activity—when determining risk versus benefit for the client with epilepsy. Each will be covered separately.

With anticonvulsant therapy approximately 50 percent of people with epilepsy are seizure-free, and an additional 25 to 30 percent have fairly good seizure control. Only about 20 percent of the people with epilepsy fail to achieve significant seizure control from anticonvulsants (Sands & Minters, 1977). Persons with poorly controlled epilepsy experience daily seizures. Generally, normal safety precautions suffice for clients who enjoy good seizure control. The TR specialist should find out how often the client has been having seizures. Ask if the client is taking the anticonvulsant medication regularly, since failure to do so can result in seizures.

The nature of the seizures also determines the need for activity restrictions. Some clients have seizures only during sleep (nocturnal seizures) and, consequently, need no restrictions. Seizures such as petit mal, elementary partial and complex partial (psychomotor) impose very few, if any, restrictions on the client's activities. Instructions may have to be repeated for the client with petit mal or psychomotor seizures, since he or she may miss hearing or seeing something during the seizure. In addition, activities such as bicycling should be confined to bike paths and parks that are away from busy streets. During swimming the therapeutic recreation specialist should make sure that the client swims with someone who is aware of the nature of the seizures and can get help if needed. Basic safety rules for everyone apply.

Grand mal seizures, however, can subject the client to harm if they occur while swimming. A grand mal seizure often begins with a quick inhalation. If the client is under water, he or she could breathe in water (Sands & Minters, 1977). Swimming can be hazardous, especially for the client with poorly controlled grand mal seizures, and should be prohibited. All personnel who are swimming with the client with epilepsy should be aware of the seizure disorder and know first aid procedures.

When a seizure does occur during swimming, the client should be supported so his or her head is out of the water to reduce the chance of getting water in the lungs. As soon as possible, the client should be taken out of the water and examined immediately to determine if artificial respiration is necessary. Even if the client seems fully recovered, medical attention should be obtained to protect the safety of the client. Seizures in the water can be very dangerous and medical attention is essential to determine if there are any ill effects for the client (*The Child with Epilepsy At Camp*, 1981).

If a client strikes his or her head forcefully against a hard object during any seizure, the client may develop a head injury. Since symptoms of a head injury such as headache, sleepiness, confusion, and weakness may be similar to symptoms occuring normally after a seizure, medical attention should be obtained for the client.

Any activities that require continued attention such as climbing or horseback riding may also need to be avoided by the client with poorly controlled grand mal seizures. If the client has occasional seizures, a hard hat may provide needed protection during bicycling or horseback riding.

The TR specialist must assess each client with epilepsy and the activity individually. Guidance from medical personnel should be sought and followed. Regardless of the type, people who have been seizure-free for 1 or 2 years usually have no restrictions and are given permission to drive an automobile (Sands & Minters, 1977).

ANTICONVULSANT DRUG THERAPY

The major treatment for seizures today is the long-term intake of anticonvulsant drugs. Other treatments have been tried with limited success. In the 1920s a ketogenic diet consisting of foods high in fat and low in carbohydrates was used. Acupuncture and biofeedback are being used experimentally today to determine their potential for use. Neurosurgery is an option for epilepsy that is very difficult to control (Sands & Minters, 1977). The majority of people with epilepsy regularly take anticonvulsant drugs. Therefore the TR specialist should be knowledgeable regarding the effects of the most common anticonvulsants.

The desired effect of the drug is to make the brain less susceptible to seizures. In other words, it raises the seizure threshold of the brain. The goal of anticonvulsant therapy is to get a sufficient amount of drug into the bloodstream to reduce seizures. Many times clients take more than one drug daily to achieve optimal seizure control. In order to maintain

194

the proper blood level, the anticonvulsant must be taken at regular intervals. Provisions must be made by the TR specialist for the client to receive drugs during prolonged activities such as field trips and overnight camping. Anticonvulsants are taken orally unless the client is unable to do so because of illness such as nausea and vomiting. If the anticonvulsant cannot be taken orally provisions must be made for medical personnel to give the drug by injection. Some anticonvulsants have serious withdrawal symptoms if too many doses are omitted.

All drugs may cause effects in addition to the desired effect for which they are being prescribed. Unfortunately, anticonvulsants have some of these side effects. It is important that the TR specialist be aware of possible side effects when assessing, planning, implementing, and evaluating activities for the client. Each client has to be assessed individually, since not everyone experiences side effects and some may only experience them temporarily. The therapeutic recreation specialist must assess which side effects the client is experiencing. For example, a client who suffers from dizziness and an unsteady gait would have difficulty with an activity that required physical agility. In addition, the TR specialist may be the first to recognize an increase in a side effect, such as extreme drowsiness, that may need medical attention.

The most commonly prescribed anticonvulsant drugs, along with their possible side effects are listed in Table 7-1. The table gives two names for each drug. The name that is listed first is the generic name. Each drug has only one generic name, which is never changed and is the same in all countries. The name that appears in parentheses is the trade name or the brand name. A drug can have many brand names. Except for phenobarbital, brand names are probably more familiar to you, since they are promoted by drug companies and are generally easier to pronounce. Generic names usually reflect the chemical makeup of the drug and are harder to pronounce and remember.

It can be seen that the therapeutic recreation specialist must be familiar with first aid and safety precautions for seizures and with possible side effects of anticonvulsant drugs in order to maintain client safety during recreation activities. The goal for anticonvulsant therapy is seizure control with a minimum of side effects. With very difficult to control seizures, some clients are forced to tolerate side effects from more than one drug. The therapeutic recreation specialist should report side effects to the client, the client's family, or medical personnel. Sometimes drugs can be changed if a side effect is potentially harmful. Assessment of side effects should be made and the information used when planning, implementing, and evaluating client care.

Table 7-1   Anticonvulsant drugs

Name	Possible Side Effects
Phenobarbital (Luminal)	Sedation, lethargy, mental dullness, anemia, skin rash; hyperactivity in children, the mentally retarded, and the elderly
Diphenylhydantion (Dilantin)	Unsteady gait, slurred speech, drowsiness, fatigue, gum swelling, skin rash, hair growth, stomach upsets, blood destruction
Primidone (Mysoline)	Sedation, nausea and vomiting, unsteady gait, temper outbursts, skin rash, slurred speech, headache
Carbamazine (Tegretol)	Double vision, slurred speech, drowsiness, nausea and vomiting, skin rash, blood destruction
Trimethadione (Tridione)	Sedation, nausea, blurred vision in bright lights, skin rash, stomach upsets, swelling of joints, blood destruction
Ethosuximide (Zarontin)	Nausea and vomiting, loss of appetite, headache, sleep disturbance, lethargy
Valproic acid (Depakene)	Loss of appetite, nausea and vomiting, decreased liver function, unsteady gait

Source. Data compiled from Meyers, Jarvety and Goldfein (1976); Solomon and Plum (1976); Sands and Minters (1977); and Hawken and Ozuna (1979).

PSYCHOTROPIC DRUGS

Many therapeutic recreation specialists provide services for clients who suffer from emotional disturbance or mental illness. In addition to other therapies such as psychotherapy and therapeutic recreation, many of these clients receive drugs to reduce the symptoms of the mental illness. These drugs have an effect on the psychic function of the client and are known collectively as **psychotropic drugs.**

In this section basic information will be presented on the four major classes of psychotropic drugs: antipsychotic, antidepressant, antimania, and antianxiety. It is important to realize that the information is what

196

usually happens when a client takes a drug regularly. The effects for any given individual may be different. Therefore individual assessment for side effects must be completed before planning therapeutic recreation strategies.

Each class of drugs will be individually covered. Names of the common major drugs will be listed. Generic names will be presented first; brand names will appear in parentheses. The desired effects, possible side effects, and potential implications for the therapeutic recreation specialist are also given.

ANTIPSYCHOTICS

Antipsychotic drugs were introduced in 1954 and have revolutionized the treatment of people with mental illness. The antipsychotics have been credited with dramatically reducing the number of patients in psychiatric institutions in the United States (Swonger & Constantine, 1976).

Chlorpromazine (Thorazine) was the first antipsychotic; it is still frequently prescribed in spite of the introduction of new drugs (Swonger & Constantine, 1976). Today there are a variety of drugs for the physician to choose from when treating the mentally ill. Table 7-2 lists some of the most commonly prescribed drugs and their common desired effects.

Antipsychotic drugs have a wide range of effects on many systems of the body in addition to the desired effects listed in Table 7-2. Not all clients experience side effects, and some clients have more pronounced side effects. Unfortunately, antipsychotic drugs have serious side effects (see Table 7-3). The extrapyramidal effects (Parkinson-like symptoms) can be so limiting for the client that a second drug (e.g., Cogentin, Artane, or Benadryl) is frequently given to counteract the extrapyramidal effects (Newton et al., 1978). The therapeutic recreation specialist must be familiar with the side effects and assess each client to determine which, if any, side effect will affect the planning of recreation activities.

Knowledge of the potential side effects of antipsychotic drugs can guide the assessment of the client by the therapeutic recreator. In addition, being aware that side effects may subside or be replaced by other side effects indicates the necessity of reassessment. When extrapyramidal symptoms (see Table 7-3) are present, activities that require physical agility such as bike riding, climbing, and gymnastics should be avoided. Even hiking down a steep hill can be potentially harmful for a client with a Parkinson-like gait. Supervision by personnel should be increased for those clients. Clients with tremors, muscle weakness, and fatigue may need to participate at a slower pace and have frequent opportunities for rest.

Table 7-2   Antipsychotic drugs

Name	Desired Effects
Chlorpromazine (Thorazine) Thioridazine (Mellaril) Trifluoperazine (Stelazine) Perphenazine (Trilafon) Fluphenazine (Prolixin) Haloperidol (Haldol) Molindine (Moban) Thiothixene (Navane) Loxapine (Loxitane)	Major actions include the reduction of symptoms of schizophrenia (i.e., hallucinations, delusions, disordered thinking processes, and social withdrawal), there are also effects of psychomotor slowing, emotional quieting, and decreased anxiety

Source. Data compiled from Bassuk and Schoononer (1977).

Some activities may not be particularly dangerous, but they subject the client to increased frustration. For example, activities that require good eye-hand coordination or clear vision can be frustrating. If the activity includes using needles or sewing with a sewing machine, the activity becomes potentially harmful. Aiming at a target, reading, and writing are potentially frustrating for clients who suffer from blurred vision or motor restlessness.

Clients who experience more than minimal sedation should not participate in activities that require alertness such as climbing, operating equipment, or driving. If a client has low blood pressure, he or she may experience lightheadedness or faintness on rising quickly from a lying position.

One side effect that occurs, especially with Thorazine, is photosensitivity, where the skin becomes increasingly sensitive to burning by the sun. The therapeutic recreation specialist should check with medical personnel before the client is allowed to participate in an outside activity with maximum exposure to sunlight such as swimming. A sunscreen can be applied or, if possible, the medication could be changed to Mellaril, which does not cause photosensitivity (Bassuk & Schoononer, 1977). For activities in the sun, clients should wear sunglasses, protective clothing, and sunscreen lotion on exposed areas if they are receiving Thorazine.

ANTIDEPRESSANTS

Antidepressant drugs, as the name implies, are widely used for the treatment of depression. They were introduced in the late 1950s and are widely prescribed for the treatment of both psychotic and psychoneurotic

198   PSYCHOTROPIC DRUGS

Table 7-3   Common side effects of antipsychotic drugs

Extrapyramidal Symptoms

Motor restlessness where the client cannot stop moving

Involuntary jerking and bizarre movements of muscles in the face, neck, tongue, eyes, arms, and legs

Tremors, muscle weakness, and fatigue

Parkinson-like symptoms such as rigidity, drooling, difficulty in speaking, slow movement, and an unusual gait when walking where the client has trouble slowing down

Other Symptoms

Sedation	Edema
Nausea	Weight gain
Vomiting	Suppression of ovulation
Rash	Reduction of sex drive
Low blood pressure	Lowered seizure threshold
Dry mouth	Blurred vision
Constipation	Photosensitivity (especially with Thorazine)
Blood destruction	

Source. Compiled from Bassuk and Schoononer (1977); and Newton et al. (1978).

episodes of depression (Swonger & Constantine, 1976). Today, antidepressant drugs are also being used on a trial basis for conditions other than depression. Phobias, manic attacks, obsessive-compulsive disorders, childhood enuresis (bed-wetting), and hyperactivity are conditions currently being treated experimentally with antidepressants (Harris, 1981).

The most commonly used group of compounds are called the tricyclic antidepressants. They are similar chemically to each other and to some of the antipsychotic drugs (e.g., Thorazine). The tricyclic antidepressants have many side effects in common with the antipsychotics (Bassuk & Schoononer, 1977). Better-known tricyclic antidepressants are listed in Table 7-4 along with their desired effects.

Tricyclic antidepressants are most helpful in the treatment of depressions where no simple precipitating cause can be identified (Swonger & Constantine, 1976). The client usually experiences a feeling of sedation rather than the mood elevation that one might expect from intake of the drug (Newton et al., 1978).

Side Effects.

The side effects of tricyclic antidepressants are very similar to those of the antipsychotic drugs listed in Table 7-3. Notable exceptions are the extra-

Table 7-4   Tricyclic antidepressants

Name	Desired Effect
Imipramine (Tofranil) Desmethyl-imipramine (Norpramin, Pertofane) Nortriptyline (Aventyl) Doxepin (Sinequan) Amitriplyline (Elavil)	Relief of feelings such as hopelessness, sadness, helplessness, worthlessness, anxiety, and fatigue that are associated with depression

pyramidal symptoms, which are greatly decreased, and the side effects such as dry mouth, constipation, and blurred vision, which are increased. The side effect of sedation can also help the client who is having trouble getting a good night's sleep. Two additional side effects include the increasing of mania in manic-depressive clients and the initiation of symptoms of schizophrenia in other clients (Newton et al., 1978).

ANTIMANIA

Lithium is presently the primary drug used for the treatment of mania and the manic phase of manic-depression psychoses. Lithium is an element that is administered as a salt. Common brand names include Eskalith, Litlane, and Lethonate (Swonger & Constantine, 1976). Lithium was approved by the Food and Drug Administration in 1970 (Ray, 1972).

Mania is a mood disorder characterized by a subjective feeling of elation. The person usually engages in endless activity and experiences a decreased need for sleep. Usually the person speaks quickly, as if under pressure to do so, and has flight of ideas where many unrelated topics are mentioned, one after another. Mania can progress to involve grandiose delusions, hallucinations, and paranoia (Bassuk & Schoononer, 1977). The exact mechanism by which lithium alleviates the symptoms of mania is unknown. However, studies reveal that long-term lithium therapy decreases the severity and frequency of manic episodes (Bassuk & Schoononer, 1977).

Side Effects

Generally, the side effects are mild and are related to the level of lithium in the bloodstream. Early side effects include thirst, increased urine, decreased appetite, nausea, vomiting, diarrhea, and a fine tremor. These side effects usually do not persist with continued therapy. However, higher lithium levels in the blood can be very dangerous; symptoms include muscular weakness, blurred vision, drowsiness, and ringing in the ears. Excessively high levels can lead to convulsions, coma, and death (Newton et al., 1978). The TR specialist's recognition of the side effects can help insure the clients' safety by encouraging the client to seek medical attention if higher-level symptoms occur.

ANTIANXIETY

Antianxiety drugs or minor tranquilizers are used to treat clients who suffer from psychoneurosis, excessive anxiety, and tension. There are two major types that are prescribed and have similar desired effects—carbamates and benzodiazepines. The common drugs are listed in Table 7-5 along with their desired effects.

Although the drugs have similar desired effects, the carbamates are more addicting and are more apt to cause death from overdose. The benzodiazepines are the most commonly prescribed drugs for anxiety. Valium given intravenously is also the treatment of choice for status epilepticus because of its anticonvulsant effect. In addition, Librium is used in the treatment of alcohol withdrawal (Swonger & Constantine, 1976; Bassuk & Schoononer, 1977; Newton et al., 1978).

Side Effects

Common side effects of the carbamates include drowsiness, impaired motor function, and lowered blood pressure in the elderly. The most common side effect of the benzodiazepines is drowsiness. Other side effects include dizziness, muscular incoordination, muscle weakness, skin rash,

Table 7-5   Antianxiety Drugs

Name	Desired Effect
Carbamates	
Meprobamate (Miltown,	Reduction of anxiety and relaxation
Equanil)	of skeletal muscles, relief of
Tybamate (Tybatran,	symptoms of psychoneurosis such as
Solacen)	tension and insomnia
Benzodiazepines	
Chlordiazepoxide (Librium)	
Diazepam (Valium)	
Oxazepam (Serax)	
Clorazepate (Tranxene)	

Source. Data compiled from Newton et al. (1978).

menstrual irregularities, and weight gain. Withdrawal reactions after prolonged use also have been known to occur (Swonger & Constantine, 1976; Newton et al., 1978).

The therapeutic recreation specialist would need to assess the individual client for side effects such as drowsiness or dizziness before planning activities that require alertness and muscular agility. Side effects of the antianxiety drugs are usually temporary and do not limit the recreational activities of the client.

PHYSICAL LIMITATIONS REQUIRING MECHANICAL AIDS

Many individuals have either permanent or temporary conditions that limit their physical mobility and require the use of mechanical aids. Mechanical aids are equipment such as braces, crutches, walkers, and wheelchairs, which assist clients in carrying out their activities of daily living. The use of mechanical aids allows the client to be as independent as possible. This section will present general guidelines for the therapeutic recreation specialist to follow when working with the client.

Safety for both the therapeutic recreation specialist and the client is the prime consideration. Every client differs in weight, disability, and size. Therefore each client should be individually assessed in order to determine his or her abilities and need for assistance. The first general rule to follow if possible is *always to consult with the client or the client's family regarding how much and what kind of assistance is needed.* Clients live with their mechanical aids and have safe and efficient routines that they follow. Even if a client has just recently developed the physical limitation, safe techniques have usually been taught to them by medical personnel prior to participating in therapeutic recreation activities.

Clients who use *braces, crutches,* or *walkers* have limited physical mobility and reduced weight-bearing ability in their legs. The therapeutic recreation specialist must assess each client's abilities prior to planning activities. Information should be sought from the chart, other medical and professional personnel, and the client. Assessment should include observation of the client in order to determine how well the client handles the mechanical aid in his or her activities of daily living. The therapeutic recreation specialist should assess how much balance the client has in various positions, whether one side of the body is weaker than the other, and how much physical endurance is present. The amount of physical endurance will affect how long the client can participate in more strenuous activities. If fatigue is present the client may be more apt to have an accident. In addition, clients who lack physical strength or mobility in both upper and lower extremities are less able to regain their balance or catch themselves if they begin to fall.

The therapeutic recreation specialist should conduct a physical inspection of the environment to insure client safety. Loose rugs, debris, and uneven or steep paths can make mobility more difficult for clients using mechanical aids. Paths that have sharp drops should be avoided.

The condition of the mechanical aid should also be observed. Equipment should be inspected to make sure that it is in safe condition and has no missing or loose pieces. Crutches and walkers should have rubber tips covering the base. Crutches should also have a rubber cover over the shoulder piece. Wheelchairs should have seat belts and wheels that lock.

Clients may develop reddened or pressure areas from lack of circulation or irritation from the mechanical aid. The therapeutic recreation specialist, especially in long-term activities such as camping, is often responsible for assessment of skin. The client cannot always be relied on to know if pressure exists because the client often has loss of feeling in the area. If any reddened or broken areas are observed, the TR specialist should call it to the attention to the client and/or medical personnel so proper measures can be taken to prevent further problems such as skin infection.

Clients who have loss of bladder function may have an indwelling urinary catheter and a collection bag. Urinary appliances are most common in the hospital setting. When working with the client, care should be taken to avoid pulling on the catheter, since the pressure may irritate the bladder opening and predispose the client to an infection. It is imperative that the tubing and collection bag always remain *below* the level of the bladder. Lifting the appliance above the bladder will cause the urine to flow back into the bladder and possibly cause an infection.

Clients who use braces, crutches, or walkers generally need minimal to moderate assistance. Ask the client or the client's family about the amount and type of assistance needed. Adequate assessment by the therapeutic recreator should result in recreational activities in which the client can participate safely. Clients may need assistance with stairs, especially if the client uses a walker. The nature of the assistance depends on the type of physical disability, the length of time the client has had the limited mobility, and other conditions. For example, an elderly client suffering from a recent stroke may need maximum assistance with stairs. When using crutches to ascend stairs, the client should place the crutches under the unaffected side and grasp the banister with the free hand. The unaffected foot is lifted to the riser above. Then, supporting the weight on the unaffected foot, the client pulls the crutches onto the riser. The process is repeated until the client reaches the top of the stairs. To go down the stairs, the client again positions himself or herself so that the banister is on the affected side and both crutches are on the other. The client places the crutches on the riser below and at the same time swings his or her affected foot out over the riser. Supporting body weight with a hand on the banister and the crutches, the client steps down with the unaffected foot. The process is repeated until the bottom of the stairs is reached.

When working with clients who are *wheelchair users,* ask them how the wheelchair works and what kind of assistance is needed, if any. Wheelchairs come in various styles. Armrests and footrests may be removable; some wheelchairs are self-propelled, depending on the needs of the clients. All wheelchairs should have brakes or locks on the wheels. Become familiar with the wheelchair before working with the client.

It is important to observe safety rules when transporting a client in a wheelchair. Safety precautions include locking the wheels of the wheelchair when it is not in motion. For example, the wheels should be locked when the client is getting in and out of the chair or when the client is being transported in the wheelchair inside a van. Always make sure that you have a good grasp on the handles of the wheelchair. Seat belts should be used to secure the client in the chair and avoid the possibility that the client can tumble forward at a sudden stop. When maneuvering over bumps and curbs, tilt the wheelchair back slightly by applying pressure on one of the tilting rods on the back of the chair. If you are pushing a wheelchair down a steep ramp, turn yourself and the chair around and proceed down the ramp backward. Your body will help control the speed of the wheelchair (National Easter Seal Society, 1980).

Wheelchair users who have full use of their arms may only need assistance when faced with an architectural barrier such as a flight of stairs. Except in the case of children, two people are usually needed to transport the client in the wheelchair up and down stairs. If the client is heavy, three people may be needed. The wheelchair is taken up the stairs backward and down the stairs frontward. The people assisting should be positioned in front and back of the wheelchair (see Figure 7-1). The chair should be balanced on the large wheels and lifted by the handgrips in back and the rods holding the footrests in front. The large wheels of the wheelchair are eased on the stairs one step at a time (National Easter Seal Society, 1980).

Some clients who are wheelchair users prefer to go it alone on the stairs. Generally, they fold up their chairs and move one step at a time by using their arms to lift their buttocks up and down the stairs taking their chair with them.

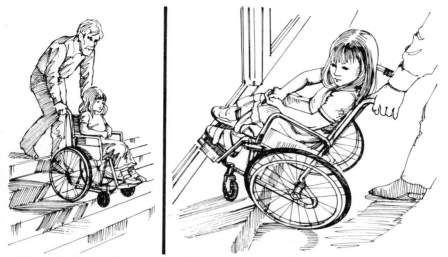

Figure 7-1 Adult assisting child in a wheelchair.

In some settings the therapeutic recreation specialist may be asked to assist a client from a bed to a wheelchair or chair. The TR specialist needs to utilize proper *lifting* and *transferring techniques* in order to protect the safety of both the client and himself or herself. According to Owen (1980), improper lifting and bending account for more than half of all back injuries. There are many methods to use. One common method that might be used by the TR specialist to transfer a client safely from a wheelchair to a bed is presented in Table 7-6 and demonstrated in Figure 7-2.

Transferring the client from the bed to the wheelchair is usually easier, since less lifting is required. Again, there are many methods. One common method to use is presented in Table 7-7 and demonstrated in Figure 7-3.

The same basic steps presented in Tables 7-6 and 7-7 can be used to transfer a client between chairs and between a wheelchair and a toilet. The distances between equipment should always be minimized. When transferring a client between chairs or between a wheelchair and a toilet, there should be about a 40-degree angle between the objects. If one side of the client's body is weaker than the other, the client should be moved toward the stronger side. The client will be able to assist more with the motion if he or she is moving toward the stronger side. The therapeutic recreation specialist should remember to keep his or her feet spread about shoulder width apart and flex the back and knees. Proper body positioning allows the muscle groups to work together and prevents injury

Table 7-6   Transferring client from a wheelchair to a bed

1. Minimize the distance between the wheelchair and the bed by placing the chair adjacent and parallel to the bed.
2. Lock the wheels on the wheelchair and the bed if the bed has wheels.
3. Raise the footrests and remove the armrest near the bed.
4. Stand in front of the client with your feet shoulder width apart. Your outside foot should be between the footrests.
5. Flex your back and knees.
6. Place your palms on either side of the client's rib cage.
7. Have the client put his or her arms on your elbows and hug your arms to assist.
8. Use your shoulder, arm, stomach, and back muscles to pull and your leg muscles to lift the client from the chair. Your knees should stabilize the client's knees.
9. Pivot your whole body to swing the client onto the bed.
10. Position the client in bed.

to the therapeutic recreation specialist. Arm, shoulder, back, and stomach muscles should be used to pull. Lifting is done with the thigh and leg muscles (Owen, 1980). The safety needs of both the client and the therapeutic recreation specialist should be considered when the TR specialist transfers clients who have reduced physical mobility.

SUMMARY

Providing therapeutic recreation services for clients from special populations requires knowing about the client's health and safety needs. Clients

Figure 7-2   Transferring a client from a wheelchair to a bed.

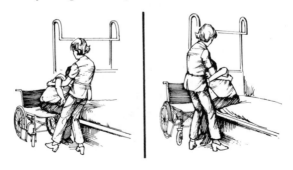

206

Table 7-7   Transferring a client from a bed to a wheelchair

---

1. Minimize the distance between the wheelchair and the bed by placing the wheelchair adjacent and parallel to the bed.
2. Lock the wheels on the wheelchair and the bed if the bed has wheels.
3. Raise the footrests and remove the armrest near the bed.
4. Face the head of the bed. Spread your feet about shoulder width apart. Place one forearm under the knees of the client and place your other forearm under the client's shoulder.
5. Assist the client to the sitting position by pivoting the client on his or her buttocks and swinging his or her legs over the edge of the bed. The client should be sitting on the edge of the bed.
6. Stand in front of the client and block his or her knees with your own. Your feet should be spread shoulder width apart. The outside foot should be midway between and in front of the footrest.
7. Place your palms on either side of the client's rib cage.
8. Have the client put his or her arms on your elbows and hug your arms to assist.
9. Use your shoulder, arm, stomach, and back muscles to lift the client off the bed.
10. At the same time, pivot the client and lower the client into the chair flexing your back and knees.
11. Position the client securely onto the wheelchair.

---

who have diabetic reactions or seizures may experience episodes that may threaten health and physical safety. Other clients who receive long-term drug therapy of psychotropic drugs may experience side effects that may affect their ability to participate in therapeutic recreation activities. Finally, clients who use mechanical aids may need assistance from the therapeutic recreation specialist. To assist the client safely and efficiently, the therapeutic recreation specialist must know proper transferring techniques. This chapter has provided general information and basic guidelines for the TR specialist to utilize when working with the clients.

KEY WORDS

Insulin Reaction. Low blood sugar resulting from too much insulin, increased physical exercise, or insufficient intake of food.

Diabetic Coma. An excessively high level of sugar in the blood resulting from insufficient insulin in the body.

Figure 7-3   Transferring a client from a bed to a wheelchair.

Desired Effect. A drug's desired or primary action on the body.

Side Effect. A drug's undesired action on the body.

Psychotropic Drugs. Pharmaceutical agents that have primary or desired effects on psychic function.

Reading Comprehension Questions

1 What are the main causes of an insulin reaction and diabetic coma?
2 What precautions should the therapeutic recreation specialist take when planning extended activities for clients with diabetes?
3 What is the first aid treatment for each type of seizure?
4 What are the main factors to consider when planning activities for the client who is subject to seizures?
5 Which side effects of anticonvulsant drugs and psychotropic drugs necessitate changes in activities due to safety considerations?
6 What are the main safety considerations for clients who use mechanical aids?
7 What are some basic principles to follow when lifting or transferring clients who have physical limitations?

REFERENCES

Bassuk, E. L., & Schoononer, S. C. 1977. *The practitioner's guide to psychoactive drugs.* New York: Plenum Publishing Co.

Epilepsy school alert. 1974. Landover, Md.: Epilepsy Foundation of America.

Epilepsy Foundation of America. 1975 *Basic statistics on the epilepsies.* Philadelphia: F. A. Davis Company.

KEY WORDS

Harris, E. 1981. Antidepressants: Old drugs, new uses. *American Journal of Nursing, 81*(7), 1308–1309.

Hawkin, M. & Ozuna, J. 1979. Practical aspects of anticonvulsant therapy. *American Journal of Nursing, 79,*(6), 1062–1068.

Krall, L. P. (Ed.). 1978. *Joslin diabetes manual* (11th edition). Philadelphia: Lea & Febiger.

Luckmann, J., & Sorensen, K. C. 1980. *Medical-surgical nursing: A psychophysiologic approach* (2nd edition). Philadelphia: W. B. Saunders Company.

National Easter Seal Society. 1980. How to handle and push a wheelchair. In D. Austin & L. Powel (eds.) *Resource guide: College instruction in recreation for individuals with handicapping conditions.* Bloomington: Indiana University.

Newton, M., Godbey, K. L., Newton, D. W., & Godbey, A. L. 1978. How you can improve the effectiveness of psychotropic drug therapy. *Nursing 78, 8*(7), 46–55.

Owen, B. D. 1980. How to avoid that aching back. *American Journal of Nursing, 80*(5), 894–897.

Ray, O. S. 1972. *Drugs, society, and human behavior.* St. Louis: The C. V. Mosby Company.

Sands, H., & Minters, F. C. 1977. *The epilepsy fact book.* Philadelphia: F. A. Davis Company.

Scott, D. J., 1978. Psychiatric aspects of epilepsy. *British Journal of Psychiatry, 132,* 417–430.

Solomon, G. E., & Plum, F. 1976. *Clinical management of seizures: A guide for the physician.* Philadelphia: W. B. Saunders Company.

Swonger, A. K., & Constantine, L. L. 1976. *Drugs and therapy.* Boston: Little, Brown and Company.

The child with epilepsy at camp. 1981. Landover, Md.: Epilepsy Foundation of America.

APPENDIX A

GLOSSARY

The glossary contains terms encountered by therapeutic recreation specialists. Many of the terms are not in the text but have been included because they may be used in agencies with therapeutic recreation services.

Assessibility Deals with meeting minimum standards of architectural design so that architectural barriers (e.g., steps) do not exist for persons with handicapping conditions.

acid Slang term for lysergic acid diethylamide (LSD).

acting-out Expression of emotional tension in actions rather than words. The term is usually used to describe impulsive, aggressive behavior in which the person is not consciously aware of the meaning of such acts.

activity analysis The process of systematically appraising what behaviors and skills are required of those who take part in a given activity.

activity therapy An umbrella term used to describe activity- or action-oriented services in psychiatric hospitals including therapeutic recreation, occupational therapy, and music therapy.

acute Of sudden onset; not chronic.

addiction Physiological dependence on a chemical substance (drug).

adjustment An individual's relation to society and to the inner self.

advocacy Working in support of the rights and needs of others. Usually used to refer to working in support of handicapped people.

affect The person's feelings, tone, or mood. One's emotional response.

ageism A word coined by Butler to describe the stigmatizing effect of society's past attitudes toward the elderly.

aggression Behavioral act with the goal of doing injury or harm to a person or object. A behavioral response that produces a harmful outcome.

Alcoholics Anonymous (AA) An organization of alcoholics that uses inspirational-supportive group methods to aid in the rehabilitation of chronic alcoholics.

ambulation Walking.

anorexia Loss of appetitie.

anomaly A malfunction or abnormality.

anticonvulsants Drugs used to control epileptic seizures.

anxiety Unpleasurable state of apprehension, tension, or uneasiness from some largely unknown or unrecognized source. Therefore the threat or danger is primarily of an intrapsychic nature in contrast to fear, which has a specific, recognizable source. It is characterized by increased heart rate, trembling, sweating, and disrupted breathing.

apathy A "don't care" feeling or affect reflected in a lack of interest or emotional involvement in one's surroundings.

aphasia Impaired ability to use or understand oral language.

assertiveness training An approach to assist people to become more assertive in sexual expression and social relationships.

assessment Collecting and analyzing information in order to determine the status of the client.

ataxia Inability to coordinate muscular movements characterized by lack of balance or unsteadiness. In psychiatry the term may be used to refer to a lack of coordination between feelings and thoughts.

atrophy Wasting away of a body tissue or organ.

attending behavior Individual responses to relevant stimuli.

attribution theories Social psychology theories dealing with attributing stable characteristics to a person after observing or knowing of his or her behavior.

aura A warning sensation that may precede a seizure (such as a flash of light, sound of a bell, etc.)

autism A developmental disability usually occuring during first 3 years of life. It is characterized by an inability to relate to others, delay in development of communication skills, abnormal responses to sensations, and ritualistic behavior.

Avedon, Elliott M. (1930–) Noted speaker and author in therapeutic recreation who left the United States for a university position in Canada during the 1970s.

Ball, Edith L. (1905–) Noted speaker and author in therapeutic recreation who served on the faculty of New York University for many years. Two-time member of the NTRS Board of Directors.

baseline information Data or observations obtained before the application of any intervention.

behaviorism An approach to psychology founded by John B. Watson that emphasizes the study or examination of overtly observable behavior. Its basis is academic learning theory.

behavior modification (behavior therapy) An approach that applies general learning principles to modify behavior through systematic manipulation of the environment. Specific behavioral techniques include operant conditioning, token economies, shaping, time-out, prompting, and fading.

Berne, Eric (1910–1970) American psychiatrist known as the founder of transactional analysis.

biofeedback A means to receive information (feedback) on various physiological processes (e.g., brainwave activity, muscle tension, heart rate, blood pressure, galvanic skin response) by use of electromechanical devices.

bisexuality Freud postulated that components of both sexes could be found in every person. Today the term is often used to describe individuals who are sexually attracted to and have sexual contact with partners of either sex. The slang terms "AC-DC" or "switch-hitter" are sometimes used to describe those who engage in bisexual behavior.

Berryman, Doris L. (1926–) Researcher and educator who developed the first standards and criteria for recreation services for residential institutions. Faculty member at New York University for many years, she served as a member of the NTRS Board of Directors and the NRPA Board of Trustees.

bestiality Sexual relations between a person and an animal.

bizarre behavior Eccentric behavior that does not conform to social expectations.

blocking Involuntary cessation of thought processes or speech brought about because of unconscious emotional factors.

cardiac Pertaining to the heart.

catchment area A term to delineate the geographic area for which a mental health facility has responsibility.

catharsis Release of impulses, thoughts, and repressed materials accompanied by an emotional response and tension release. Often used in connection with the release of aggression.

central nervous system (CNS) The brain and spinal cord.

cerebral palsy A condition characterized by the inability to control muscular movements due to injury, infection, or faulty development of the motor controls of the brain. Movement is impaired for many parts of the body or for only a limited group of muscles. It may be characterized by involuntary movements, rigidity, paralyses, facial grimacing, and speech disturbances. Associated problems frequently accompany the condition, resulting in multiple handicaps.

chemotherapy Drug therapy. The use of chemical substances in the treatment of illness.

chronological age Age in years.

client-centered therapy A type of growth-oriented therapy developed by Carl Rogers that is based on the concept of offering clients unconditional positive regard.

clinical psychologist An individual with a Ph.D. in clinical psychology who aids in the diagnosis, treatment, and prevention of mental and emotional disorders.

cognitive processes The higher mental processes pertaining to thinking and knowing, including learning, reasoning, intelligence, memory, imagination, concept formation, comprehension, decision making, and problem solving. They provide the ability to understand and deal with the environment and the self.

commitment Legally hospitalizing persons for psychiatric treatment.

communications Verbal and nonverbal transmission of ideas, feelings, beliefs, and attitudes that permits a common understanding between the sender of the message and the receiver.

congenital Present at or before birth.

conjoint psychotherapy Psychotherapy involving couples or entire families who see the therapist together.

continuum A continuous whole whose parts cannot be completely separated, such as the continuum of therapeutic recreation service.

compulsion Uncontrollable impulse to perform an act repetitively.

cope To deal or contend with problems successfully.

countertransference Idea from psychoanalysis in which the therapist unconsciously responds to the client as though he or she was a significant other from the therapist's past.

criterion level Predetermined standard of acceptable performance.

defense mechanisms A psychoanalytic construct to explain strategies that take place unconsciously to protect oneself from a threat to the integrity of the ego or to protect oneself against painful negative feelings. Examples are denial, sublimation, and rationalization. Sometimes referred to as ego defense mechanisms.

delusion A fixed false belief or conviction without foundaiton; often regarding one's status (delusions of grandeur), persecution (delusions of persecution), or oversupiciousness (paranoid delusions).

dependency Reliance on another (usually a helping professional) for psychological support.

depression A wide-range feeling running from unhappiness to extreme dejection. As a clinical syndrome it involves deep sadness or despair, feelings of worthlessness, morbid thinking, and greatly reduced psychomotor activity.

detoxification Process of the removal of the toxic effects of a drug.

developmental disability A handicap originating before age 18 that may be expected to continue for an indefinate period and that constitutes a substantial impairment. Developmental disabilities include epilepsy, cerebral palsy, mental retardation, and autism.

diabetic coma An excessively high level of sugar in the blood resulting from insufficient insulin in the body.

diplegia Paralysis of corresponding parts on both sides of the body (i.e., both arms or both legs).

Down's syndrome A common type of mental retardation brought on by a congenital condition resulting from a chromosomal abnormality. At one time referred to as mongolism. Down's syndrome children are characterized by widely spaced and slanted eyes, a flat face, small ears, and congenital anomalies of the heart.

dyslexia Impairment in the ability to read.

electroencephalogram (EEG) A graphic record of the electrical activity of the brain.

ego A part of the psychoanalytic personality (along with the id and superego). It is the rational part that mediates between the id and superego.

eclectic approach The utilization of therapeutic approaches and techniques selected from various sources or theoretical orientations.

electrocardiogram (EKG) The graphic record of the electrical activity of the heart.

electroconvulsive therapy (ECT) A treatment used to combat depression and schizophrenia in psychiatric patients. An electric current is applied to the brain through electrodes on the scalp, causing convulsions. Sometimes termed electroshock treatment (EST).

elopement "Running" (unauthorized departure) from a psychiatric hospital.

empathy The ability to perceive the world from the client's frame of reference or to put oneself in another person's place and understand the client's feelings and behaviors.

encounter group The major goals of the encounter group are awareness and genuineness. Concern is not so much with the transfer of learning but with the encounters among members. Sessions tend to be emotionally charged, dealing with extreme feelings of love and aggression.

epilepsy A disorder characterized by recurrent seizures caused by disturb-ances of the electrical activity of the brain.

etiology Cause of a disease or disorder.

euphoria Altered state of consciousness characterized by an exaggerated feeling of well-being, with or without foundation.

euthanasia "Mercy killing," or putting to death painlessly.

fixation The arresting of personality development prior to full maturity due to either excessive frustration or gratification. In Freudian theory the individual may become fixated at any of the psychosexual stages.

flaccid Soft, relaxed.

folie á deux Emotional illness shared by two closely related persons that involves sharing of the same delusions.

Freud, Sigmund (1856–1939) Austrian psychiatrist and founder of psychoanalysis.

Frye, Mary Virginia (1918–   ) From her beginnings as a Red Cross hospital recreation worker during World War II to her retirement from the position of chairperson of leisure studies at Iowa State University, Virginia Frye was a key national figure in TR. Among her accomplishments were the advancement of the national registration program and serving as coauthor of a major TR textbook.

functional blindness The inability to read newsprint even with corrective lenses or to perform ordinary tasks of daily living.

genital organs The male and female sex organs.

geriatrics Branch of medicine dealing

214

with the aging process and medical problems of aging.

gerontology The study of aging.

gestalt therapy Type of psychotherapy developed by Frederic Perls that focuses on sensory awareness and here-and-now experiences.

group A collection of individuals who coordinate their activities toward a common goal or cooperate to fulfill some purpose. Group members relate to one another and are interdependent.

group dynamics Group process. Phenomena that occur in groups.

growth psychology A humanistic psychology that perceives people as being self-aware, able to accept or reject environmental influences, and generally capable of being in conscious control of their own destiny. It emphasizes the development of unused potentials.

hallucination A false sensory perception involving any of the senses, without corresponding stimuli. Hearing voices that do not exist, for example, would be termed an auditory hallucination.

hedonic Seeking pleasure and avoiding pain.

helping relationship An interpersonal relationship between a person(s) with special problems or needs and a person skilled in techniques to help meet these problems or needs.

helplessness A feeling that results when events and behaviors are perceived to be uncontrollable. Helplessness is learned through environmental interactions and therefore may be altered.

hemiplegia Loss of power of one side of the body.

heredity Transmitted genetically from parent to child.

heterosexuality Sexual attraction or contact between opposite-sex individuals.

high-level wellness An approach that centers around the wholeness of the individual, calling for wellness or health enhancement in contrast to the illness orientation often found in the medical community.

Hillman, William A., Jr. (1929–   ) National leader in therapeutic recreation as the consultant for therapeutic recreation in the Office of Special Education and Rehabilitative Services, U.S. Department of Education. Past president of the National Therapeutic Recreation Society and editor of *Therapeutic Recreation Journal.*

holistic The view that an integrated whole has a reality independent of and greater than the sum of its parts.

homosexuality Sexual attraction or contact between individuals of the same sex.

hopelessness A feeling that often accompanies helplessness in which the individual feels doomed to live with a condition with no opportunity for change.

humanistic perspective A view that perceives the delivery of human services as a human enterprise in which the dignity and rights of clients are fully recognized. People are seen as striving to realize their individual potentials, yet capable of growing beyond themselves in order to care about others.

Humphrey, Fred (1922–   ) Active in the development of therapeutic recreation services in the evolutionary days of the field. Initiated TR curriculum at the University of Iowa, Pennsylvania State University, and Temple University. Past president of NTRS and member of the Board of Trustees of NRPA.

Hutchinson, Ira J. (1926–   ) First President and first executive secretary of NTRS.

hydrotherapy Use of water in the treatment of disease.

hyperactiviy Overreaction to stimuli leading to greatly increased muscular movement. Also known as hyperkinesis.

hypochondriasis A psychological disorder characterized by anxiety and a preoccupation with somatic concerns and symptoms that do not exist.

hypoglycemia Low blood sugar.

id A part of the psychoanalytic personality (along with the ego and superego). It contains the primative biological urges that demand immediate gratification and is ruled by the pleasure principle.

idiopathic Of unknown etiology.

illusion A misperception of an actual sensory stimulus.

individual program plan A plan flowing out of an established goals set that takes into consideration each client's unique background, psychological makeup, and personal needs and expectations.

insight Self-understanding. Awareness of the origin, nature, and mechanisms of attitudes and behaviors.

instinct Unlearned, biologically determined behavior.

insulin reaction Low blood sugar resulting from too much insulin, increased physical exercise, or insufficient intake of food.

intervention The carrying out of a plan of action derived during the planning stage to bring about changes in the client.

Journal of Therapeutic Recreation The quarterly journal of the National Therapeutic Recreation Society. It first appeared in 1967.

kinesthesis Muscle sense. The feel that accompanies any movement.

labeling The act of assigning a categorical term to an individual, often causing a stigmatization. An example would be to label persons "mentally ill" and, as a result, have them be perceived by others as inadequate persons possessing negative traits.

labile Unstable, liable to change.

laterality Awareness of the right and left sides of the body.

learning disability A condition affecting persons of normal or above normal intellect characterized by specific difficulties in learning. Examples include dyslexia (difficulty in reading) and dysgraphia (difficulty in writing).

legal blindness The legal definition of blindness is visual acuity for a distance of 20/200 or less in the better eye with correcting lenses or a visual field of less than an angle of 20 degrees. Thus the legally blind person can see no more at a distance of 20 feet than a person with normal vision can see at 200 feet.

Leisure counseling A helping process

216

in which the counselor attempts to assist the client to discover and change leisure attitudes or behaviors. Various verbal and nonverbal techniques are utilized in a counseling setting to help the client cope effectively with leisure problems and concerns, make decisions and develop plans for future leisure participation, become self-aware regarding perceptions toward leisure, and explore options for leisure.

lesbianism Female homosexuality.

lethargy Mental dullness or drowsiness.

LSD Lysergic acid dielhylamide. A potent psychotogenic drug.

mainstreaming The concept of integrating people who are exceptional (i.e., special populations) into society instead of segregating them.

malingering Simulation or exaggeration of an illness to avoid an unpleasant situation or duty or to obtain some type of personal gain.

marathon group The main goal of the marathon group is to break down defenses. The major distinguishing feature of this type of group is the time the group consumes. Ordinarily, marathons are uninterrupted meetings of 20 hours or more.

masturbation Achievement of sexual gratification by manual stimulation.

Medicaid A medical care program for United States citizens who cannot afford regular medical services. It is financed jointly by state and federal governments.

milieu therapy A psychiatric treatment approach that emphasizes socioenvironmental manipulations or the effect of the total environment on the client. It is usually employed in psychiatric hospitals.

mental retardation Subnormal general intellectual functioning existing concurrently with deficits in adaptive behavior, evident at birth or manifested during childhood.

meta- A prefix meaning "going beyond," "higher," "transcending," and so forth.

minimal brain damage Minimal or mild neurological abnormality that may lead to learning difficulties.

MMPI Minnesota Multiphasic Personality Inventory. Psychological instrument often administered to psychiatric patients. It provides a profile reflecting nine dimensions of personality.

muscular dystrophy A chronic, inherited disease of the muscles characterized by gradual weakening and degeneration of the voluntary muscles.

multiple sclerosis A chronic, slowly progressive disease of the central nervous system that usually occurs between the ages of 20 and 35. It is unpredictable, often punctuated by remissions and exacerbations. Weakness of the extremities is the most common symptom of the disease.

Narcissism Self-love. Preoccupation with self.

nervous breakdown. A lay term. It is a nonspecific euphemism for a mental disorder.

Nesbitt, John A. (1933–) A past president of both the National Therapeutic Recreation Society and the National Consortium on Physical

Education and Recreation for the Handicapped. Noted author, advocate, and educator in TR.

neurology The diagnostic study and treatment of organic diseases of the nervous system.

neurosis A group of mental disorders characterized by anxiety and maladaptive ways of dealing with it. In contrast to psychosis, the person does not experience an overt distortion of reality, but neurosis can be severe enough to impair functioning in dealing with reality.

nonverbal communications Messages passing between the sender and receiver that do not use the spoken word.

obese Overweight.

observational learning Behavior is learned by an individual by approximating the behavior of a model.

obsession A fixed idea or impulse that cannot be eliminated by logic or reasoning.

Office of Special Education and Rehabilitative Services An office within the Department of Education, within the federal government, that provides funding (i.e., grants) to support inservice and preservice training of various helping professions including therapeutic recreation.

O'Morrow, Gerald S. (1929–) A past president of NTRS, NRPA trustee, major textbook author, noted educator, and early advocate for leisure counseling.

orientation Awareness of oneself in terms of time, place, and person.

overt Observable, not hidden. Can be observed by other people.

palsy Paralysis.

para- A prefix meaning "alongside."

paraplegia Paralysis of the lower extremities.

paranoid disorders A class of mental disorders that involves delusions of persecution or jealousy.

Parkinsonism Once called Parkinson's disease, it is currently perceived to be a clinical syndrome and not one specific disease. It usually begins with a tremor in one of the upper limbs accompanied by "pill-rolling" movements of the thumb and fingers, a masklike appearance to the face, and slowed speech. It usually affects older persons and is slowly progressive.

partial hospitalization A type of psychiatric service often provided by community mental health centers for clients who require hospitalization only during the day, overnight, or on weekends.

pediatrician A physician (medical doctor) who specializes in the development and care of children and the treatment of children's diseases.

perception The process of becoming aware of, attending to, or interpreting stimuli, usually by visual, auditory, or kinesthetic senses.

phantom pain Perception of pain in a body part that has been surgically or accidently removed from the body.

pheylketonuria (PKU) A genetic disorder resulting in the buildup of concentrations of chemicals that interfere with brain development, leading to severe mental retardation. It is detectable by a simple test administered shortly after birth and is treatable by diet when detected early.

phobia A morbid fear associated with a specific object or situation.

physical disability Physical degeneration or loss to an individual caused by either congenital or adentitious factors. Often used interchangeably with the term physical handicap.

Piaget, Jean (1896–1980) Swiss psychologist noted for his theory of cognitive development.

placebo A material prepared to resemble an active drug but that has no pharmacologic activity. Thus any response is due to the psychological effect of taking a pill and not to any pharmacological property.

play therapy A type of psychotherapy that utilizes play activities and toys with children.

poly- A prefix meaning "many."

Pomeroy, Janet (unknown–   ) Founder and Director of the Recreation Center for the Handicapped in San Francisco. Perhaps the most instrumental figure in the development of community recreation for special populations.

professional helping A process where assistance is given by a professional person, working from a knowledge base, in which client needs are paramount and the ultimate aim is to facilitate the highest possible level of independence in the client.

prosthesis An artificial limb.

PSRO The Professional Standards Review Organization (PSRO) is an organization of physicians and other health care providers in a community, region, or state; they review the quality of health care services delivered in their jurisdiction. PSRO reviews are required by federal law under Medicare and Medicaid.

psyche The mind.

psychiatrist A physician (medical doctor) who specializes in the diagnosis, treatment, and prevention of mental and emotional disorders.

psychoanalysis A long, drawn-out therapy based primarily on exploring the unconscious to make it conscious. It is based on Freudian constructs.

psychoanalytic theory A psychological theory developed by Freud. It is a conflict model involving three systems of personality (id, ego, and superego) and two instinctual drives (sex and aggression).

psychodrama Psychotherapy approach originated by J. L. Moreno. It utilizes a dramatized acting out of the client's problems.

psychogenic Having emotional or psychological origin in contrast to an organic basis.

psychologist Individual who holds a degree (usually a Ph.D.) in psychology. Psychologists engage in psychological testing, diagnosis, counseling, and other therapies.

psychomotor Manipulative and motor acts requiring voluntary human movement (neuromuscular coordination) in contrast to involuntary reflex movement.

psychosis A major mental disorder that seriously disrupts a person's ability to recognize reality, think rationally, remember, communicate, and relate to others. It so involves all forms of adaptive behavior that it interferes with the capacity to meet the everyday demands of life.

It is often characterized by bizarre behavior, inappropriate mood, regressive behavior, delusions, and hallucinations.

psychosomatic Pertaining to the interaction of the mind and body. Commonly used to refer to bodily symptoms having at least a partial emotional cause.

psychotherapy A process of personal contact between a therapist and client involving verbal and nonverbal communication through which the client attempts to alleviate maladaptive behaviors or problems in living or to seek personal growth.

psychotropic drugs Pharmaceutical agents that have a special action on the psyche.

quadriplegia Paralysis of all four limbs.

rapport The feeling of a close and harmonious relationship between two persons. It is often used to describe the client's confidence in the helper and a willingness to work cooperatively with the helper. Having "good rapport" indicates a level of trust and ease in communicating with the helper.

rational-emotive therapy (RET) A cognitively oriented therapeutic approach developed by Albert Ellis.

reality orientation (RO) A technique used with confused elderly people involving regular repetition of basic facts and constant orientation to time, place, names, events, and things in the environment.

reality therapy A therapeutic approach developed by William Glasser that emphasizes present behavior,

facing reality, and taking responsibility for one's needs.

Recreation Center for the Handicapped Pioneering effort in the provision of special centers to offer recreation services to physically and mentally disabled people. It was founded by Janet Pomeroy in San Francisco, California, in 1952.

referral Occurs when a client is assisted to gain help from another helping professional.

rehabilitation To restore or return the person to maximum functioning and optimal adjustment.

relaxation training A means to help clients who are experiencing stress and tension to develop a feeling of deep relaxation.

remission Abatement of symptoms.

remotivation A group technique to encourage moderately confused elderly clients to take a renewed interest in their environment.

residential facility A site where residents (clients) live and receive educational, recreational, and therapeutic services appropriate for their particular needs. Examples include psychiatric hospitals and state schools for the mentally retarded.

resocialization A group technique to increase the social functioning of residents in geriatric settings. Its aim is to increase the awareness of self and others by helping clients form relationships, establish friendships, and develop new interests.

risky shift The phenomenon, studied by social psychologists, that people in groups behave with greater risk than those not in a group.

220

Rorschach test A projective psychological test sometimes referred to by laypersons as the inkblot test.

Rush, Benjamin (1745–1813) The father of American psychiatry.

self-actualization The process of becoming everything one is capable of becoming.

self-concept How individuals see themselves and how they feel about themselves. It contains both self-awareness and affective elements.

self-esteem One's self-regard or the value placed on oneself by oneself. Equates roughly to terms such as "self-respect" and "personal worth."

self-fulfilling prophecy A belief or expectation that operates to bring about its own fulfillment.

schizophrenia A term used to designate a large group of severe mental disorders of a psychotic level that are characterized by disturbances of thinking, emotionality, and behavior. The thinking disturbance is marked by distortion of reality, often with accompanying delusions, hallucinations, and incoherent speech. The mood disturbance is marked by inappropriate affective responses. Behavior may be withdrawn, regressive, and bizarre.

sensory training A group technique directed toward maintaining and improving the functioning of regressed patients through a program of stimulus bombardment.

side effect A drug's undesired action on the body.

significant other A parent, teacher, coach, recreation leader, or other person whose relationship is regarded to be especially important. Significant others influence feelings and behavior.

social facilitation theory A social psychology theory centered on the effect of the presence of others on behavior, particularly performance and learning. Robert B. Zajonc has been responsible for much of the research on this theory.

social reinforcement A behavioral term indicating attention (e.g., smile, affection, approval) from a significant other.

somatic Pertaining to the body.

somatic therapy Treatment of psychiatric clients by physiological means.

spasticity A tendency to spasm or violent contractions.

special populations Groups of people who are not usually included in the mainstream of society because of some impairment. Special populations served by therapeutic recreators include (but are not limited to) persons with mental retardation, individuals with physically handicapping conditions, persons with problems in mental health, and old people.

spina bifida A congenital closure defect that generally occurs in the lower lumbar region of the spine. In mild forms there may be no obvious deformity, but in severe forms parts of the spinal canal ballon out through the defect, although the defect remains covered with skin.

stereotypes Assumptions and beliefs about a group of people that have been assigned to every member of that group.

stroke A transactional analysis term

meaning a unit of recognition one person receives from another. Equates roughly with the behavioristic concept of reinforcement.

syndrome A complete picture of a disease, including all symptoms.

superego A part of the psychoanalytic personality (along with the id and ego). It contains internalized parental and societal controls and acts as the conscience.

tactile Related to the sense of touch.

terminal illness A disease that results in death.

T-group (training group) The purpose of T-groups is to allow "normal" people to gain increased awareness and increased skills in interpersonal relations. The groups consist of 10 to 15 members who work together for 20 to 30 hours in an unstructured environment. Members are urged to try new behaviors and to share emotional reactions to behaviors.

theory A systematically related set of statements stipulating relationships or underlying principles, including some lawlike generalizations from which testable hypotheses may be drawn.

therapeutic agent Anything (people or drugs) that brings about therapeutic outcomes.

therapeutic community A way of operating a relatively small unit within a hospital or institution in which the entire social milieu is used as an intervention.

therapeutic recreation process A systematic method of problem solving employed in therapeutic recreation. The process contains four phases:

assessment, planning, implementation, and evaluation.

therapeutic recreation specialist A person prepared for the responsibility of applying appropriate strategies to facilitate growth and development and help prevent or relieve problems of clients from special population groups through the provision of recreation and leisure services.

total blindness No light perception in either eye. Only 12 percent of legally blind persons fall into this category.

transactional analysis (TA) A theory of personality and social interaction developed by Eric Berne. It is commonly used as a basis for group therapy.

transfer Movement of a person from one piece of equipment (e.g., wheelchair) or furniture to another.

transference Idea from psychoanalysis in which the therapist is unconsciously perceived as a significant figure from the client's past. The therapist is attributed the attitudes and feelings the client holds toward that significant other. Transference may be hostile or affectionate.

trauma Injury.

trauma (emotional) An emotional shock having long-lasting effects.

type A personality A personality type characterized by excessive drive, competitiveness, and overscheduling. It is thought that this personality type is correlated with coronary heart disease.

type B personality A personality type characterized by a relaxed, easygoing manner.

usability Deals with going beyond

minimum legal architectural standards (for accessibility) to insure that the facility may be utilized by handicapped persons.

values Individualized beliefs and principles by which people live their lives. Values govern and influence the way people behave.

values clarification A technique to help people explore their values and make decisions regarding their values.

ventilation A free, uninterrupted flow of thoughts and feelings by the client during which the helping professional accepts feelings expressed and listens in a nonjudgmental manner; usually leads to the release of tension.

APPENDIX B

LIST OF ABBREVIATIONS

ā.ā.	of each
AA	Alcoholics Anonymous
AAHPERD	American Alliance for Health, Physical Education, Recreation, and Dance
AALR	American Association for Leisure and Recreation
a.c.	before meals
ACA	American Camping Association
AFB	American Foundation for the Blind
ADL	activities of daily living
AMA	against medical advice
ANS	autonomic nervous system
ARC	Association for Retarded Citizens of the United States
b.i.d.	twice a day
B.P.	blood pressure
B.R.	bed rest
c̄.	with
caps.	capsules
cc	cubic centimeter
CNS	central nervous system
CMHC	community mental health center
CP	cerebral palsy
CVA	cerebrovascular accident; stroke

224

dil.	dilute
D.D.S.A.	Developmental Disability Services Administration
DMH	Department of Mental Health
DSM III	Diagnostic and Statistical Manual of Mental Disorders (third edition)
DTs	delirium tremens
ECT	electroconvulsive treatment
EEG	electroencephalogram
EKG	electrocardiogram
EMR	educable mentally retarded
est	Erhard seminar training
EST	electroconvulsive treatment
Gm.	gram
gr.	grain
h.	hour
HMO	health maintenance organization
h.s.	hours of sleep
IEP	Individualized Educational Program
IQ	intelligence quotient
IRUC	Information and Research Utilization Center
JCAH	Joint Commission on Accreditation of Hospitals
JLR	Journal of Leisure Research
JOPERD	Journal of Physical Education, Recreation and Dance
Kg.	kilogram
L.D.	learning disability
LP	lumbar puncture
LPN	licensed practical nurse
LSD	lysergic acid diethylamide
MBD	minimal brain dysfunction
mg.	milligram
MHA	Mental Health Association
MS	multiple sclerosis
MMPI	Minnesota Multiphasic Personality Inventory
NAMH	National Association for Mental Health
NCPERH	National Consortium on Physical Education and Recreation for the Handicapped

NHSRA	National Handicapped Sports and Recreation Association
NRPA	National Recreation and Park Association
NTRS	National Therapeutic Recreation Society
NWAA	National Wheelchair Athletic Association
NWBA	National Wheelchair Basketball Association
NIHR	National Institute of Handicapped Research
OB	obstetrics
OBD	organic brain disease
OBS	organic brain syndrome
O.D.	right eye
O.O.B.	out of bed
O.S.	left eye
OT	occupational therapy
per.	by
PKU	phenylketonuria
p.r.n.	when required
PSRO	Professional Standards Review Organization
PT	physical therapy
q.	every
q.d.	every day
q.h.	every hour
q.i.d.	four times a day
q.o.d.	every other day
RET	rational-emotive therapy
RN	registered nurse
RO	reality orientation
RT	recreation therapy
s̄.	without
Sol.	solution
SRA	Social & Rehabilitation Administration
Stat.	immediately
TA	transactional analysis
tab.	tablet
t.i.d.	three times a day
TM	transcendental meditation

226

TMR	trainable mentally retarded
TR	therapeutic recreation
TRIC	Therapeutic Recreation Information Center
TRJ	Therapeutic Recreation Journal
VA	Veterans' Administration
WHO	World Health Organization

APPENDIX C

SELECTED AUDIOVISUALS

A DAY IN THE LIFE OF BONNIE CONSOLO (16 mm, color, 17 minutes)
An inspirational film about a woman born without arms who leads a normal and productive life. Mrs. Consolo seems to be a thoroughly mentally healthy person. Barr Films, 3490 East Foothill Road, Pasadena, California 91107.

A DIFFERENT APPROACH (16 mm, color, 21 minutes)
Humorous, fast-paced film that utilizes television personalities and persons with handicapping conditions to present the message that handicapped persons represent an untapped pool of productive workers. Serves as a good introduction to the physically handicapped and their abilities. Marsha Savat, Los Angeles Harbor College, 11 Figuera Place, Wilmington, California 90744.

A FILM ABOUT PEOPLE (16 mm, color, 12 minutes)
Film describes types of epilepsy and problems of persons with epilepsy. Indiana Department of Mental Health, Division of Developmental Disabilities, 429 N. Pennsylvania, Indianapolis, Indiana 46204.

AGING (16 mm, color, 25 minutes)
Attempts to dispel negative stereotypes of aging. Presents activity theory and disengagement theory. Audio-Visual Center, Indiana University, Bloomington, Indiana 47405.

AGING IN AMERICA (audio cassette)
Bert Kruger Smith interview on problems among the aged and ways of meeting some of their needs. Hogg Foundation Library, Hogg Founda-

228

tion for Mental Health, P.O. Box 7998, University of Texas, Austin, Texas 78712.

A MATTER OF CONVENIENCE (16 mm, color, 10 minutes)
Film about an exceptional group of young skiers who are either blind or amputees. Stanfield House, 900 Euclid Avenue, P.O. Box 3208, Santa Monica, California 90403.

ASSERTIVENESS TRAINING (audio cassette)
Tape explains the theory and practice of assertiveness training. *Psychology Today*, P.O. Box 278, Pratt Station, Brooklyn, New York 11205.

BEHAVIOR THERAPY (audio cassette)
Joseph Wolpe explains the methods of behavior therapy. *Psychology Today*, P.O. Box 278, Pratt Station, Brooklyn, New York 11205.

CAMPING AND RECREATIONAL PROGRAMS FOR THE HANDICAPPED (16 mm, color, 17 minutes)
Film shows the activities of campers at Camp Riley for handicapped children, a summer camp at Bradford Woods. Audio-Visual Center, Indiana University, Bloomington, Indiana 47405.

CAST NO SHADOW (16 mm, color, 27 minutes)
Film produced for the Recreation Center of the Handicapped. It depicts activities of severely mentally retarded, physically handicapped, multihandicapped, and emotionally disturbed children. Academic Support Center, Film Library Scheduling, 505 East Stewart Road, Columbia, Missouri 65211.

CLIENT-CENTERED THERAPY (audio cassette)
Carl Rogers explains his client-centered therapy approach. *Psychology Today*, P.O. Box 278, Pratt Station, Brooklyn, New York 11205.

COUNT ME IN (16 mm, color, 20 minutes)
Film illustrates the process of mainstreaming. Depicts disabled persons involved in independent living, work, and recreation. Stanfield House Film/Media, 12381 Wilshire Boulevard, Suite 203, Los Angeles, California 80025.

DEEP RELAXATION (audio cassette)
Dr. Daniel Goleman leads listeners through a deep relaxation procedure. *Psychology Today*, P.O. Box 278, Pratt Station, Brooklyn, New York 11205.

FOCUS ON ABILITY (16 mm, color, 22 minutes)
Basic techniques, sensitivity, and understanding in swimming instruction with persons with orthopedic, mental, emotional, and sensory disabilities. Academic Support Center, Film Library Scheduling, 505 East Stewart Road, Columbia, Missouri 65211.

FREUD: THE HIDDEN NATURE OF MAN (16 mm, color, 29 minutes)
Analyzes Freud's theories, including the power of the unconscious and the ego, superego, and id of human personality. Audio-Visual Center, Indiana University, Bloomington, Indiana 47405.

GESTALT THERAPY (audio cassette)
Robert W. Resnick talks of self-awareness and gestalt therapy. *Psychology Today,* P.O. Box 278, Pratt Station, Brooklyn, New York 11205.

HANDS FOR THE HANDICAPPED (16 mm, color, 23 minutes)
Demonstrates a number of devices used by young man with cerebral palsy. International Rehabilitation Film Review Library, 20 West 40th Street, New York, New York 10018.

LIKE OTHER PEOPLE (16 mm, color, 37 minutes)
Controversial British film on the pleasures, frustrations, and prejudices encountered by a young couple both of whom have cerebral palsy. Academic Support Center, Film Library Scheduling, 505 East Stewart Road, Columbia, Missouri 65211.

LITTLE MARTY (16 mm, color, 5 minutes)
Marty, 8-year-old poster boy of the National Foundation—March of Dimes, has artificial arms and built-up shoes, yet feeds himself, paints, types, swims and plays softball, soccer, and cards. National Foundation—March of Dimes, 800 Second Avenue, New York, New York 10017.

MOVING AND LIFTING THE DISABLED PERSON (16 mm, color, 13 minutes)
Methods of moving and lifting persons with disabilities. International Rehabilitation Film Review Library, 20 West 40th Street, New York, New York 10018.

NOT JUST A SPECTATOR (16 mm, color, 26 minutes)
Film shows 40 to 50 recreation activities that challenge and give satisfaction to persons with different handicapping conditions. Includes mountain climbing, basketball, angling, sailing, kyaking, caving, wheelchair dancing, and more. International Rehabilitation Film Library, 20 West 40th Street, New York, New York 10018.

ODYSSEY INTO LUNACY (audio cassette)
Psychologist David Rosenhan describes a unique research experiment in which a psychologist and his student admit themselves as psychiatric patients. *Psychology Today,* P.O. Box 278, Pratt Station, Brooklyn, New York 11205.

ONE STEP AT A TIME: AN INTRODUCTION TO BEHAVIOR MODIFICATION (16 mm, color, 31 minutes)
Illustrates the use of behavior modification techniques in state mental

hospitals, special schools, and with multiply handicapped persons. Audio-Visual Center, Indiana University, Bloomington, Indiana 47405.

ONLY HUMAN (16 mm, color, 29 minutes)
Film produced by the National Association for Mental Health. It uses everyday language to discuss attitudes toward emotional problems, tension, and anxiety. National Association for Mental Health Film Service, P.O. Box 7316, Alexandria, Virginia 22307.

OUT OF LEFT FIELD (16 mm, color, 7 minutes)
Film shows how blind and visually impaired youths can be integrated with sighted peers. American Foundation for the Blind, 15 West 16th Street, New York, New York 10011.

OUT OF THE SHADOW (16 mm, color, 25 minutes)
Film produced by the Recreation Center for the Handicapped. Shows persons with a variety of handicapping conditions in recreation activities. Recreation Center for the Handicapped, 207 Skyline Boulevard, San Francisco, California 94132.

PARALYMPICS, HEIDELBERG 1972 (16 mm, color, 15 minutes)
Film on the 1972 Paralympics held in Heidelberg, Germany. National Wheelchair Athletic Association, 40-24 62nd Street, Woodside, New York 11377.

RATIONAL-EMOTIVE THERAPY (audio cassette)
Dr. Albert Ellis discusses RET and its effectiveness in dealing with problems of children and adults. (Tape also contains information by William Glasser on reality therapy.) Hogg Foundation Library, Hogg Foundation for Mental Health, P.O. Box 7998, University of Texas, Austin, Texas 78712.

REALITY THERAPY (audio cassette)
Dr. William Glasser, originator of reality therapy, is interviewed regarding his approach. (Tape also contains information by Albert Ellis on rational-emotive therapy.) Hogg Foundation Library, Hogg Foundation for Mental Health, P.O. Box 7998, University of Texas, Austin, Texas 78712.

RECREATION CENTER FOR THE HANDICAPPED (16 mm, color, 23 minutes)
Film illustrates programming for handicapped participants at the Recreation Center for the Handicapped. Recreation Center for the Handicapped, 207 Skyline Boulevard, San Francisco, California 94132.

STROKES (16 mm, color, 30 minutes)
Presents a combination of dramatized situations and group discussions to illustrate the concept of strokes and stroking in the content of transac-

tional analysis. Audio-Visual Center, Indiana University, Bloomington, Indiana 47405.

TO SERVE A PURPOSE (16 mm, color, 15 minutes)
Depicts scope of therapeutic recreation services and populations served. Academic Support Center, Film Library Scheduling, 505 East Stewart Road, Columbia, Missouri 65211.

THE SEVEN-MINUTE LESSON (16 mm, color, 7 minutes)
Film for anyone who may ever act as a sighted guide. Demonstrates proper techniques involved in acting as a sighted guide. American Foundation for the Blind, 15 West 16 Street, New York, New York 10011.

THE SEXUALLY DISADVANTAGED (audio cassette)
Dr. Harvey Gochros discusses the need to accept handicapped people as sexual beings and some of the problems handicapped persons face in dealing with their own sexuality. Hogg Foundation Library, Hogg Foundation for Mental Health, P.O. Box 7998, University of Texas, Austin, Texas 78712.

THE THERAPEUTIC COMMUNITY (16 mm, color, 28 minutes)
Shows milieu therapy approach utilized with geriatric patients in a hospital setting. University of Michigan Television Center and Division of Gerontology, Ann Arbor, Michigan, 48103.

SPECIAL OLYMPICS (16 mm, color, 25 minutes)
Professionally produced documentary on the Special Olympics sports training and competition for the mentally retarded. Academic Support Center, Film Library Scheduling, 505 East Stewart Road, Columbia, Missouri 65211.

STEP ASIDE, STEP DOWN (16 mm, color, 20 minutes)
Film on the problems of aging in America. General Services, National Archives and Records, National Audiovisual Center, Washington, D.C. 20409.

THERAPY THROUGH PLAY (16 mm, color, 17 minutes)
Shows adapted sports for physically handicapped children. Human Resources Center, Albertson, New York 11507.

THEORY AND PRACTICE OF TRANSACTIONAL ANALYSIS (audio cassette)
Claude Steiner explains concepts of transactional analysis. *Psychology Today*, P.O. Box 278, Pratt Station, Brooklyn, New York 11205.

TOKEN ECONOMY: BEHAVIORISM APPLIED (16 mm, color, 21 minutes)
B. F. Skinner defines the term "token" and explains how they can be

used in reinforcement therapy. Audio-Visual Center, Indiana University, Bloomington, Indiana 47405.

TRANSACTIONS (16 mm, color, 30 minutes)

Presents a combination of dramatized situations and group discussions to illustrate the basic concepts of transactions in the content of transactional analysis. Audio-Visual Center, Indiana University, Bloomington, Indiana 47405.

WE'RE OK (16 mm, color, 11 minutes)

Cartoon characters are used to exemplify the three ego states as explained by transactional analysis: parent, child, and adult. Audio-Visual Center, Indiana University, Bloomington, Indiana 47405.

WHAT DO YOU DO WHEN YOU SEE A BLIND PERSON (16 mm, color, 13 minutes)

Humorous film demonstrating the right and wrong ways of dealing with blind persons. American Foundation for the Blind, 15 West 16th Street, New York, New York 10011.

AUTHOR INDEX

Anderson, R. A., 37, 38
Ardell, B., 57, 58
Armstrong, H. 39
Austin, D. R., 11, 19, 94
Avedon, E. M., 58, 75, 149, 151, 152
Axline, V., 13

Barker, L. L., 167
Barns, E. K., 35, 42, 43, 44, 45
Bassuk, E. L., 198, 200, 201
Bates, B. J., 43, 45, 144, 167
Beal, B. M., 156
Berkowitz, L., 14, 17
Berne, E., 29
Bernstein, D. A., 36, 37
Bernstein, L., 137
Binkley, A. L., 94
Blackham, G. J., 13, 175
Bohlen, J. M., 156
Borden, G. A., 22, 56, 97, 105, 178
Borkovec, T. D., 36, 37
Brammer, L. M., 38, 92, 119, 121, 122, 123
Brill, N. I., 91, 95, 103, 130, 131
Bullock, C. C., 128, 130, 174
Burgess, W., 81

Campos, L., 32
Carkhuff, R. R., 92
Carlson, P. V., 17, 94, 95
Cartwright, D., 152
Chapman, H. H., 56
Chapman, J. E., 56, 94, 95
Chartier, M. R., 114, 115
Clarke, W., 42
Coffey, F., 174
Cohen, R. G., 34

Coleman, J. C., 12, 34, 43
Compton, D., 177
Connolly, M. L., 40
Constantine, L. L., 197, 199, 200, 201
Cooper, J., 160
Coopersmith, S., 96
Cormier, L. S., 120, 123, 134, 137, 138, 175

Delaney, D. J., 34, 40, 93, 94
Diebert, A. N., 17, 19
Dunn, H. L., 57, 58
Dusek-Girdano, D., 38

Egan, G., 122, 125
Eisenberg, S., 34, 40, 93, 94, 96, 97
Ellis, A., 26, 27
Ellis, M. J., 13
Eubanks, R. E., 91
Everly, G., 37, 38

Fikes, C. R., 177
Folsom, J. C., 42
Ford, D. H., 10
Freedman, A. M., 25
French, J., 145
Frye, M. V., 103

Gergen, K. J., 96
Gibson, J. L., 113
Girdano, D., 37, 38
Glasser, W., 28
Gordon, C., 96
Gordon, T., 150
Gray, D. E., 55, 56
Gronlund, N. E., 72, 73, 74
Guba, E. G., 171, 172

236

SUBJECT INDEX

Activity analysis, 77
Adult ego state, 29, 30, 31, 32
Aggression, 14, 15
Anticonvulsant drugs, 194–196
Assertiveness training, 39, 40
Attribution theory, 129

Behavioral domains: affective domain, 79
  cognitive domain, 79
  psychomotor domain, 79
  social domain, 80
Behavioristic approach, 15–21
  techniques: chaining, 19
    fading, 20
    modeling, 19, 20
    Premack principle, 20, 21
    prompting, 20
    shaping, 19
    time-out, 20
    token economies, 20
Behavior modification, *see* Behavioristic
  approach
Behavior therapy, *see* Behavioristic
  approach
Bibliotherapy, 34

Cathartic notion, 14
Characteristics: of effective helpers, 91–93
  of therapeutic recreation specialists, 94
Child ego state, 29, 30, 31, 32, 33
Classical conditioning, 16, 17
Client-centered therapy, 23, 24
Client involvement: in evaluation, 84
  in planning, 71
Communications, 110–141
  elements in process, 113

exercises, 122, 123, 127, 128, 130, 134,
  135, 136, 138
defined, 138
guidelines for improvement, 114–119
nonverbal, 130–136, 139
in success-failure situations, 128–130
verbal responses, 124–128
Confidentiality, 162
Conformity, 160
Countertransference, 13

Defense mechanisms, 12, 14, 15, 23
Dependency, 149–150
Diabetic reactions, 186, 188–190

Eclectic approach, 9, 46
Education of ALL Handicapped Children
  Act (PL 94-142), 75
Ego, 10–12, 15
Epilepsy, 186, 190–194
  and physical activity, 193, 194
Evaluation: client, 82–84
  formative, 170
  naturalistic, 171
  program, 170–175
  summative, 170

Gestalt therapy, 24, 25
Goals: defined, 85
  formulation of, 72, 73
Groups: analysis of, 155–158
  leader functions, 150, 151
  stages of development, 152, 153
  structures for therapeutic recreation,
    151, 152
Growth psychology approach, 21–26

Gunn/Peterson model, 59

Helping professional: characteristics, 91–94
   distinction with layman, 2, 3
   training, 101, 102
Helping relationship: aim, 91
   defined, 5
   professional helping, 90–91
High-level wellness, 57, 58, 85
   and therapeutic recreation, 58, 59
Humanistic perspective, 55, 56, 84
   and therapeutic recreation, 56, 57
Humanistic psychology, 22
   and behavioristic psychology, 22
   and psychoanalytic psychology, 22

Id, 10–12, 15
Illness-wellness continuum, 58, 59
Implications for therapeutic recreation of:
   assertiveness training, 40
   bibliotherapy, 34
   client-centered therapy, 25
   diabetes, 188–190
   Gestalt therapy, 25, 26
   mechanical aids, 202–206
   physical activity and stress reduction, 39
   psychodrama, 34
   psychotropic drug effects, 197–201
   rational-emotive therapy, 27
   reality orientation, 42
   reality therapy, 28, 29
   relaxation training, 35
   remotivation, 43
   resocialization, 44
   seizures, 191–194
   sensory training, 45
   therapeutic community, 35
   transactional analysis, 33
   values clarification, 41
Individual program plans, 75–77, 85
Influence, 145, 146
Instincts: aggression, 10, 11, 15
   self-preservation, 10
   sexual, 10, 11, 15
Instrumental conditioning, see Operant
     conditioning
Interviews, 63–67, 136
   children, 65, 66
   phases, 137, 138
   setting, 136

Johari window, 97, 98

Labeling, 179, 180
Leadership: levels of, 144, 145
   principles of group, 160–162
   roles, 149
   styles, 146–149
Learned helplessness, 178, 179
Leisure counseling, 175–178
   conclusions regarding, 177–178
   orientations, 175, 176
Leisure interest instruments, 64, 65
Libido, 10
Listening, 117–124
   attending, 119
   clarifying, 121
   paraphrasing, 121
   perception checking, 121

Maslow's needs hierarchy, 71, 98, 99
Mechanical aids, 187, 201–206
   braces, 203
   crutches, 203, 204
   walkers, 203
   wheelchairs, 204–206

Objective assessment data, 70
Objectives, 73–75
   defined, 85
   rules for stating, 73
Observation methods, 62, 63
Operant conditioning, 16, 17

Parent ego state, 29, 30, 31
Philosophical base, 103–104
Play therapy, 13
Pleasure principle, 11
Power, 145, 146
Progress notes, 163–167
Psychoanalysis, 12, 13
Psychoanalytic approach, 9–15
Psychodrama, 33–34
Psychotropic drugs, 186, 187, 196–201
   antianxiety, 201
   antidepressant, 198–200
   antimania, 200, 201
   antipsychotic, 197, 198

Rational-emotive therapy, 26–27
Reality orientation, 41, 42